GUIDE TO
PERTH &
FREMANTLE

LIZ GLASS & SUE SCOTT

NEW
HOLLAND

First published in Australia in 1999 by
New Holland Publishers (Australia) Pty Ltd
Sydney • Auckland • London • Cape Town

14 Aquatic Drive Frenchs Forest NSW 2086 Australia
218 Lake Road Northcote Auckland New Zealand
24 Nutford Place London W1H 6DQ United Kingdom
80 McKenzie Street Cape Town 8001 South Africa

National Library of Australia Cataloguing-in-Publication Data:

Scott, Sue, 1951-
Guide to Perth & Fremantle

ISBN 1 86436 537 4

1. Perth region (W.A.) - Guidebooks. I. Glass, Liz, 1953-.
II. Title.

919.411

Photograph credits (colour section): Australian Pinnacle Tours, photographs
30, 31; Boat Torque 2000, photograph 29; Cameleer Park Camel Farm,
photograph 28; Cohunu Wildlife Park, photograph 21; Hillarys Boat Harbour,
photograph 24; Shaen Adey/NHIL, photographs 1, 14, 15, 16, 18; Anthony
Johnson/NHIL, photographs 3, 6, 9, 22; Jaime Plaza Van Roon/NHIL ,
photographs 8, 20; unknown/NHIL, photograph 10; Underwater World,
photograph 25; Rottnest Island Authority, photograph 17.

Commissioning Editor: Anouska Good
Project Editor: Monica Ban
Designer: Robyn Latimer
Artwork: Colin Wynter Seton
Reproduction: DNL Resource Pty Ltd
Printer: Times Offset (m) Sdn. Bhd.

Disclaimer
The authors and publishers have made every effort to ensure the
information in this book was correct at the time of going to press.
Prices, opening times, facilities, locations or amenities can change over
time so it is recommended that the reader call the operator or service
and confirm any information that might be required.

CONTENTS

ACKNOWLEDGEMENTS

The authors wish to thank their families and friends for their support and encouragement during the writing of this book. Many thanks also to those who supplied photographs for inclusion in the book—Underwater World, Cohunu Koala Park, Cameleer Park Camel Farm, Hillarys Boat Resort, Australian Pinnacle Tours, Rottnest Island Authority and Boat Torque 2000.

HOW TO USE THIS BOOK

The *Guide to Perth & Fremantle* is a user-friendly book that caters to the independent traveller, as well as people who like to be organised when they travel and sightsee. A quick glance at the Contents page should inform the reader how to access whatever information they need, be it where to stay, where to eat or what to see and do. The entries are arranged alphabetically throughout the book in relation to their subject matter with plenty of cross-references to maps and related subjects in other chapters. Chapter 20: General Information provides information on various amenities, opening hours, rules and regulations within the state of Western Australia. For specific attractions or activities please refer to the index at the back of this book. On a final note, the maps have a grid system that allows the reader to quickly find all sites listed in the key. The maps are to serve as a guide and are intended to complement detailed street directories, which are available at bookshops and newsagencies.

PERTH AND SURROUNDS

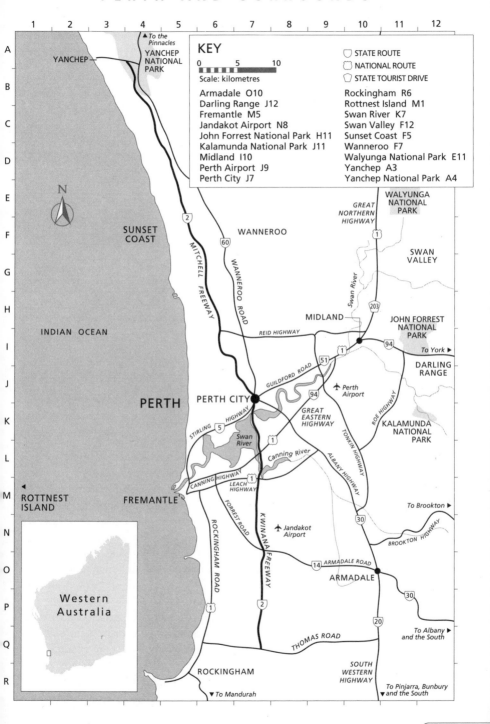

KEY

Scale: kilometres 0 5 10

STATE ROUTE
NATIONAL ROUTE
STATE TOURIST DRIVE

Armadale O10
Darling Range J12
Fremantle M5
Jandakot Airport N8
John Forrest National Park H11
Kalamunda National Park J11
Midland I10
Perth Airport J9
Perth City J7

Rockingham R6
Rottnest Island M1
Swan River K7
Swan Valley F12
Sunset Coast F5
Wanneroo F7
Walyunga National Park E11
Yanchep A3
Yanchep National Park A4

YANCHEP

To the Pinnacles

YANCHEP NATIONAL PARK

N

SUNSET COAST

INDIAN OCEAN

WANNEROO

MITCHELL FREEWAY

WANNEROO ROAD

GREAT NORTHERN HIGHWAY

WALYUNGA NATIONAL PARK

SWAN VALLEY

Swan River

MIDLAND

REID HIGHWAY

JOHN FORREST NATIONAL PARK

To York ▶

DARLING RANGE

GUILDFORD ROAD

PERTH

PERTH CITY

STIRLING HIGHWAY

Swan River

GREAT EASTERN HIGHWAY

Perth Airport

Canning River

ROE HIGHWAY

KALAMUNDA NATIONAL PARK

CANNING HIGHWAY

LEACH HIGHWAY

TONKIN HIGHWAY

ALBANY HIGHWAY

ROTTNEST ISLAND

FREMANTLE

ROCKINGHAM ROAD

FORREST ROAD

Jandakot Airport

KWINANA FREEWAY

To Brookton ▶

BROOKTON HIGHWAY

Western Australia

ARMADALE ROAD

ARMADALE

To Albany and the South ▶

THOMAS ROAD

ROCKINGHAM

SOUTH WESTERN HIGHWAY

To Mandurah ▼

To Pinjarra, Bunbury and the South ▼

1

CHAPTER 1

PERTH AND FREMANTLE

Perth, the capital of Western Australia, is a clean, modern, high-rise city, built on the banks of the spectacular Swan River. By contrast, 15 kilometres downstream lies the historic port city of Fremantle with its charming old buildings and cosmopolitan atmosphere. The Mediterranean climate in combination with Perth and Fremantle's proximity to the Indian Ocean and its diverse and beautiful natural attractions, make this an ideal tourist destination.

The city of Perth straddles the sprawling yet picturesque Swan River estuary. Its suburbs spread from the Darling Range escarpment in the east to the pristine white beaches of the Indian Ocean in the west, from Yanchep in the north, to the port city of Fremantle, at the mouth of the Swan River, some 15 kilometres to the south. Western Australia, the largest state in Australia, occupies approximately one third of the continent's land mass. The whole of Europe, including the United Kingdom, could fit into its 2.5 million square kilometres—with room to spare! Western Australia is separated from the rest of Australia by the Kimberleys to the north, largely uninhabited deserts and mountain ranges in the centre, and the Nullarbor Plain to the south.

Perth is probably the most isolated capital city in the world. Its nearest neighbour Adelaide, South Australia's capital, is well over 2700 kilometres away. This is about the same distance as its closest Asian neighbour, Indonesia.

HISTORY

Aboriginal people have occupied the Australian continent since time immemorial. Apart from their northern origin, and the certainty that they discovered Australia more than 30 000 years ago, no-one knows who they were or from whence they came.

Although shipwrecks litter the West Australian coast, the first known landing by a white man was in 1616. A Dutch captain, Dirk Hartog, sailing the Eendracht, discovered an island which still bears his name, at what is now Shark Bay. Then in 1696, a Dutch navigator, Willem de Vlamingh, aboard the frigate Geelviack, discovered the

Swan River, naming it after the black swans which were found there. Visiting Rottnest Island, he also named it after its unique fauna. This time the unusual 'rats' (actually quokkas) were its namesake. However, Vlamingh was unimpressed with the region, and the Dutch lost interest.

It was not until the late 18th century that Australia was colonised by white settlers. In 1787, the British government sent a fleet to establish settlements on the east coast. Then, in 1827 Captain James Stirling was sent to assess the suitability of the Swan River estuary for colonisation. On his recommendation, in May 1829, Captain Fremantle arrived with orders to formally take possession of this land, and a month later, Captain James Stirling established the sites for the port city of Fremantle, and the city of Perth some 15 kilometres further up the Swan River. By 1830, there were 1500 settlers but development was slow. In 1850 the first convicts arrived, and were set to work constructing buildings and roads. The discovery of gold in the late 1880's increased the population and by the turn of the century it reached 180 000. Since then, Perth has continued to expand and flourish.

PERTH AND FREMANTLE TODAY

The prosperous and culturally diverse cities of Perth and Fremantle have a combined population of about 1.3 million. Of the State's 1.8 million inhabitants, less than half a million live outside the Perth metropolitan area.

Western Australia's prosperity is due in part to the wealth of oil and natural gas found off its northern shores, and the gold, iron ore, diamonds, nickel, alumina and other minerals mined elsewhere in the State. Perth's skyline, with its state-of-the-art high-rise office blocks, includes many head office buildings of large mining companies. The affluent riverside and coastal suburbs and the high standard of living enjoyed by many residents reflect this State of prosperity.

TOURISM

Besides the importance of mineral resources and commerce, Perth is a tourism centre and the gateway to Australia for many Asian, African and European tourists.

It has domestic and international airports, and is well provided with a range of accommodation from five-star hotels, international chains, boutique hotels, middle range and budget motels, serviced apartments and guesthouses through to backpackers' hostels and lodges. The restaurants, nightlife and entertainment are varied and generally of high quality.

Western Australia is well-endowed with natural resources ranging from ancient forests and dramatic coastlines in the south, to the ruggedness of the Kimberley and the grandeur of the Hamersley Range in the north. In spring, the arid interior and the southern regions come alive after winter rains germinate up to 8 000 species of wildflowers—more species than in the rest of the world put together! Nature's magnificent display is a popular tourist attraction.

CLIMATE

Perth's Mediterranean climate too, is a natural attraction. It is the sunniest Australian capital and averages eight hours of sunshine per day, encouraging an informal, relaxed, outdoor lifestyle. In summer, when the weather is hot and dry, the ocean and river become playgrounds for all to enjoy. There is an endless variety of recreational activities. Eating out means just that. Al fresco dining is popular, with pavement cafés and garden restaurants in many suburbs, and lets not forget the well-known backyard Aussie BBQ!

The equable climate and fertile soils of the Swan Valley allow a wide range of fruit and vegetables to be grown and these, combined with plentiful local seafood and Western Australian wines, provide Perth's restaurants and shops with produce of the highest quality.

COSMOPOLITAN POPULATION

Perth's close proximity to Asia and the diverse origins of its immigrants are key influences on the city's development. Initially settled by the British and Irish, many other Europeans made Perth their home after the Second World War. Italians, Greeks and Yugoslavs were just some of the people drawn to Western Australia to start a new life. Their Mediterranean influence is seen in the vineyards, olive groves and market gardens around Perth and Fremantle, and also in the diversity of restaurants and foods available. More recently, increasing numbers of immigrants from nearby Asian countries, including Vietnam, Thailand, Malaysia, Indonesia, China and Japan, have brought their

cultural and gastronomic influences to the city. Areas like Northbridge and Fremantle abound with both European and Asian restaurants and shops.

ATTRACTIONS

From historical sites to cultural centres; from shopping malls to specialty boutiques; from waterside marinas to bustling markets, Perth and Fremantle offer attractions to suit all tastes.

Subiaco and Claremont's Bay View Terrace precincts offer up-market boutiques, specialty shops and trendy cafés, not forgetting the Subiaco Markets! The Northbridge area is legendary for its restaurants and nightlife, and is adjacent to Perth Cultural Complex which includes the Art Gallery of Western Australia, the Western Australian Museum, the Alexander Library and PICA, an exhibition and performance centre for local artists.

Across the Swan River, via the Narrows Bridge, is South Perth's restaurant strip where you can dine on whatever takes your fancy, while gazing over Perth's skyline. Wending your way to Fremantle along the river foreshore takes you past some magnificent homes in the prestigious suburbs of Applecross, Attadale and East Fremantle.

Fremantle is a treasure trove! Its rich history can be seen through the convict built Roundhouse, the oldest public building in Western Australia, and Fremantle Prison, as well as streets lined with beautifully restored 19th century buildings. For casual dining, Fishing Boat Harbour is lined with restaurants, including the famous Cicerello's fish 'n chip joint, and the Cappuccino Strip

PERTH CITY AND SUBURBS

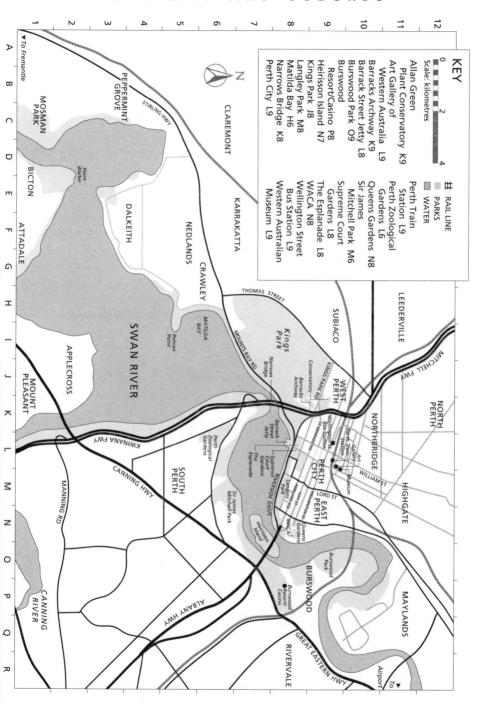

FREMANTLE

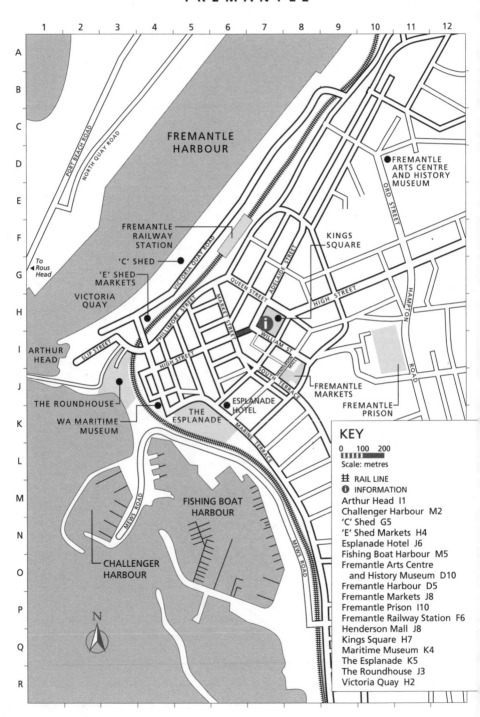

KEY

```
0   100   200
```
Scale: metres

╫ RAIL LINE
ℹ️ INFORMATION

Arthur Head I1
Challenger Harbour M2
'C' Shed G5
'E' Shed Markets H4
Esplanade Hotel J6
Fishing Boat Harbour M5
Fremantle Arts Centre
  and History Museum D10
Fremantle Harbour D5
Fremantle Markets J8
Fremantle Prison I10
Fremantle Railway Station F6
Henderson Mall J8
Kings Square H7
Maritime Museum K4
The Esplanade K5
The Roundhouse J3
Victoria Quay H2

has many great cafés and eateries. The Freo Markets are always a hive of activity and are still held in the original building constructed during the gold rush days of the last century.

The coastal drive back to Perth takes you past some of the best known city beaches, Cottesloe and Swanbourne, and through Kings Park, 400 hectares of bushland preserved by the city founders. The city centre is compact and modern with shopping malls, commerce centres and a focal point at Forrest Place where you often see buskers and live street theatre.

The East Perth redevelopment at Claisebrook is inner city dwelling at its stylish best. On the opposite river bank is Burswood, home of the Resort Hotel and Casino complex which includes restaurants, a theatre and an enormous entertainment dome which stages events as varied as trade fairs, tennis tournaments and pop concerts.

With such diverse attractions and natural attributes, Perth is an ideal place for a holiday or, as many have discovered, for a more permanent stay.

CHAPTER 2

GETTING AROUND

Travelling around Perth, Fremantle and their suburbs is comparatively easy. The road network is extensive and generally uncongested. The public transport system is reliable, clean and inexpensive. Over 300 bus routes, four rail lines and numerous major arterial roads ensure easy access to all suburbs.

This chapter covers a wide range of transport options for the Perth and Fremantle region, including public transport, the hiring of a variety of vehicles or simply getting around on foot.

PUBLIC TRANSPORT SYSTEM

Transperth is the umbrella name for all public transport services in Perth; that is the bus, train and ferry. Information services include:

TRANSPERTH INFOLINE

Phone: 13 62 13.
Internet: www.transperth.wa.gov.au.
This provides: bus times, numbers, routes and destinations. Operating hours: weekdays 6.30 am to 9.00 pm; Saturday, Sunday and Public Holidays 7.00 am to 7.00 pm.

TRANSPERTH INFORMATION CENTRES

Transperth has information centres located at City Busport, Wellington Street Bus Station, Plaza Arcade and Perth Train Station. Timetables for all bus routes, trains and ferries can be obtained at these locations.

TRANSPERTH FASTCARDS

- MultiRider, MultiRider Plus, DayRider and MaxiRider are tickets which allow more travel at cheaper rates. They can be purchased from Newspower newsagents, and Transperth InfoCentres (see above).

BUSES

On weekdays and Saturdays Transperth bus services run from 6.00 am to 6.00 pm, though on heavily used routes services continue until approximately 11.00 pm. On Sunday, buses run from 10.00 am to 7.30 pm. Services cover most of the metropolitan area.

FREE TRAVEL IS AVAILABLE ON:

Transperth buses around the Central Business District (CBD). The Free Transit Zone (FTZ) boundaries are Barrack Street Jetty, the Causeway, Newcastle Street, Thomas Street and Kings Park Road.

CAT (Central Area Transit) system is a free bus service around central Perth. The routes are:

Red CAT: east-west from the WACA Ground in East Perth to Outram Street in West Perth, operating Monday to Friday from 6.00 am to 7.00 pm, departing every five minutes.

Blue CAT: north-south from Northbridge to the Barrack Street Jetty on the Swan River, operating Monday to Friday from 6.00 am to 7.00 pm at seven and a half minute intervals.

Weekend CAT: runs over a modified Blue CAT route, operating on Friday from 6.00 pm to 1.00 am, Saturday from 8.30 am to 1.00 am and Sunday from 10.00 am to 5.00 pm. Just hop on at any CAT bus stop.

Fremantle Clipper Service which circles Fremantle city centre allows you to park a little further away and catch the bus. This service operates on Saturdays, Sunday and public holidays, every 15 minutes, between 10.00 am and 6.00 pm. Buses stop at Fremantle Station and other places of interest, such as the Fremantle Markets, Cinemas, the Esplanade Hotel, the Esplanade Reserve, the Round House, the E Shed Markets, Historic Boats Museum, Rottnest Ferry Terminal, Shell and Rock Museum, Leisure Centre, Samson House Museum, Energy Museum and Fremantle Prison. Maps showing the route covered can be obtained from the Tourist Information Office by the Fremantle Town Hall.

COMPANIES OPERATING OUTSIDE THE METROPOLITAN AREA INCLUDE:

Greyhound Pioneer. Phone: 13 20 30. Transport available to destinations throughout Australia except for south-west Western Australia.

South West Coach Lines. Phone: 08 9324 2333. Daily express services from Perth to the south-west of Western Australia.

Westrail. Phone: 13 10 53. Coach services north to Kalbarri, inland to Kalgoorlie and Meekatharra, and to south-west destinations, such as Albany and Margaret River.

FERRIES

A ferry service operates between Barrack Street Jetty and the Mends Street Jetty, South Perth. From there it is only a short walk to Perth Zoo. Two ferries leave simultaneously from opposite sides of the river at quarter past and quarter to every hour, more frequently during the rush hour. The last ferry is at 7.15 pm. Timetables are available from Transperth Information Centres (see previous page) and also from the Barrack Street and Mends Street Jetties. For further information contact Transperth Infoline: 13 62 13.

TRAINS

Suburban trains are fast, clean and well supervised, but the network is not extensive. The Perth Train Station is in the central city block in Wellington Street. Trains run from here to Armadale, Midland, Fremantle and Currambine (Joondalup Line). Details of all services can be obtained from Transperth Information Centres and Transperth InfoLine: 13 62 13.

Intrastate and interstate trains depart from the East Perth Terminal, except for the Australind to Bunbury, which leaves from Perth Train Station. Westrail operates intrastate services (the Australind to Bunbury, the Prospector to Kalgoorlie and the Avonlink to Northam). Great Southern Railways operates the 'Indian Pacific', which is an interstate service crossing the Nullarbor Plain from Perth to Adelaide and Sydney, a distance of 4352 kilometres. This is one of the longest rail routes in the world and includes the longest straight stretch of track—478 kilometres or 300 miles. This marvellous train journey takes three days and the one way fare costs between $424.00 ('coach' class) and $1350.00 ('first' class). Phone: 13 22 32 or 13 21 47. Westrail also acts as a booking agent for this service. Westrail has a Travel Centre at the East Perth Rail Terminal. Phone: 08 9326 2222 or 13 10 53.

CARS

Perth is a car-oriented city, which is easy to navigate. Most adult residents own or have access to a vehicle, and it is not uncommon for a family with mature children to have three or four cars in their driveway.

Taxis are readily available at the airports. There are taxi stands throughout the city but from other destinations it is easier to phone and pre-book a cab:

Black & White Taxis.
  Phone: 08 9333 3333.

Swan Taxis. Phone: 13 13 88.
Yellow Cab Co. Phone: 13 19 24.
Coastal Cabs (Fremantle) 13 10 08.

Hiring any vehicle is possible and reasonable prices are available.

Newsagents, department stores and bookshops all sell Perth street directories which are essential for newcomers to Perth, as signposting is not always adequate.

Major car hire companies have offices in Perth city and suburbs, and pick-up facilities at Perth Airport. There are also numerous smaller companies with cars ranging from family saloons to four-wheel-drive vehicles and campervans. Prices vary, starting around $17.00 per day. Check the *Yellow Pages* for a full list of companies and their locations. Some well-known companies include:

Avis. Phone: 1800 225 533.
Bayswater Car Rentals.
  Phone: 08 9325 1000.
Britz Australia Rentals. Phone: 1800 331 454. Campervans, four-wheel-drive vehicles, bushcampers and motor homes available.
Budget. Phone: 13 27 27 or 1800 649 800.
Budget Four-Wheel-Drive Rentals. Phone: 08 9479 1919 or 1800 444 808.
City Car Rentals. Phone: 08 9322 1887 or 1800 806 141.
Drive-A-Ute Rentals.
  Phone: 08 9228 2212. Utes, cars and trucks available.
Hertz. Phone: 13 30 39.
Koala Campervan Rentals. Phone: 1800 998 029 or 08 9277 1000.
Maui. Phone: 1300 363 800 or

SUBURBAN BUS AND TRAIN SERVICES

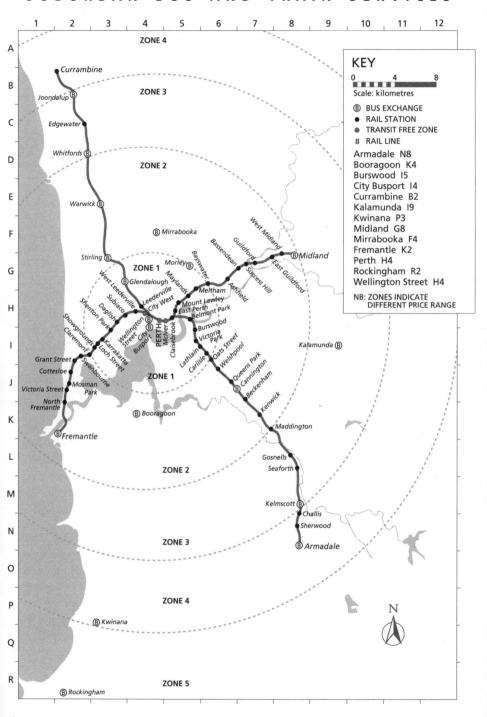

KEY

Scale: kilometres
0 4 8

Ⓑ BUS EXCHANGE
● RAIL STATION
● TRANSIT FREE ZONE
RAIL LINE

Armadale N8
Booragoon K4
Burswood I5
City Busport I4
Currambine B2
Kalamunda I9
Kwinana P3
Midland G8
Mirrabooka F4
Fremantle K2
Perth H4
Rockingham R2
Wellington Street H4

NB: ZONES INDICATE
DIFFERENT PRICE RANGE

08 9277 5696. Campervans and motor homes available.

AAA Bateman Rent an Oldie. Phone: 08 9322 7715. Older model cars.

Swiss Aussie Holidays. Phone: 08 9359 1746. Many vehicles available: station wagons, panel vans, campervans, Toyota Land Cruisers, and bushcampers or vehicles with a roof-tent which are fully equipped with camping, cooking and sleeping equipment.

Toy Shop Classic Car Hire. Phone: 08 9228 0554. Classic and prestige car hire, for example Porsche, Ferrari, Mercedes (from $75.00 per day).

ON FOOT

As the city of Perth is flat and the main shopping area confined to a few blocks, it is safe and easy to explore on foot. Numerous arcades and malls filled with cafés, food halls and shops of every conceivable variety, crisscross the area bounded by Wellington Street, William Street, St. Georges Terrace and Barrack Street. Adjacent streets also offer a wide variety of shopping and eating experiences.

A variety of walking tours are described in Chapter 17: Activities on the Land, page 114.

BIKES

Wearing helmets is compulsory when cycling in Perth. Bike hire companies include a helmet and lock as part of the hire cost. See also: Bicycling in Chapter 17: Activities on the Land.

■ Note: Bikewest puts out free booklets of recreational cycle tours with excellent maps and suggested routes, for example *Along the Coast Ride* and *Around the Rivers Ride*. These can be obtained from the WA Tourist Centre in Forrest Place, Perth, or Bikewest. Phone: 08 9320 9320.

BIKE HIRE

Venues include:

About Bike Hire: No 4 Car Park, Riverside Drive, Perth. Phone: 08 9221 2665. Open seven days: weekdays 10.00 am to 4.00 pm; Saturday 10.00 am to 5.00 pm; Sunday 9.00 am to 5.00 pm. Quality bicycles and tandems are available for hire on an hourly, daily, weekly or monthly basis. They supply helmets, panniers and baby carriers as required.

Activity Booking Centre: Kiosk 3, Old Perth Port, Barrack Street Jetty, Perth. Phone: 08 9221 1828. Open seven days: 8.00 am to 6.00 pm. Quality bicycles and tandems are available for hire on an hourly, daily, weekly or monthly basis. They supply helmets, panniers and baby carriers as required. It is also possible to book bikes for Rottnest Island.

Boat Torque Cruises: Pier 4, Barrack Street Jetty, Perth. Phone: 08 9221 5844. This company operates ferries to Rottnest Island, where bikes are the main form of transport. You can hire bikes to take to Rottnest at a cost of $15.00 per day (a week costs $45.00). See also Chapter 11: Rottnest Island.

Koala Bike Hire: Fraser Avenue Car Park, Kings Park, West Perth. Phone: 08 9321 3061. Open seven days: weekdays 9.30 am to 4.00 pm; weekends 9.30 am to 6.00 pm. Cost:

$4.00 for the first hour, $7.00 for two hours, $10.00 for three hours and $15.00 for one day. Tandems and kids bikes are available. This is an inexpensive and fun way to explore the wide expanses of Kings Park.

SCOOTER HIRE

A driving licence is required to hire a motor scooter. Hire venues include:
Scootabout: 37 Cliff Street, Fremantle. Phone: 08 9336 3471. Open seven days. Costs: $15.00 for the first hour, $5.00 per hour thereafter. There is a bond of $250.00, which is fully refundable on safe return of the scooter.

MOTOR CYCLE HIRE

Companies include:
Exclusive Motorcycle Hire: 1/108 Beechboro Road, Bayswater. Phone: 08 9371 1122. This company hires Harley Davidsons.
H Bombs Motorcycle Hire: 6/9 Hayden Court, Myaree. Phone: 08 9330 6789. Japanese and European bikes for short or long term hire.
Motts Motorcycle World: 115 Albany Highway, Victoria Park. Phone: 08 9470 1234. BMWs for hire.

Consult the *Yellow Pages* directory: Motor Cycles Hire and Tours, for other hire companies.

If you wish to be driven around on a motorcycle, see Chapter 18: Organised Tours, for Motor Bike Tours, page 132.

TRAMS

CITY TRAM TOURS ARE AVAILABLE FROM:
Perth Tram Company. Phone: 08 9322 2006.

TOURS INCLUDE:
The City Explorer Tour is a round trip visiting Kings Park, Burswood Resort Casino, Barrack St Jetty, Perth Mint, city shopping areas and Perth's major tourist attractions. The full tour with commentary lasts one and a half hours with the option to break and resume your tour at any stop. No booking is necessary. Cost: adults $12.00, pensioners $10.00, children $6.00, family pass $30.00.
Kings Park and University Tour. Kings Park provides unspoilt Australian bush near the centre of the city, and wonderful panoramic views of the city and river. See Chapter 13: Parks and Gardens, page 84, for details. The tour also visits the University of Western Australia with its historic buildings and gardens. It takes approximately one hour and departs from Kings Park at 11.00 am, 12.15 pm, 1.00 pm and 2.15 pm. Cost: adults $10.00, pensioners $8.00, children $5.00, family $25.00.
Combined Tour. This is a combination of the above two tours. Cost: adults $20.00, pensioners $16.00, children $10.00, family $50.00.
Tourist Trifecta. This tour consists of a return cruise from Perth to Fremantle plus tram tours of both cities with three hours free to lunch or shop in Fremantle. The Perth tram will pick you up at or near your city hotel. Cost: adults $45.00, children four to 14 $22.50; or for $75.00 adults, and $37.50 children, you can experience the above tour plus a guided tour of Fremantle Prison, and lunch at the Esplanade Hotel.

FREMANTLE TRAM TOURS ARE AVAILABLE FROM:

Trams West: 39A Malsbury St, Bicton. Phone: 08 9339 8719 or 018 094 361. Operates every day, leaving on the hour from 10.00 am to 5.00 pm from Fremantle Town Hall. Cost: adults $8.00, pensioners and senior citizens $6.00, children six to 15 years $3.00, family passes $16.00, with reduced prices for combined tours. There are four tours to choose from including full commentary, and you can hop on and off the tram whenever you like. Tours include:

Historical Trail Tour

Top of the Port Spectacular

Four Harbours Tour

Twilight Fish and Chips Dinner Tour (Thursdays). This tour costs $20.00 for adults with children half price, and includes fish and chips and a cool drink.

The Tourist Quartet leaves at 10.00 am and 2.00 pm and includes the Historical Trail Tour of Fremantle, a River Cruise to Perth and a tour of the city by tram, after which you return to Fremantle at your leisure by Transperth train or bus. Cost: adults $35.00, children (aged four to 15) $17.50.

SUBIACO SCENIC TRAM TOURS ARE AVAILABLE FROM:

Trams West: 39A Malsbury St, Bicton. Phone: 08 9339 8719. Mobile: 018 094 361. Operates Monday to Friday leaving from Linneys Jewellers, 37 Rokeby Road, Subiaco, at 11.00 am, 1.00 pm and 3.00 pm for the Historical City Tour; and at 12 noon and 2.00 pm for the Outer City and Lakes Tour. Cost: adults $6.00, concession $5.00, children $3.00.

WATER TAXI

A water taxi is available to take you to a riverfront restaurant or location of your choice. It leaves from the Old Perth Port, or Kiosk No 3, Barrack Street Jetty. Phone: 08 9221 9191 or 015 478 608. Prices start at $30.00 return.

CHAPTER 3

ACCOMMODATION

Visitors to Perth and Fremantle will find a wide range of accommodation available, from the humble caravan park or backpackers hostel to five star luxury hotels of a world class standard. The accommodation listings which follow provide a broad cross-section of places to stay to suit every taste and budget.

Most of the budget accommodation is centred around Northbridge, whilst the better hotels, other than the Burswood and Rendezvous Observation City, are in the centre of Perth. Prices do vary, even within the same category of accommodation. For example a double room at a five-star hotel could cost anything between $200.00 and $500.00, whilst a double room at a budget hotel on the beach could cost as little as $60.00. A bed in a dormitory at a backpackers or youth hostel costs between $10.00 and $15.00 per night.

The Royal Automobile Club of Western Australia (RAC) produce an accommodation guide called the *WA Touring and Accommodation Guide*, and has a free booking service on 08 9421 4488 or 1800 807 011. The Western Australian Tourist Centre publish the *Western Australia Accommodation and Tours Listing* annually and also has a booking service on 08 9483 1111 or 1300 361 351. Similarly, the Fremantle Tourist Bureau offer an accommodation booking service on 08 9431 7878.

HOTELS
FIVE-STAR: ★★★★★
Burswood Resort Hotel: Great Eastern Highway, Burswood.
Phone: 08 9362 7777.
Hyatt Regency: 99 Adelaide Terrace, Perth. Phone: 08 9225 1234.
Joondalup Resort: Country Club Boulevard, Connolly.
Phone: 08 9400 8888.
Parmelia Hilton: Mill Street, Perth.
Phone: 08 9322 3622.
Rendezvous Observation City: The Esplanade, Scarborough.
Phone: 08 9245 1000.
Sheraton: 207 Adelaide Terrace: Perth.
Phone: 08 9224 7777.

FOUR-STAR: ★★★★
Duxton Hotel (four star de luxe): 1 St Georges Terrace, Perth. Phone: 08 9261 8000.
The Esplanade Hotel: 46 Marine Terrace, Fremantle.
Phone: 08 9432 4000.
The Holiday Inn: 778 Hay Street, Perth. Phone: 08 9261 7200.

Hotel Grand Chancellor: 707 Wellington Street, Perth. Phone: 08 9327 7000.

The Melbourne Hotel: cnr Hay and Milligan Streets, Perth. Phone: 08 9320 3333.

Mercure Hotel: 10 Irwin Street, Perth. Phone: 08 9325 0481.

Novotel Langley: cnr Hill Street and Adelaide Terrace, Perth. Phone: 08 9221 1200.

Novotel Vines Resort: Verdelho Drive, The Vines. Phone: 08 9297 3000.

Parkroyal: 54 Terrace Road, Perth. Phone: 08 9325 3811.

Rydges Hotel: cnr King and Hay Streets, Perth. Phone: 08 9263 1800.

Sebel of Perth: 37 Pier Street, Perth. Phone: 08 9325 7655.

THREE-AND-A-HALF-STARS: ★★★☆

Chateau Commodore: cnr Victoria Ave and Hay Street, Perth. Phone: 08 9325 0461.

Criterion Hotel: 560 Hay Street, Perth. Phone: 08 9325 5155.

Hotel Ibis: 334 Murray Street, Perth. Phone: 08 9322 2844.

Indian Ocean Hotel: 23–27 Hastings Street, Scarborough. Phone: 08 9341 1122.

Kings Perth Hotel: 517 Hay Street, Perth. Phone: 08 9325 6555.

Metro Inn: 61 Canning Highway, South Perth. Phone: 08 9367 6122.

Mindarie Marina Hotel: Ocean Falls Boulevard, Mindarie. Phone: 08 9305 1057.

Perth Ambassador: 196 Adelaide Terrace, Perth. Phone: 08 9325 1455.

Rottnest Lodge Resort: Rottnest Island. Phone: 08 9292 5161.

Trade Winds Hotel: 59 Canning Highway, East Fremantle. Phone: 08 9339 8188.

THREE-STAR: ★★★

Miss Maud Swedish Hotel: 97 Murray Street, Perth. Phone: 08 9325 3900.

Park Inn International: cnr Murray and Pier Streets, Perth. Phone: 08 9325 2133.

Sullivans: 166 Mounts Bay Road, Perth. Phone: 08 9321 8022.

Wentworth Plaza Hotel: 300 Murray Street, Perth. Phone: 08 9481 1000.

TWO-AND-A-HALF-STAR: ★★☆

Ascot Inn: 1 Epsom Avenue, Ascot. Phone: 08 9277 8999.

Raffles Riverfront Hotel: cnr Canning Highway and Kintail Road, Applecross. Phone: 08 9364 7400.

BUDGET:

Carlton Hotel: 248 Hay Street, Perth. Phone: 08 9325 2092.

Cottesloe Beach Hotel: 104 Marine Parade, Cottesloe. Phone: 08 9383 1100.

Fremantle Hotel: cnr High and Cliff Streets, Fremantle. Phone: 08 9430 4300.

Ocean Beach Hotel: cnr Eric Street & Marine Parade, Cottesloe. Phone: 08 9384 2555.

Royal Hotel: 300 Murray Street, Perth. Phone: 08 9324 1510.

SELF-CATERING ACCOMMODATION
FIVE-STAR: ★★★★★

Observation Rise: 183 West Coast Highway, Scarborough. Phone: 08 9245 0800.

FOUR-AND-A-HALF-STAR: ★★★★☆

Arlington Quest Apartments: cnr Arlington Ave and Mill Point Road, South Perth. Phone: 08 9474 0200.

Broadwater Pagoda-Perth: 112 Melville Parade, Como. Phone: 08 9474 5999.

Harbour Village Quest Apartments: Mews Road, Fremantle. Phone: 08 9430 3888.

Hillarys Harbour Quest Resort: Hillarys Boat Harbour, Hillarys. Phone: 08 9262 7888.

Holiday Inn Park Suites: cnr Hay and Bennett Streets, East Perth. Phone: 08 9267 4888.

Sandcastles on Scarborough: 170 The Esplanade, Scarborough. Phone: 08 9245 2030.

Scarborough Seashells Resort: 178 The Esplanade, Scarborough. Phone: 08 9341 6644.

St James Quest Establishment (Apartment Hotel): 228 James St, Northbridge. Phone: 08 9227 2888.

Victoria Quest Apartments: 222 Hay Street, Subiaco. Phone: 08 9380 0800.

West End Quest Establishment: cnr Milligan and Murray Streets, Perth. Phone: 08 9480 3888.

FOUR-STAR: ★★★★

Barbara's Cottage: 26 Holdsworth Street, Fremantle. Phone: 08 9430 8051.

Executive Apartments: 19 Charles Street, South Perth. Phone: 08 9474 2255.

Fremantle Biscuit Factory Apartments: 330 South Terrace, Fremantle. Phone: 08 9430 5255.

Lawson Apartments: 2 Sherwood Court, Perth. Phone: 08 9321 4228.

Observation Villas: 7 Manning Street, Scarborough. Phone: 08 9245 3111.

Ocean Villas: 17–19 Hastings Street, Scarborough. Phone: 08 9245 1066.

THREE-AND-A-HALF-STAR: ★★★☆

City Stay Apartments: 875 Wellington Street, Perth. Phone: 08 9322 6061.

Emerald Court and Mews Apartments: 46 Scarborough Beach Road, Scarborough. Phone: 08 9245 2350.

Emerald Hotel: 24 Mount Street, Perth. Phone: 08 9481 0866.

Florina Lodge: 6 Kintail Road, Applecross. Phone: 08 9364 5322.

Metro Inn Apartments, 22 Nile Street, Perth. Phone: 08 9325 1866.

Pier 21 Resort: 7–9 John Street, North Fremantle. Phone: 08 9336 2555.

Sorrento Beach Resort: 1 Padbury Circle, Sorrento. Phone: 08 9448 7133.

Terrace Hotel, 195 Adelaide Terrace, Perth. Phone: 08 9492 7777.

THREE-STAR: ★★★

Adelphi Apartments: 130A Mounts Bay Road, Perth. Phone: 08 9322 4666.

Cottesloe Beach Chalets: 6 John Street, Cottesloe. Phone: 08 9385 4111.

Cottesloe Waters Holiday Units: 8 MacArthur Street, Cottesloe. Phone: 08 9242 2600.

Elsinore Holiday Units: 51 Pearl Parade, Scarborough. Phone: 08 9245 1272.

Fremantle Colonial Accommodation Cottages: 2,4,6 The Terrace, Fremantle. Phone: 08 9430 6568.

Fremantle Cottages and Apartments: 50 Money Road, Melville. Phone: 08 9317 2314.

Kingswood College Apartments:
Stirling Highway, Nedlands
Phone: 08 9423 9423.

Lyall Holiday Apartments: 2 Lyall
Street, cnr Melville Parade, South
Perth. Phone: 08 9387 1711.

Park Lane Auto Lodge: 45 Angelo
Street, South Perth. Phone:
08 9367 7588.

West Beach Lagoon: 251 West Coast
Highway, Scarborough. Phone:
08 9341 6122.

TWO-AND-A-HALF-STAR: ★★☆

Brownlea Holiday Apartments: 166
Palmerston Street, Perth. Phone:
08 9227 1710.

Canning Bridge Auto Lodge: 891
Canning Highway, Applecross.
Phone: 08 9364 2511.

City Waters Lodge: 118 Terrace Road,
Perth. Phone: 08 9325 1566.

Riverview on Mount Street: 44 Mount
Street, Perth. Phone: 08 9321 8963.

MOTELS
THREE-AND-A-HALF-STAR: ★★★☆

Great Eastern Motor Lodge: 81 Great
Eastern Highway, Rivervale. Phone:
08 9362 3611.

Kings Park Motel: 255 Thomas Street,
Subiaco. Phone: 08 9381 0000.

Windsor Lodge Motel: 3 Preston
Street, Como. Phone: 08 9367 9177.

THREE-STAR: ★★★

Murray Lodge Motel: 718 Murray
Street, West Perth. Phone:
08 9321 7441.

The Regency Motel: 61 Great Eastern
Highway, Rivervale. Phone:
08 9362 3000.

Swan View Motel: 1 Preston Street,
Como. Phone: 08 9367 5755.

TWO-AND-A-HALF-STAR: ★★☆

Pacific Motel: 111 Harold Street, Mt.
Lawley. Phone: 08 9328 5599.

Toorak Lodge Motel: 85 Great Eastern
Highway, Rivervale. Phone:
08 9361 5522.

BED AND BREAKFAST
FOUR-STAR: ★★★★

**Applecross Bed and Breakfast by the
River**: Canning Beach Road,
Applecross. Phone: 08 9364 7742.

Danum House: 6 Fothergill Street,
Fremantle. Phone: 08 9336 3735.

Westerly: 74 Solomon Street,
Fremantle. Phone: 08 9430 4458.

THREE-AND-A-HALF-STAR: ★★★☆

Fothergills of Fremantle: 20–22 Ord
Street, Fremantle. Phone:
08 9335 6784.

Mino's Homestay: 138 Seacrest Drive,
Sorrento. Phone: 08 9447 8355.

Palms Bed and Breakfast: 24
Dorchester Avenue, Warwick. Phone:
08 9246 9499.

Perth Bed and Breakfast: 7 Forbes
Road, Applecross. Phone:
08 9364 4498.

Rosemoore Bed and Breakfast: 2
Winifred Street, Mosman Park.
Phone: 08 9384 8214.

Swanbourne Guest House: 5 Myera
Street, Swanbourne. Phone:
08 9383 1981.

THREE-STAR: ★★★

Kalamunda Bed and Breakfast: 195
Orange Valley Road, Kalumunda.

Phone: 08 9291 9872.

BACKPACKERS
FOUR-STAR: ★★★★
Britannia International YHA: 253 William Street, Perth. Phone: 08 9328 6121.

Hay Street Backpackers: 266–268 Hay Street, Perth. Phone: 08 9221 9880.

Lancelin Lodge: 10 Hopkins Street, Lancelin. Situated one hour north of Perth. Phone: 08 9655 2020.

THREE-STAR: ★★★
Backpackers Inn: 11 Packenham Street, Fremantle. Phone: 08 9431 7065.

Kingstown Barracks: Rottnest Island. Phone: 08 9372 9780.

12.01 East: 195 Hay Street, Perth. Phone: 08 9221 1666.

Mandarin Gardens Scarborough Beach Resort YHA: 20–28 Wheatcroft Street, Scarborough. Phone: 08 9341 5431.

Northbridge YHA: 46 Francis Street, Northbridge. Phone: 08 9328 7794.

Ozi Inn: 282 Newcastle Street, Northbridge. Phone: 08 9328 1222.

Rainbow Lodge International: 133 Summers Street, Perth. Phone: 08 9227 1818.

Rory's Backpackers: cnr Lake and Brisbane Streets, Northbridge. Phone: 08 9328 9958.

The Shiralee: 107 Brisbane Street, Northbridge. Phone: 08 9227 7448.

Western Beach Lodge: 6 Westborough Street, Scarborough. Phone: 08 9245 1624.

TWO-STAR: ★★
Aberdeen Lodge: 79–81 Aberdeen Street, Northbridge. Phone: 08 9227 6137.

Cheviot Lodge: 30 Bulwer Street, North Perth. Phone: 08 9227 6817.

Djaril-Mari YHA: Mundaring Weir Road, Mundaring. Phone: 08 9295 1809.

Globe Hotel: 497 Wellington Street, Perth. Phone: 08 9321 4080.

Lone Stars Perth City Backpackers HQ: 156–158 Aberdeen Street, Northbridge. Phone: 08 9328 6667.

Murray Street Hostel: 119 Murray Street, Perth. Phone: 08 9325 7627.

NO-STAR:
Budget Backpackers International Hostel: 342 Newcastle Street, Northbridge. Phone: 08 9328 9468.

Port City Backpackers: 5 Essex Street, Fremantle. Phone: 08 9335 6635.

OTHER BUDGET ACCOMMODATION:
Beatty Lodge: 235 Vincent Street, North Perth. Phone: 08 9227 1521.

City Holiday Apartments: 537 William Street, Mount Lawley. Phone: 08 9227 1112.

Jewell House (YMCA): 180 Goderich Street, Perth. Phone: 08 9325 8488.

Mountway Holiday Units: 36 Mount Street, Perth. Phone: 08 9321 8307.

The Witch's Hat: 148 Palmerston Street, Northbridge. Phone: 08 9228 4228.

CARAVAN PARKS AND CAMP SITES
FOUR-AND-A-HALF-STAR: ★★★★☆
Perth Holiday Park: 911 Benara Road, Caversham. Phone: 08 9279 6700.

Perth International Tourist Park: Hale Road, Forrestfield. Phone: 08 9453 6677.

Woodman Point Caravan and Camping Resort: Lot 132 Cockburn Road, Woodman Point. Phone: 08 9434 1433.

FOUR-STAR: ★★★★

Banskia Tourist and Park Home Village: 219 Midland Road, Hazelmere. Phone: 08 9250 2398.

Burns Beach Caravan Resort: 35 Ocean Parade, Iluka, Burns Beach. Phone: 08 9305 5000.

Kingsway Caravan Park: cnr Kingsway and Wanneroo Roads, Landsdale. Phone: 08 9409 9267.

THREE-AND-A-HALF-STAR: ★★★☆

Coogee Beach Caravan Resort: Cockburn Road, Coogee. Phone: 08 9418 1810.

Fremantle Village Caravan Park and Chalet Centre: cnr Cockburn and Rockingham Roads, Fremantle. Phone: 08 9430 4866.

Karrinyup Waters Resort: 467 North Beach Road, Gwelup. Phone: 08 9447 6665.

Swan Valley Tourist Village: West Swan Road, West Swan. Phone: 08 9274 2828.

THREE-STAR: ★★★

Springvale Village (Caravan Park): Lot 10 Maida Vale Road, High Wycombe. Phone: 08 9454 9454.

NO-STAR:

Scarborough Star Haven Caravan Park: 18 Pearl Parade, Scarborough. Phone: 08 9341 1770.

CHAPTER 4

RESTAURANTS AND CAFÉS

Perth has a thriving restaurant scene. This is due to its multicultural population and the abundance of fresh seafood, fruit, vegetables and other produce which can be readily obtained in Western Australia. This, coupled with its relatively affluent population and Mediterranean climate, has led to a proliferation of restaurants representing almost every cuisine possible. Many of Western Australia's migrants are from Mediterranean countries as well as from nearby Asian countries, and the influences of their cuisines are evident in many restaurants.

As in most large cities, there are many of the international fast food chains such as McDonald's and Kentucky Fried Chicken (KFC). However, it is possible to eat just as cheaply in many of the international food halls which are located in and around Perth, for example the Carillon Food Hall, downstairs in the Carillon Arcade in central Perth; the Northbridge Pavilion and The Old Shanghai in Northbridge; the E Shed Markets and The Old Shanghai in Fremantle; Wanneroo Weekend Markets, Wanneroo; and Subiaco Pavilion Markets, Subiaco. These food halls usually consist of a central area containing dining tables and chairs, surrounded by stalls offering food from a variety of different countries. Six or seven dollars is usually sufficient to buy a large plate of food, be it curry and rice, spaghetti bolognese, sushi or sweet and sour pork. Most food halls allow you to bring your own alcohol, although you may have to pay a small corkage fee.

The Perth *Yellow Pages* has a comprehensive list of restaurants. Detailed descriptions of a selection of Perth's restaurants, in *The Western Table* by Peter Forrestal and Margaret Johnson, will have your mouth watering.

Licensed restaurants normally charge more for wines than the local bottle shop. Some BYO (bring your own alcohol) restaurants are happy to open your wine at no extra charge, while others charge corkage fees which range from $1.00 per bottle to $5.00 per person. It is worth inquiring about this when making a booking. Some restaurants are completely non-smoking whilst others have designated non-smoking and smoking areas. Once again, enquire on making your booking.

The following list of restaurants, which are categorised by cuisine or situation (for example, those with river or ocean views), includes only a small number of Perth's restaurants and cafés. Selections of restaurants to suit all wallets and tastes, and in various locations, are included. A rough guide to the system of costing we have used is:

$ means you should be able to buy a main course for under $10.00;

$$ means you should be able to buy a main course between $10.00 and $20.00;

$$$ and $$$$ restaurants are regarded as Perth's most exclusive, and include the Loose Box, Gershwin's, Frasers and Windows.

It goes without saying that the number of courses you eat and whether you choose sardines or crayfish, will affect the cost of your meal.

LIST OF RESTAURANTS
ASIAN CUISINE (MIXED)

Bibik Chan: 134B Stirling Highway, Nedlands. Phone: 08 9386 8492. Open: Lunch (Wed–Fri) Dinner (Mon–Sun) BYO. Cost: $

Joe's Oriental Diner: Hyatt Regency, 99 Adelaide Terrace, Perth. Phone: 08 9225 1268. Open: Lunch (Mon–Fri) Dinner (Mon–Sat) Licensed. Cost: $$

Overseas Noodle House: 62 High Street, Fremantle. Phone: 08 9430 4032. Open: Lunch & Dinner (Mon–Sun) BYO. Cost: $ to $$

Ten Ten Kitchen: 852 Albany Highway, East Victoria Park. Phone: 08 9362 1713. Open: Lunch & Dinner (Wed–Mon) BYO. Cost: $

Yen Do: 416 William Street, Perth. Phone: 08 9227 8833. Open: Lunch & Dinner (Mon–Sun) BYO. Cost $

AUSTRALIAN CUISINE
Features 'bush tucker' such as kangaroo, emu and crocodile.

Brown's Restaurant: 218 Nicholson Road, Subiaco. Phone: 08 9382 4763. Open: Lunch (Thurs–Fri) Dinner (Tues–Sat) BYO & Licensed. Cost: $$$

The Plum: 134 West Coast Drive, Sorrento. Phone: 08 9246 9221. Open: Lunch (Mon–Fri) Dinner (Mon–Sat) Licensed. Cost: $$ to $$$

Prickle's Café: cnr South Terrace and Douro Road, South Fremantle. Phone: 08 9336 2194. Open: Lunch & Dinner (Mon–Sat) BYO. Cost: $$

CHINESE CUISINE
Dragon Palace: Rendezvous Observation City, The Esplanade, Scarborough. Phone: 08 9340 5723. Open: Dinner (Wed–Sun) Licensed. Cost: $$

Emperor's Court: 66 Lake Street, Northbridge. Phone: 08 9328 1628. Open: Lunch (Daily Yum Cha) Dinner (Mon–Sun) Licensed. Cost: $$ to $$$

Genting Palace: Burswood International Resort Casino, Great Eastern Highway, Burswood. Phone:

08 9362 7777. Open: Lunch (Yum Cha Sat & Sun) Dinner (Mon–Sun) Licensed. Cost: $$$ to $$$$

Han Palace: 73 Bennett Street, East Perth. Phone: 08 9325 8883. Open: Lunch (Mon–Fri) Dinner (Mon–Sun) Licensed. Cost: $$$

Harbour View: 393 William Street, Northbridge. Phone: 08 9228 3688. Open: Lunch (Fri–Wed) Dinner (Mon–Sun) BYO. Cost: $ to $$

Jade Court: cnr Jarrad Street and Stirling Highway, Cottesloe. Phone: 08 9383 3431. Open: Lunch (Tues–Fri) Dinner (Tues–Sun) BYO & Licensed. Cost: $$

Canton Restaurant: 532 Hay Street, Perth. Phone: 08 9325 8865. Open: Lunch (Mon–Sat) Dinner (Mon–Sun) BYO & Licensed. Cost: $ to $$

FRENCH CUISINE

Ambrosia: 292 Hay Street, Subiaco. Phone: 08 9388 1638. Open: Lunch (Fri) Dinner (Tues–Sat) BYO. Cost: $$

Frenchy's: 125 Melville Parade, Como. Phone: 08 9367 7411. Open: Lunch (Fri & Sun) Dinner (Mon–Sun) BYO & Licensed. Cost: $$

La Cascade: 149 Stirling Highway, Nedlands. Phone: 08 9386 4547. Open: Dinner (Mon–Sun) BYO. Cost: $$ to $$$

L'escargot: 71 Bennett Street, East Perth. Phone: 08 9325 1660. Open: Dinner (Tues–Sat) BYO & Licensed. Cost: $$

INDIAN CUISINE

Annalakshmi (Vegetarian): 2nd Floor, CTA Building, 12 The Esplanade,

Perth. Phone: 08 9221 3003. Open: Lunch & Dinner (Mon–Fri) Alcohol not served. Cost: $$

Bombay Garden: 88 Rokeby Road, Subiaco. Phone: 08 9382 2941. Open: Lunch (Tues–Fri) Dinner (Mon–Sun) BYO & Licensed. Cost: $$

Maya Indian Restaurant: 75 Market Street, Fremantle. Phone: 08 9335 2796. Open: Dinner (Tues–Sun) BYO. Cost: $$

Mughal: 622 Stirling Highway, Mosman Park. Phone: 08 9383 1116. Open: Dinner (Mon–Sat) BYO. Cost: $ to $$

Royal India: 1134 Hay Street, West Perth. Phone: 08 9324 1368. Open: Lunch (Mon–Fri) Dinner (Mon–Sun) Licensed. Cost: $$

The Shalimar: 209 Oxford Street, Leederville. Phone: 08 9443 4567. Open: Dinner (Wed–Sat) BYO. Cost: $$

The Taj Tandoor: 442 Murray Street, Perth. Phone: 08 9322 3542. Open: Lunch (Mon–Fri) Dinner (Mon–Sat) BYO & Licensed. Cost: $$

The Turban: 248 Stock Road, Melville. Phone: 08 9330 1985. Open: Dinner (Tues–Sun) BYO. Cost: $$

ITALIAN CUISINE

Bellissimo: 3 Bay View Terrace, Claremont. Phone: 08 9385 3588. Open: Breakfast, Lunch & Dinner (Mon–Sun) BYO. Cost: $ to $$

Campo de Fiore: 22 Kearns Crescent, Ardross. Phone: 08 9316 3600. Open: Lunch (Mon–Fri) Dinner (Mon–Sat) Licensed. Cost: $$$

Chianti on Collins: 23 Colin Street, West Perth. Phone: 08 9322 2120.

Open: Lunch (Mon–Fri) Dinner (Mon–Sat) Licensed. Cost: $$ to $$$

E Cucina: Shop 10, Central Park, 777 Hay Street, Perth. Phone: 08 9481 1020. Open: Breakfast, Lunch & Dinner (Mon–Sat) Licensed. Cost: $$

Giardini: 135 Oxford Street, Leederville. Phone: 08 9242 2602. Open: Breakfast, Lunch & Dinner (Mon–Sun) BYO & Licensed. Cost: $$

Perugino: 77 Outram Street, West Perth. Phone: 08 9321 5420. Open: Lunch (Mon–Fri) Dinner (Mon–Sat) Licensed. Cost: $$$

Pizza Bella Roma: 14 South Terrace, Fremantle. Phone: 08 9335 1554. Open: Lunch (Sun) Dinner (Tues–Sun) BYO. Cost: $$

Primavera: 72 Marine Terrace, Fremantle. Phone: 08 9335 1744. Open: Lunch & Dinner (Tues–Sun) Licensed. Cost: $$

Roma: 9 High Street, Fremantle. Phone: 08 9335 3664. Open: Lunch & Dinner (Mon–Sat) BYO. Cost: $ to $$

Ruoccos: 213 South Terrace, Fremantle. Phone: 08 9335 6939. Open: Lunch & Dinner (Tues–Sun) BYO. Cost: $$

Santorelli's: 22 Viveash Road, Midland. Phone: 08 9274 3430. Open: Lunch (Mon–Fri) Dinner (Mon–Sat) BYO & Licensed. Cost: $$ to $$$

The Sicilian: 47 Mews Road, Fremantle. Phone: 08 9430 7024. Open: Breakfast (Sun) Lunch & Dinner (Mon–Sun) BYO & Licensed. Cost: $$; and 480 Hay Street, Subiaco. Phone. 08 9380 4554. Open: Lunch & Dinner (Mon–Sun) BYO & Licensed. Cost: $$

Spaghi's: 35 Mends Street, South Perth. Phone: 08 9474 3339. Open: Lunch

(Fri) Dinner (Tues–Sun) BYO. Cost: $$ to $$

Uncle Vince's: 71 Lake Street, Northbridge. Phone: 08 9328 4498. Open: Dinner (Mon–Sun) BYO. Cost: $ to $$

Villa D'este: 49 Outram Street, West Perth. Phone: 08 9322 6262. Open: Lunch (Mon–Fri) Dinner (Mon–Sat) Licensed. Cost: $$$

JAPANESE CUISINE

Chunagon: 46 Mews Road, Fremantle. Phone: 08 9336 1000. Open: Lunch & Dinner (Mon–Sun) Licensed. Cost: $$$ to $$$$

Edo Kirin: Burswood International Resort Casino, Great Eastern Highway, Burswood. Phone: 08 9362 7777. Open: Dinner (Mon–Sun) Licensed. Cost: $$$ to $$$$

Hayashi: 107 Pier Street, Perth. Phone: 08 9325 6009. Open: Lunch (Mon–Fri) Dinner (Mon–Sat) BYO. Cost: $$ to $$$; and 15 Ogilvie Road, Applecross. Phone: 08 9316 3384. Open: Lunch (Fri) Dinner (Mon–Sat) BYO & Licensed. Cost: $$ to $$$

Jaws: (Revolving sushi bar) 726 Hay Street, Perth. Phone: 08 9481 1445. Open: Daily 11.30 am to 6.00 pm. BYO. Cost: $ to $$

Matsuri Restaurant: 900 Hay Street, Perth. Phone: 08 9322 7737. Open: Lunch (Tues–Fri) Dinner (Tues–Sun) BYO. Cost: $$

Matsuri Sushi Bar: 903 Hay Street, Perth. Phone: 9324 2420. Open: Lunch (Mon–Fri) Dinner (Mon–Sat) BYO. Cost: $ to $$

Midori Japanese & Korean Restaurant: Hotel Grand Chancellor, cnr Milligan and Wellington Streets, Perth. Phone: 08 9322 5688. Open: Lunch (Fri) Dinner (Mon–Sun) Licensed. Cost: $$$

Nippon Café (karaoke and snacks): 564-568 Hay Street, Perth. Phone: 08 9325 5980. Open: Dinner (Mon–Sat) Licensed. Cost: $

Sado Island: 2/1 Seddon Street, Subiaco. Phone: 08 9381 4931. Open: Lunch (Tues–Sat) Dinner (Tues–Sun) BYO & Licensed. Cost: $$; and 57B Bay View Terrace Claremont. Phone: 08 9284 6667. Open: Lunch (Tues–Fri) Dinner (Tues–Sun) BYO & Licensed. Cost: $$

Sushi Station Fuji: 233 Albany Highway, Victoria Park. Phone: 08 9362 3796. Open: Lunch & Dinner (Wed–Mon) BYO. Cost: $$

Sakura Ya: (Downstairs) 566 Hay Street, Perth. Phone: 08 9325 5980. Open: Lunch (Mon–Fri) Dinner (Mon–Sat) BYO & Licensed. Cost: $$

Tansawa Tei: cnr Shenton and James Street, Northbridge. Phone: 08 9228 0258. Open: Lunch & Dinner (Mon–Sat) BYO & Licensed. Cost: $$ to $$$

MALAYSIAN CUISINE

Ann's Malaysian: 137 Barrack Street, Perth. Phone: 08 9325 8696. Open: Lunch & Dinner (Mon–Sat) BYO. Cost: $

Hawker's Hut: 150 Oxford Street, Leederville. Phone: 08 9444 6662. Open: Lunch & Dinner (Tues–Sun) BYO. Cost: $ to $$

Mahsuri Satay: 313 Albany Highway,

Victoria Park. Phone: 08 9362 5062. Open: Lunch (Mon–Fri) Dinner (Mon–Sat) BYO. Cost: $ to $$

Melati Satay: 38 Pier Street, Perth. Phone: 08 9421 1685. Open: Lunch & Dinner (Mon–Sun) BYO. Cost: $

Sri Melaka 313 William Street, Northbridge. Phone: 08 9328 6406. Open: Lunch & Dinner (Tues–Sun) BYO. Cost: $ to $$

Tak Chee: 182 William Street, Northbridge. Phone: 08 9328 9445. Open: Lunch (Mon–Sun) Dinner (Thurs–Tues) BYO. Cost: $

MEDITERRANEAN CUISINE

Apicus: 2 Wray Avenue, Fremantle. Phone: 08 9335 9892. Open: Lunch (Wed–Sat) Dinner (Tues–Sat) BYO. Cost: $$

Barocco: 318 William Street, Northbridge. Phone: 08 9228 3888. Open: Lunch & Dinner (Mon–Sun) Licensed. Cost: $$ to $$$

SEAFOOD RESTAURANTS

Aristos: 151 Broadway, Nedlands. Phone: 08 9386 4243. Open: Lunch & Dinner (Mon–Sun) BYO & Licensed. Cost: $$$

The Bridges: 22 Tydeman Road, North Fremantle. Phone: 08 9430 4433. Open: Lunch (Sun–Fri) Dinner (Mon–Sun) BYO & Licensed. Cost: $$ to $$$

Harry's Seafood Grill: 94 Aberdeen Street, Northbridge. Phone: 08 9328 2822. Open: Lunch (Mon–Fri) Dinner (Mon–Sun) BYO & Licensed. Cost: $$

Jessica's: Hyatt Regency Hotel, 23 Plain Street, Perth. Phone: 08 9325 2511. Open: Lunch (Sun–Fri) Dinner

(Mon–Sun) Licensed. Cost: $$$

Jo Jo's: Nedlands Jetty, Broadway, Nedlands. Phone: 08 9386 8757. Open: Lunch & Dinner (Mon–Sun) Licensed. Cost: $$$

Mead's Fish Gallery: 15 Johnson Parade, Mosman Park. Phone: 08 9383 3388. Open: Lunch & Dinner (Wed–Sun) Licensed. Cost: $$$ to $$$$

The Oyster Bar: 20 Roe Street, Northbridge. Phone: 08 9328 7888. Open: Lunch (Mon–Fri) Dinner (Mon–Sun) BYO & Licensed. Cost: $$ to $$$

Sails Seafood Restaurant: 1st Floor, 47 Mews Road, Fremantle. Phone: 08 9430 5151. Open: Lunch & Dinner (Mon–Sun) BYO & Licensed. Cost: $$ to $$$

Simon's Seafood Restaurant: 73 Francis Street, Northbridge. Phone: 08 9227 9055. Open: Lunch (Mon–Fri) Dinner (Mon–Sun) BYO & Licensed. Cost: $$ to $$$

Surf Club Restaurant & Café: Port Beach Road, North Fremantle. Phone: 08 9430 6866. Open: Breakfast (Café–every day, Restaurant–Sun). Lunch (Mon–Sun) Dinner (Mon–Sun) Licensed. Cost: $$ to $$$

THAI CUISINE

Bangkok Thai: 569 Stirling Highway, Cottesloe. Phone: 08 9384 2908. Open: Lunch (Thurs & Fri) Dinner (Tues–Sun) BYO. Cost: $$ to $$$

Dusit Thai: 249 James Street, Northbridge. Phone: 08 9328 7647. Open: Lunch (Tues–Fri) Dinner (Mon–Sun) BYO. Cost: $$

Erawan: 251 West Coast Highway, Scarborough. Phone: 08 9341 6477. Open: Dinner (Tues–Sun) BYO & Licensed. Cost: $$

Individual Thai Restaurant: 101 Edward Street, East Perth. Phone: 08 9227 6122. Open: Lunch (Wed–Fri) Dinner (Mon–Sun) BYO. Cost: $$

River Kwai Thai: 28A Chapman Road, Bentley. Phone: 08 9356 1378. Open: Dinner (Tues -Sun) BYO. Cost: $$

Sala Thai: 12 Norfolk Street, Fremantle. Phone: 08 9335 7749. Open: Dinner (Mon–Sun) BYO. Cost: $$

Sawadee: 279 Rokeby Road, Subiaco. Phone: 08 9381 8398. Open: Dinner (Mon–Sun) BYO. Cost: $ to $$

Taste of Thai: 324 Stirling Highway, Claremont. Phone: 08 9384 1934. Open: Dinner (Tues–Sun) BYO. Cost: $$

Thai Corner: 893–897 Canning Highway (cnr Sleat Road), Mount Pleasant. Phone: 08 9364 3435. Open: Lunch (Mon–Fri) Dinner (Mon–Sun) BYO & Licensed. Cost: $$

White Elephant: Shop 3, 323 William Street, Northbridge. Phone. 08 9227 5738. Open: Dinner (Mon–Sun) BYO. Cost: $$

VEGETARIAN CUISINE

George Street Café: 73 George Street, East Fremantle. Phone: 08 9339 6352. Open: Lunch & Dinner (Mon–Sun) BYO. Cost: $ to $$

Lotus Vegetarian Restaurant: 2/220 James Street, Northbridge. Phone: 08 9228 2882. Open: Lunch & Dinner (Buffets) (Tues–Sun) BYO. Cost: $$

Peppers Vegetable Eating House: Shop 3, 685 Beaufort Street, Mt. Lawley.

Phone: 08 9371 7331. Open: Dinner
(Mon–Sat) BYO. Cost: $$

VIETNAMESE CUISINE

Hung Long Noodle House: 344
William Street, Perth. Phone:
08 9227 9541. Open: Lunch & Dinner
(Thurs–Tues) BYO. Cost: $

Thach's Quan (TQR): 27 Stirling
Highway, Nedlands. Phone:
08 9386 2889. Open: Dinner
(Mon–Sat) BYO. Cost: $ to $$

Viet Hoa: 349 William Street,
Northbridge. Phone: 08 9328 2127.
Open: Lunch & Dinner (Mon–Sun)
BYO. Cost: $

Viet's Quan: 72 Bennett Street, East
Perth. Phone: 08 9325 8288. Open:
Lunch (Tues–Sat) Dinner (Mon–Sat)
BYO. Cost: $

Vu's Kitchen: 27 Mt. Hawthorn Plaza,
148 Scarborough Beach Road, Mt.
Hawthorn. Phone: 08 9242 2535.
Open: Lunch (Fri) Dinner (Tues–Sun)
BYO. Cost: $

RESTAURANTS WITH RIVER VIEWS

Note: Meads, Jessica's, and Jo Jo's,
which are listed under **Seafood
Restaurants** are also on the riverfront or
have river views.

Ascot Inn (Brasserie): 1–13 Epsom
Avenue, Ascot. Phone: 08 9277 8999.
Open: Lunch & Dinner (Mon–Sun)
Licensed. Cost: $$

Boardwalk: Aquarama Marina, 10
Riverside Road, East Fremantle.
Phone: 08 9339 8022. Open:
Breakfast (Sun) Lunch (Tues–Sun)
Dinner (Tues–Sat) BYO & Licensed.
Cost: $$ to $$$

Boat Shed Café: Coode Street Jetty,
Coode Street, South Perth. Phone:
08 9474 1314. Open: Breakfast,
Lunch & Dinner (Mon–Sun). BYO.
Cost: $$ to $$$

Coco's: 85 The Esplanade, South Perth.
Phone: 08 9474 3030. Open: Lunch &
Dinner (Mon–Sun) Licensed.
Cost: $$ to $$$

Frasers: Fraser Avenue, Kings Park,
Perth. Phone: 08 9481 7100. Open:
Breakfast, Lunch & Dinner (Mon–Sun)
Licensed. Cost: $$$ to $$$$

Hi-Lite 33 (Revolving): St. Martins
Tower, 44 St Georges Terrace, Perth.
Phone: 08 9325 4844. Open: Lunch
(Sun–Fri) Dinner (Mon–Sun)
Licensed. Cost: $$$

Matilda Bay: 3 Hackett Drive, Crawley.
Phone: 08 9386 6355. Open:
Breakfast (Sat & Sun) Lunch & Dinner
(Mon–Sun) Licensed. Cost: $$ to $$$

Moorings Café: Old Perth Port, Barrack
Street Jetty, Perth. Phone:
08 9325 4575. Open: Breakfast,
Lunch & Dinner (Mon–Sun) Licensed.
Cost: $$ to $$$

Plantation Estate: 79 South Perth
Esplanade, South Perth. Phone:
08 9474 5566. Open: Breakfast,
Lunch & Dinner (Mon–Sun) Licensed.
Cost: $$$

Point Walter Café: Point Walter
Reserve, Bicton. Phone:
08 9317 1478. Open: Breakfast (Sat &
Sun) Lunch & Dinner (Mon–Sun but
closed for dinner in winter) BYO.
Cost: $ to $$

Red Herring: 26 Riverside Road, East
Fremantle. Phone: 08 9339 1611.
Open: Breakfast (Sat & Sun), Lunch &
Dinner (Mon–Sun) Licensed.

Cost: $$ to $$$

Stephenies: Upstairs, Steve's Nedlands Park Hotel, The Esplanade, Nedlands. Phone: 08 9386 8351. Open: Lunch (Mon–Fri & Sun.) Dinner (Mon–Sat) Licensed. Cost: $$ to $$$

Shun Fung on the River: Old Perth Port, Barrack Street Jetty, Perth. Phone: 08 9221 1868. Open Lunch & Dinner (Mon–Sun) Licensed. Cost: $$$

Windows: Burswood International Resort Casino, Great Eastern Highway, Burswood. Phone: 08 9362 7551. Open: Lunch (Fri) Dinner (Tues–Sat) Licensed. Cost: $$$ to $$$$

RESTAURANTS WITH OCEAN VIEWS

Note: **The Dragon Palace** (listed under Chinese Cuisine) and **Sails** and the **Surf Club Restaurant & Café** (listed under Seafood) also have ocean views.

Blue Duck: 151 Marine Parade, Cottesloe. Phone: 08 9385 2499. Open: Breakfast, Lunch & Dinner (Mon–Sun) BYO & Licensed. Cost: $$

Cicerello's (Fish & Chips): Fishing Boat Harbour, Fremantle. Phone: 08 9335 1911. Open: Breakfast, Lunch & Dinner (Mon–Sun) Licensed. Cost: $ to $$

Indiana Tea House: 99 Marine Parade, Cottesloe. Phone: 08 9385 5005. Open: Breakfast, Lunch & Dinner (Mon–Sun) Licensed. Cost: $$ to $$$

Joe's Fish Shack: Fishing Boat Harbour, Mews Road, Fremantle. Phone: 08 9336 7161. Open: Lunch & Dinner (Mon–Sun) BYO & Licensed. Cost: $$

Kailis (Fish & Chips): Fishing Boat Harbour, Mews Road, Fremantle. Phone: 08 9335 7755. Open: Lunch & Dinner (Mon–Sun) BYO. Cost: $ to $$

Savannahs: Rendezvous Observation City, The Esplanade, Scarborough. Phone: 08 9340 5753. Open: Dinner (Mon–Sun) Licensed. Cost: $$ to $$$

Jetty's Restaurant: Sorrento Quay, Hillarys Boat Harbour, Sorrento. Phone: 08 9448 9066. Open: Breakfast (Fri, Sat & Sun) Lunch & Dinner (Buffets: Mon–Sun) Licensed Cost: $$ to $$$

Trigg Island Café: 360 West Coast Drive, Trigg. Phone: 08 9447 0077. Open: Breakfast (Sat & Sun) Lunch & Dinner (Mon–Sun) BYO & Licensed. Cost: $$ to $$$

SWAN VALLEY/COUNTRY RESTAURANTS

Dear Friends Garden Restaurant: 100 Benara Road, Caversham. Phone: 08 9279 2815. Open: Lunch (Wed, Fri & Sun) Dinner (Wed–Sun) Licensed. Cost: $$$ to $$$$

Farmhouse: 955 Chittering Road, Lower Chittering. Phone: 08 9571 8227. Open: Lunch (Fri, Sat & Sun) Dinner (Fri & Sat) BYO & Licensed. Cost: $$

Hunter's Lodge: 39 Moor Street, Wungong (near Armadale). Phone: 08 9399 3256. Open: Lunch (Sun) Dinner (Wed–Sat) Licensed. Cost: $$$

Lamonts: Lamonts Winery, Bisdee Road, Millendon. Phone: 08 9296 4485. Open: Lunch (Wed–Sun) Dinner (Sat) Licensed. Cost: $$$

Loose Box: 6825 Great Eastern

Highway, Mundaring. Phone: 08 9295 1787. Open: Lunch (Fri & Sun) Dinner (Wed–Sat) Licensed. Cost: $$$ to $$$$

Sugar Gums: 105 Terrace Road, Guildford. Phone: 08 9377 2262. Open: Lunch (Wed–Fri & Sun) Dinner (Tues–Sat) BYO. Cost: $$$

Verandahs: Araluen Country Club, Country Club Avenue, Roleystone. Phone: 08 9397 9000. Open: Breakfast (Sun) Lunch (Mon–Fri & Sun) Dinner (Wed–Sat) Licensed. Cost: $$ to $$$

MISCELLANEOUS RESTAURANTS AND CAFÉS

Note: The following are restaurants and cafés which do not fit into any of the above categories. In some cases the cuisine is mixed, that is, international or 'east meets west'.

Chez Uchino (French/Japanese): 120 Wellington Street, Mosman Park. Phone: 08 9385 2202. Open: Dinner (Tues–Sat) Licensed. Cost: $$$

Court Wine Bar (Macedonian): 84 Beaufort Street, Perth. Phone: 08 9227 1200. Open: Lunch (Mon–Fri) Dinner (Wed–Sat) Licensed. Cost: $$

44 King Street (International): 44 King Street, Perth. Phone: 08 9321 4476. Open: Breakfast, Lunch & Dinner (Mon–Sun) BYO & Licensed. Cost: $$ to $$$

Friends (International): Hyatt Centre, Terrace Road, East Perth. Phone: 08 9221 0885. Open: Lunch &

Dinner (Tues–Sat) Licensed. Cost: $$$

Gershwins (International): Hyatt Regency, 99 Adelaide Terrace, Perth. Phone: 08 9225 1274. Open: Dinner (Tues–Sat) Licensed. Cost: $$$ to $$$$

The Globe (International): Parmelia Hilton Hotel, Mill Street, Perth. Phone: 08 9322 3622. Open: Breakfast, Lunch & Dinner (Mon–Sun) Licensed. Cost: $$$

Istanbul (Turkish): 19b Essex Street, Fremantle. Phone: 08 9335 6068. Open: Lunch & Dinner (Mon–Sun) BYO. Cost: $ to $$$

Kafeneon (Greek): 31A Hampden Road, Nedlands. Phone. 08 9386 6181. Open: Lunch (Tues–Fri) Dinner (Sat) BYO. Cost: $$

Oriel (International) Open 24 hours: 483 Hay Street, Subiaco. Phone: 08 9382 1886. Open: Breakfast, Lunch & Dinner (Mon–Sun) Licensed. Cost: $$

Origins (International): Sheraton Hotel, 207 Adelaide Terrace, Perth. Phone: 08 9224 7777. Open: Dinner (Mon–Sat) Licensed. Cost: $$$

Toledo Café (Spanish–Tapas): 35 Lake Street, Northbridge. Phone: 08 9227 5282. Open: Lunch & Dinner (Mon–Sun) Licensed. Cost: $$

Witches Cauldron (Reef & Beef): 89 Rokeby Road, Subiaco. Phone: 08 9381 2508. Open: Lunch (Mon–Fri) Dinner (Mon–Sun) Licensed. Cost: $$

ENTERTAINMENT AND NIGHTLIFE

Visitors to Perth and Fremantle will find plenty to do in the evening as there is a wide range of theatres, pubs and clubs to sample. Although, generally speaking, Perth is a safe city by night, as in any large city care needs to be taken. A NightSafe card, available at most pubs and clubs and some police stations, offers information such as the location of train stations, taxi ranks, well-lit car parks and public phone boxes, as well as maps of relevant areas.

The West Australian Ballet and the West Australian Opera are both based at His Majesty's Theatre in Perth. The West Australian Symphony Orchestra (WASO) has its home at the Concert Hall, but also performs at a variety of venues. The Perth Theatre Trust produces plays at venues such as His Majesty's Theatre, the Playhouse and the Subiaco Theatre Centre. There are also many other troupes and companies which provide a wide range of different entertainment at Perth's numerous theatres.

The Festival of Perth welcomes a variety of entertainers from around the world. It provides a smorgasbord of entertainment ranging through every imaginable interpretation of theatre, dance, music and film, at venues throughout the metropolitan area and outdoor concerts as far afield as Margaret River's famous Leeuwin Estate Winery. The Festival is held annually from mid-February to mid-March.

The Film Festival, screened at the unique open air Somerville Theatre at the University of Western Australia, runs from the beginning of December until the end of March.

In addition, there is an ever-increasing range of cinemas, nightclubs and pubs to visit, and a casino which operates 24 hours a day. Artists of international renown perform in Perth on a frequent basis and there is a constantly expanding entertainment industry.

The *West Australian* newspaper has a comprehensive daily listing of cinemas and live entertainment. Several free booklets, such as the *West Coast Visitors' Guide, What's On in Perth and Fremantle,*

Your Guide to Perth and Fremantle and *Hello Perth* advertise events in Perth. They are available at the Western Australian Tourist Centre, in hotels, at airports and also in many shops and tourist venues.

BOOKING SERVICES (THEATRE, SPORTS AND OTHER EVENTS)

BOCS. Phone: 08 9484 1133 or 1800 193 300 (for calls from outside the Metropolitan area). Tickets for theatres, the Concert Hall, some rock concerts (but not at the Entertainment Centre), the Hopman Cup (tennis), all University Theatres, including tickets for the Somerville Auditorium (outdoor cinema), and the Sunset Cinemas in Kings Park. BOCS produce a monthly pamphlet called *What's on BOCS* with a schedule of the month's entertainment, which can be booked by them and locations of BOCS ticket offices.

Red Tickets. Phone: 08 9484 1222; 1902 291 502 (information line); or 1800 199 991 (for calls from outside the Metropolitan area). Tickets for events at the Entertainment Centre, sporting events and live bands at some of the nightclubs.

CINEMAS

Cinema complexes abound in and around Perth, especially in some of the bigger shopping centres. Consult the *Yellow Pages*, or the *West Australian* newspaper for a guide to current films and locations. Most cinemas have half price days, often Tuesday.

FILM CLASSIFICATIONS

G: Suitable for all ages

PG: Parental guidance recommended

M: Mature—recommended for 15 years and over

MA: Restricted to 15 years and over

R: Restricted to 18 years and over.

Some cinema locations are:

PERTH

Greater Union Cinecentre: cnr Murray and Barrack Streets, Perth. Phone: 08 9325 2844.

Hoyts Centre: St. Martins Arcade, Perth. Phone: 08 9325 4992.

Hoyts Cinema City: 580 Hay Street, Perth. Phone: 08 9325 2377.

Piccadilly Cinema Centre: 700 Hay Street, Perth. Phone: 08 9322 3577.

FREMANTLE

Essex Street Cinema: Essex Street, Fremantle. Phone: 08 9430 5999.

Queensgate Cinema: 6 William Street, Fremantle. Phone: 08 9430 6988.

Port Cinema: 86 Adelaide Terrace, Fremantle. Phone: 08 9335 1839.

CINEMAS OF SPECIAL INTEREST

Megaplex (Greater Union) Innaloo: cnr Scarborough Beach Road and Liege Street, Innaloo. Phone: 08 9446 8222, or 24 hour movie information line, 08 9244 3000. This huge cinema complex offers 16 screens and 4200 seats.

Omni Theatre: City West, Railway Parade, West Perth. Phone: 08 9481 6481. The Omni Theatre is one of only a handful of these unique domed-screen cinemas, in the world. It has the largest screen in Australia (10 times larger than conventional screens). Special Omnimax films and conventional movies are projected onto the huge domed-ceiling (screen). The dome is also used as a planetarium, but generally only for school groups. The Omni Theatre is in the same complex as Scitech Discovery Centre. See Scitech, Chapter 8: Attractions, page 51.

DRIVE-IN CINEMAS

Galaxy Drive-in Theatre: Lot 26, Goollelal Drive, Kingsley. Phone: 08 9409 9664.

OUTDOOR CINEMAS

Outdoor cinemas only operate during the summer months (usually from the beginning of December to the end of March), and are in delightful settings and offer some unusual films. Seating is often in deckchairs, so it is advisable to take cushions with you. Many people take their own picnic hamper and a rug to sit on. It can get chilly after dark so take a jacket.

Some venues are:

Camelot Outdoor Picture Garden: 16 Lochee Street, Mosman Park. Phone: 08 9385 3827. There is a licensed bar with refreshments for sale.

Luna Cinemas: 155 Oxford Street, Leederville. Phone: 08 9444 4056. Includes both outdoor and indoor cinemas, but bring your own refreshments for outdoors.

Somerville Auditorium: University of Western Australia. Phone: 08 9380 2691. Offers deckchair seating in a picturesque setting amongst the pine trees. There is a licensed bar and kiosk, but you can also take your own

food and drinks. Locals often take gourmet picnic hampers and bottles of wine to consume before the films starts. Festival of Perth films are shown and queues for popular movies can be long, so arrive early to claim your deckchair and get a good picnic spot. Alternatively pre-book your entry ticket by phoning BOCS on 08 9484 1133 or 1800 193 300 and avoid the queue.

Sunset Cinemas: Kings Park. Phone: 08 9430 9714.

ENTERTAINMENT VENUES

Major indoor concert venues and large capacity venues are:

Burswood Dome: Great Eastern Highway, Burswood. Phone: 08 9484 7000. This is a huge indoor entertainment centre which has staged concerts by artists such as Mick Jagger and Mariah Carey. There are also periodical exhibitions (for example Auto Expo), and the Hopman Cup Tennis tournament is played here every January.

Burswood Resort Casino: Great Eastern Highway, Burswood. Phone: 08 9362 7777. The Casino operates 24 hours a day, has 130 gaming tables, 1110 gaming machines and three private rooms for high rollers. Games played include baccarat, blackjack, craps, keno, mini dice, money wheel, roulette and Two-Up (a unique Australian game involving throwing two coins into the air). Dress standards apply: no jeans may be worn in the Casino after 8.00 pm, and shorts are only acceptable during the day. The Cabaret Lounge has free entertainment most nights and there are bars, restaurants, a five-star luxury hotel, beautiful gardens and a challenging 18 hole golf course.

Perth Entertainment Centre: Wellington Street, Perth. Phone: 08 9322 4766 or for bookings phone Red Tickets on 08 9484 1222. This is Perth's largest entertainment venue seating up to 8000 people. Many of the world's premier entertainers and best-known rock groups perform here. The Perth Wildcats Basketball team is based at the Entertainment Centre. From time to time there are family concerts, productions on ice, musicals, circuses and expos.

Perth Concert Hall: 5 St Georges Terrace, Perth. Phone: 08 9231 9900 or ring BOCS on 08 9484 1133. This is the home of the WA Symphony Orchestra, but it also stages concerts by visiting performers from overseas.

THEATRES

Most theatre tickets can be booked through BOCS. See Booking Services, Chapter 5: Entertainment and Nightlife, page 31.

Belvoir Valley Amphitheatre (outdoor theatre): 1155 Great Northern Highway, Upper Swan. Phone: 08 9296 1817.

Burswood Show Room (theatre or cabaret): Burswood Resort, Great Eastern Highway, Burswood. Phone: 08 9484 7000.

Deckchair Theatre Inc: Victoria Hall, 179 High Street, Fremantle. Phone: 08 9430 4771.

Dolphin Theatre (small conventional theatre): University of Western Australia. Phone: 08 9380 2691.

Effie Crump Theatre (intimate theatre): cnr Beaufort and Brisbane Streets, Northbridge (above the Old Brisbane Hotel). Phone: 08 9227 7226.

Garrick Theatre: 16 Meadow Street, Guildford. Phone: 08 9377 3358.

Hayman Theatre Co: Curtin University, Kent Street, Bentley. Phone: 08 9266 7026.

His Majesty's Theatre: 825 Hay Street, Perth. Phone: 08 9322 2929. Perth's original and best-known theatre. A lovely Edwardian building, originally opened in 1904, and beautifully restored. The WA Opera Company and the WA Ballet perform here.

Hole in the Wall: 267 William Street, Northbridge. Phone: 08 9328 1130.

Parkerville Amphitheatre (outdoors): 1745 Falls Road, Hovea. Phone: 08 9295 4269.

Patch Theatre: Suite 30, 443 Albany Highway, Victoria Park. Phone: 08 9362 4399. Specialises in children's theatre, especially pantomimes.

Playhouse Theatre: 3 Pier Street, Perth. Phone: 08 9325 3344. Home of the Perth Theatre Company, this theatre seats 427 people and is situated in central Perth.

Quarry Amphitheatre (outdoors): Oceanic Drive, City Beach. Phone: 08 9385 7144. Built around an abandoned limestone quarry, this outdoor theatre provides a venue for drama, ballet and concerts during the summer.

Regal Theatre: 474 Hay Street, Subiaco. Phone: 08 9381 5522. Former art deco cinema converted to a theatre.

Spare Parts Puppet Theatre: 1 Short Street, Fremantle. Phone: 08 9335 5044. Mainly for children, families and school groups.

Subiaco Theatre Centre: 180 Hamersley Road, Subiaco. Phone: 08 9382 3385. There are two indoor stages and an outdoor amphitheatre. The Barking Gekko Theatre Company is based here.

Tivoli Theatre: cnr Canning Beach and Kintail Roads, Applecross. Phone: 08 9364 5463.

University of Western Australia: Stirling Highway, Nedlands. Phone: 08 9380 2691 or 08 9380 2432. The University is home to three theatres, The New Fortune, The Octagon and The Dolphin.

Yirra Yaakin Aboriginal Theatre: 65 Murray Street, Perth. Phone: 08 9202 1966. Performances here are written, produced and acted solely by Aboriginal people.

THEATRE RESTAURANTS

Blarney Castle: cnr Newcastle and Stirling Streets, Perth. Phone: 08 9328 7996. Irish music and comedy with audience participation.

Civic Theatre Restaurant: 380 Beaufort Street, Perth. Phone: 08 9328 1455. Usually variety shows, for example, singing, dancing and comedy. Performances are on Thursday, Friday and Saturday evenings.

OTHER NIGHTLIFE

Many areas in Perth come alive at night, but none more so than Northbridge, across the railway line from the city centre, and within easy walking distance. Footbridges are at the Wellington Street Bus Station, at Perth Train Station, and the Entertainment Centre. This last one has a ramp.

A stroll around the square formed by William Street, Aberdeen Street, Lake Street and James Street will give a taste of the bustling crowds and cosmopolitan atmosphere which make Northbridge a favourite after-dark playground. It abounds with restaurants, cafés, food halls, pubs and nightclubs. Almost every cuisine from Asia can be sampled here, some at incredibly low prices: $5.00 or $6.00 for a main meal. However, there are also many European restaurants, especially Italian, and restaurants which specialise in local seafood. Perth's Chinatown is situated in Northbridge, between James and Roe streets, but many more Asian restaurants line William Street, from Brisbane to Roe streets.

Since the Americas Cup, Fremantle offers some beautifully renovated pubs, a cappuccino strip in South Terrace, and restaurants reflecting a multitude of nationalities. There are a particularly large number of Italian restaurants, many of which include the abundant fresh seafood from Fisherman's Harbour on their menus. Fremantle also boasts nightclubs, theatres and cinemas. You can travel by train, from Perth Train Station to Fremantle, in 30 minutes. At night, trains run at half hourly intervals. Every night the last train from Fremantle to Perth departs at midnight, except on Sunday when it leaves at 11.30 pm.

Oxford Street, Leederville, is popular for restaurants and pavement cafés, particularly between Vincent and Aberdeen streets. Asian and Italian restaurants are well represented here and parking is less of a problem than in Northbridge. There are also cinemas and a pub.

Five kilometres west of the city centre lies one of Perth's older suburbs, Subiaco, with its restored colonial buildings such as the Subiaco Hotel, and the art deco Regal Theatre. Its wide variety of shops, restaurants, pubs and nightclubs and easy accessibility from the city, by road and rail, make it a very popular place to visit by day or night.

A detailed list of restaurants is given in Chapter 4: Restaurants and Cafés, page 21.

A sample of pubs and nightclubs in the metropolitan area and Fremantle is listed below, but there are pubs in almost every suburb. There is a free weekly magazine called X-press, available at bottle shops, cafés, fashion shops, record shops. This serves as a guide to live music and night club gigs.

NIGHTCLUBS

The list that follows is merely a selection of the numerous nightclubs in Northbridge, Perth City, Fremantle and the suburbs.

Bronsons: 49 Boas Avenue, Joondalup. Phone: 08 9300 3733.

Club A: The Esplanade, Scarborough (underneath the Rendezvous Observation City). Phone: 08 9340 5652.

Club Bayview: 20 St. Quentin's Avenue, Claremont. Phone: 08 9385 1331. Small, upmarket and trendy. Expect to queue after midnight.

Connections: 81 James Street, Northbridge. Phone: 08 9328 1870. Perth's best-known gay and lesbian nightclub.

Dual Control DC: 105 Francis Street, Northbridge. Phone: 08 9227 7950. Gay and lesbian bar, but all welcome.

Excapade: 187 Stirling Street, Perth. Phone: 08 9227 8200.

Fly By Nite Club: Parry Street, Fremantle. Phone: 08 9430 5976. Live blues, jazz and rock (smoke free).

Frostbites: Shafto Lane, 397 Murray Street, Perth. Phone: 08 9321 3258. Novelty bar specialising in frozen drinks. Great in summer.

Go Club: 80 High Street, Fremantle. Phone: 08 9335 3933.

Gobbles: 613 Wellington Street, Perth. Phone: 08 9322 1221.

Greenwich Bar: basement, His Majesty's Theatre, Hay Street, Perth. Phone: 08 9321 5324.

Hip-E-Club: 663 Newcastle Street, Leederville. Phone: 08 9227 8899. Popular with travellers and surfies. Plays 60s and 70s music.

The Jackal: 230 William Street, Northbridge. Phone: 08 9328 2885.

Kazbah: 298 Hay Street, Subiaco. Phone: 08 9380 4470.

Krush: 135A James Street, Northbridge. Phone: 08 9328 9808.

Metropolis Concert Club:
- 58 South Terrace, Fremantle. Phone: 08 9336 1880 (live music).
- 146 Roe Street, Northbridge. Phone: 08 9228 0500. Biggest nightclub in Perth. Three storeys, live entertainment, very popular).

O² Bar and Club: 139 James Street, Northbridge. Phone: 08 9328 7447. Features both live entertainment and DJs.

Post Office: cnr Aberdeen and Parker Streets, Northbridge. Phone:

08 9228 0077. Live bands and entertainment.

Red Sea: 83 Rokeby Road, Subiaco. Phone: 08 9382 2022. Chic lounge bar with an oriental feel.

Redheads: 44 Lake Street, Northbridge. Phone: 08 9228 2888. Beer garden, pool tables and pin ball, and a late night dance bar.

The Church: 69 Lake Street, Northbridge. Phone: 08 9328 1065.

The Clink: 14–16 South Terrace, Fremantle. Phone: 08 9336 1919. Popular with mature clientele.

PUBS AND BARS

The list below is only a sample of the many pubs and bars in Perth and Fremantle.

Albion Hotel (with Ogdens Bar and Grill): 535 Stirling Highway, Cottesloe. Phone: 08 9384 0021. Popular with all ages, including family groups. Cook your own steak at Ogdens Grill.

Brass Monkey: cnr William and James Streets, Northbridge. Phone: 08 9227 9596. Bar and brasserie. Boutique beers on tap. Good meals, central location and live music.

The Bog: 361 Newcastle Street, Northbridge. Phone: 08 9228 0900. Irish pub selling a wide variety of beers including 11 on tap. Irish music most nights and dancers occasionally.

Black Tom's Bar: 222 Hay Street, Subiaco. Phone: 08 9380 0878. Popular for after-work or pre-show drinks.

Breakwater Tavern: Southside Drive, Sorrento Quay, Hillarys Boat Harbour. Phone: 08 9448 9055. On the boardwalk at Sorrento Quay.

Bridie O'Reilly's: 328 Barker Road, Subiaco. Phone: 08 9381 8400. An Irish pub with 23 beers on tap. Live Irish music on some nights.

Brooklyn Tavern: 161 James Street, Northbridge. Phone: 08 9328 7200. Very trendy and particularly popular on Friday evenings with the business crowd. New York warehouse theme.

Captain Stirling Hotel: 80 Stirling Highway, Nedlands. Phone: 08 9386 2200. Two bars, one sporting, one formal. Popular with the over 30s on Friday nights. Good meals available.

CBD Restaurant and Bar (in Rydges Hotel): 815 Hay Street, Perth. Phone: 08 9263 1859. This restaurant converts to a trendy pub for city workers on Friday nights.

Clancy's Fish Pub: 51 Cantonment Street, Fremantle. Phone: 08 9335 1351. Draught beers and fish and chips every day of the week.

The Como: 241 Canning Highway, South Perth. Phone: 08 9367 6666. The bar offers boutique beers and an extensive wine list. There is a brasserie and courtyard.

Cottesloe Beach Hotel: 104 Marine Parade, Cottesloe. Phone: 08 9383 1100. Well known for its Sunday session. Overlooks Cottesloe Beach and Rottnest Island. Has a beer garden, pool tables and a fully licensed café.

The Court Hotel: 50 Beaufort Street, Northbridge. Phone: 08 9328 5292. This gay hotel offers live music at weekends, a Sunday beer garden and DJs every night.

Darling Range Brewing Co: Broadway Fair Shopping Centre, Broadway,

Nedlands. Phone: 08 9386 5147. Recently refurbished and selling boutique beers. Family atmosphere.

Elephant and Wheelbarrow: 53 Lake Street, Northbridge. Phone: 08 9228 4433. An extremely popular British pub offering traditional British food, live entertainment and drinks (including 27 beers on tap).

Fenians Pub: 221 Adelaide Terrace, Perth. Phone: 08 9221 1200. An Irish pub in the heart of Perth offering live entertainment, beers on tap and a beer garden.

Fremantle Hotel: cnr High and Cliff Streets, Fremantle. Phone: 08 9430 4300. Mainstream jazz is played here every Sunday. There is a Jazz Hotline on 08 9357 2807 giving information about who is playing at this hotel and also at the Hyde Park Hotel (see below).

Hyde Park Hotel: 331 Bulwer Street, Northbridge. Phone: 08 9328 6166. Jazz evenings on Monday and Tuesday, and occasional lunchtime jazz concerts.

Inglewood Hotel: 803 Beaufort Street, Inglewood. Phone: 08 9370 5511. Good food and live entertainment in attractive surroundings.   .

Lawleys: 639 Beaufort Street, Mount Lawley. Phone: 08 9328 6200. Eight beers on tap. Boutique beers available.

Leederville Hotel: 742 Newcastle Street, Leederville. Phone: 08 9444 8388. Has five bars, a beer garden and live entertainment most nights. Half-a-dozen beers on tap. Very busy on Wednesday nights and Sunday sessions.

Left Bank Bar and Café: 15 Riverside Road, East Fremantle. Phone:

08 9319 1315. Situated on the banks of the Swan River with large outdoor seating area. Popular Sunday session. Good food available.

The Lookout (in Rendezvous Observation City): The Esplanade, Scarborough. Phone: 08 9340 5738. Popular pub overlooking Scarborough Beach. Free live entertainment Thursday to Sunday.

Moon and Sixpence (next to the Wentworth Plaza Hotel): 300 Murray Street, Perth. Phone: 08 9481 0727. English style pub with all the English ales, and pub food, in the heart of the city.

Newport Hotel: 2 South Terrace, Fremantle. Phone: 08 9335 2428. In the main street of Fremantle, this colonial style hotel has live bands Wednesday to Sunday.

Norfolk Hotel: 47 South Terrace, Fremantle. Phone: 08 9335 5405. Nine beers on tap. Popular all year round but particularly on warm summer evenings. Try to get an outdoor table.

Ocean Beach Hotel (OBH): Marine Parade, Cottesloe. Phone: 08 9384 2555. Has magnificent ocean views. This hotel is famous for its Sunday Session, particularly in the summer. People drift in from lunchtime and it closes at 9.00 pm.

Paddington Ale House: 141 Scarborough Beach Road, Mount Hawthorn. Phone: 08 9242 3077. Sixteen beers on tap and sells 61 international beers.

Paddy Hannan's Irish Pub: Burswood International Resort Casino, Great Eastern Highway, Burswood. Phone:

08 9362 7777. Irish pub with
traditional food, beers and live
entertainment on Friday, Saturday and
Sunday evenings.

Phillimore's: cnr Phillimore and Mouat
Streets, Fremantle. Phone:
08 9335 9596. Beer garden, bar and
restaurant serving a good range of
meals. Live jazz Sunday evenings.

Queens Tavern: 520 Beaufort Street,
Highgate. Phone: 08 9328 7267.
Boutique beers and great meals
available in very pleasant
surroundings.

Raffles: Kintail Road, Applecross (at
Canning Bridge). Phone:
08 9364 7400. Live rock and roll
music every night except Monday.

Rigbys Bar and Bistro: rear 221 St
Georges Terrace, Perth. Phone:
08 9324 1196. Irish pub catering for
the business/city crowd. Free sausages
on Friday night!

Red Rock Hotel: cnr Bay View Terrace
and Gugeri Streets, Claremont.
Phone: 08 9384 0977. Live music
Thursday, Friday (Jazz Club),
Saturday and Sunday nights. A place
to be seen!

Rose and Crown: 105 Swan Street,
Guildford. Phone: 08 9279 8444.
Built in 1841, this is the oldest trading
hotel in WA. There are a couple of
bars and a beer garden and good food
is available throughout the day.
Though they sell a wide range of
other beers, their Inchant Brewery
produces four of their own brews.

Rosie O'Grady's:
- 203 James Street, Northbridge.
Phone: 08 9328 1488.
- 23 William Street, Fremantle.
Phone: 08 9335 1645.
- 71 Canning Highway, South Perth.
Phone: 08 9474 1964.

The three Irish pubs above offer
traditional Irish beer, music and food.

Sail & Anchor Pub Brewery: 64 South
Terrace, Fremantle. Phone:
08 9335 8433. Between 12 and 15
beers, five of which are brewed on the
premises. Situated in the heart of
Fremantle in a beautiful old heritage
listed building, the pub has several
bars, a beer garden and a bottle shop.
You can ask to tour the brewery.

Subiaco Hotel: 465 Hay Street,
Subiaco. Phone: 08 9381 3069. This
colonial style hotel has about 10 beers
on tap, a popular restaurant, and live
music on Saturday nights.

Steves (Nedlands Park Hotel): 171
Broadway, Nedlands. Phone:
08 9386 3336. Situated by the river
close to the University of Western
Australia, popular with University
students (and ex University students).
The beer gardens have river views and
good food is available.

Swanbourne Hotel: 141 Claremont
Crescent, Swanbourne. Phone:
08 9384 2733. Live bands regularly.
Pool and indoor basketball.

Universal Bar and Grill: 221 William
Street, Northbridge. Phone:
08 9227 6771. Live bands.

CHAPTER 6

MUSEUMS

Perth and Fremantle have over 20 museums. Those who are interested in Aboriginal culture, early shipwrecks along the Western Australian coast, the Royal Flying Doctor service, lifestyles of the early settlers and other aspects of Western Australia's history, will not be disappointed. Planes, trains and automobiles have museums dedicated to them and Perth has a law museum, one of only two found in the world.

The Western Australian Museum, which is centrally located close to Perth Train Station, is the largest museum and has a wide variety of exhibits. Others are either in Fremantle or the suburbs and can be easily accessed by public transport.

MUSEUMS INCLUDE:

Army Museum of Western Australia: Artillery Barracks, Burt Street, Fremantle. Phone: 08 9335 2077. Open Saturday and Sunday 12.30 pm to 4.30 pm. Cost: adults $3.00, children $1.00. There is an Education Centre showing old newsreels, a display of military activity from the founding of the Swan Colony to the Boer War, sections on World Wars One and Two, and a Prisoner of War Gallery.

Aviation Museum: Bullcreek Drive, Bullcreek. Phone: 08 9311 4470. Open daily 10.00 am to 4.00 pm. Closed Good Friday and Christmas Day. Cost: adults $6.00, children

$2.50, concession $4.00. There are 28 planes, including a Spitfire, Tiger Moth and a Lancaster Bomber, on display in two large hangars. Also other aviation exhibits including engines and model planes.

Berndt Museum of Anthropology: Social Sciences Building, University of Western Australia, Hackett Drive Entrance No 1, Crawley. Phone: 08 9380 2854. Open Monday and Wednesday 2.00 pm to 4.30 pm, Friday 10.00 am to 2.00 pm. Closed from about 10th December to 26th January. Admission free. Exhibits are about early Aboriginal life, traditional and contemporary Aboriginal art and artefacts, and also items from Papua New Guinea and Asia.

Claremont Museum: 66 Victoria Avenue, Claremont. Phone: 08 9386 3352. Open Monday to Thursday 10.00 am to 4.00 pm and Sunday 1.00 pm to 4.00 pm. Cost: adults $2.00, concession $1.00. Local history museum with exhibits on early

Claremont businesses, commerce and local government. It also has an 1860's school room, a display of kitchens and kitchen utensils and a washhouse.

Francis Burt Law Education Centre: 33 Barrack Street, Perth. Phone: 08 9325 4787. Located in the Supreme Court Gardens. Open Monday to Friday 10.00 am to 2.30 pm. Admission is free. The Museum is in the Old Courthouse (one of the oldest buildings in Perth) and is one of only two Law Museums in the world. Displays feature the history of law in Western Australia including regalia, books, documents, a noose and many other artefacts. Local schools occasionally use the premises to run mock trials.

Fremantle History Museum (Fremantle Arts Centre): cnr Ord and Finnerty Streets, Fremantle. Phone: 08 9430 7966. Open Sunday to Friday 10.30 am to 4.30 pm, Saturday and Anzac Day 1.00 pm to 5.00 pm. Closed Christmas and Boxing days and Good Friday. Admission by donation. This Museum is housed in a magnificent convict built building which was the colony's first lunatic asylum. Displays include 'Foundations of Fremantle', describing the founding of the Swan River colony; and 'A New Australia' about post-war migration to Western Australia. There are also changing community exhibitions and travelling exhibitions from elsewhere in Australia. The Fremantle Arts Centre is housed in the same building and there are galleries, a courtyard café, bookshop and craft shop.

Geological Museum: University of Western Australia, Stirling Highway, Nedlands. Phone: 08 9380 2681. Open 10.00 am. to 4.30 pm. Monday to Friday, 2.00 pm. to 5.00 pm. on Sunday. Admission is free. Display of rocks, minerals and fossils, and exhibits on how earthquakes and volcanoes occur.

Historic Boats Museum: B Shed, Victoria Quay, Fremantle. Phone: 08 9430 4680. Open Monday to Friday 10.00 am to 3.00 pm, Saturday, Sunday and Public Holidays 11.00 am to 4.00 pm. Closed Good Friday and Christmas Day. This is a sub-branch of the Western Australian Maritime Museum and houses old vessels, such as the *Lady Forrest* (Western Australia's first pilot boat), fishing dinghies and yachts, including Jon Sanders' (solo circumnavigation of the world) yachts *Parry Endeavour* and *Perie Banou*. There are also model boats, a hands-on area where kids can climb the ratlines, and Australia's largest collection of marine engines.

It's a Small World: 12 Parliament Place, West Perth. Phone: 08 9322 2020. Open Sunday to Friday 10.00 am to 5.00 pm, Saturday 2.00 pm to 5.00 pm. Cost: adults $5.00, children and pensioners $4.00, family $16.00 (two adults/two children). Museum devoted to toys, miniatures and animated displays of nursery rhymes and children's stories, some of which are interactive. Also has a model railway which children can operate.

Kalamunda History Village: 56 Railway Road, Kalamunda. Phone: 08 9293 1371. Open Monday to

Thursday and Saturday 10.00 am to 3.00 pm and Sunday 1.30 pm to 4.30 pm. Cost: adults $3.00, children $1.00, seniors $2.00. Western Australia's largest folk museum. Re-live the early days in Kalamunda by visiting genuine original Kalamunda buildings: post office, school house and a couple of cottages. These have been rebuilt and furnished to reflect the pioneer days.

Mineral Museum of Western Australia: 100 Plain Street, Perth. Phone: 08 9222 3333. Open Monday to Friday 8.30 am to 4.30 pm. Admission is free. Display of mainly Western Australian rocks and minerals such as gold, iron-ore and manganese.

Museum of Childhood: Edith Cowan University, Bay Road, Claremont. Phone: 08 9442 1373. Open Sunday and Tuesday to Friday 10.00 am to 4.00 pm. Closed mid-December to mid-January and Public Holidays. Australia's most comprehensive collection of historical childhood items, including dolls, toys and games. There are many hands-on exhibits and displays which depict an Australian childhood through the years.

Museum of Western Australian Sport: Challenge Stadium, Stephenson Avenue, Mt Claremont. Phone: 08 9387 8542. Entrance is free. This is a small, changing exhibition of sportsmen and women, their equipment, clothing and prizes including medals. Over 40 different sports are represented.

The O'Connor Museum: Mundaring Weir, Mundaring. Phone: 08 9295 2455. Open weekdays, except Tuesday 10.30 am to 3.00 pm Sunday 12 noon to 5.00 pm. Cost: adults $1.00, children 50 cents. The Museum is named after CY O'Connor, the engineer who, commencing in 1902, built the pipeline which carries water from Mundaring Weir to the Goldfields. You can see the original steam pump, learn about the history of the pipeline and the tragic suicide of CY O'Connor. Information about Mundaring Weir is also available.

Rail Transport Museum and Heritage Train: 136 Railway Parade, Bassendean. Phone: 08 9279 7189. Open Sunday and public holidays 1.00 pm to 5.00 pm. Displays of over 28 old diesel and steam locomotives, and other rolling stock. There are also historic carriages and railway memorabilia.

Samson House: 61 Ellen St, Fremantle. Phone: 08 9335 2553. This historic house, completed in 1900, was built entirely from limestone quarried on site. It is furnished with antiques belonging to the Samson family, one of Fremantle's leading families at that time, and is a good example of a wealthy family home of the era. Open Thursday and Sunday 1.00 pm to 5.00 pm. Cost: $3.00, or for $5.00 you can have a guided tour.

Telecommunications Museum (Wireless Hill): Almondbury Road, Ardross. Phone: 08 9364 7067. Open Saturday and Sunday 2.00 pm to 5.00 pm. Cost: adults $1.50, children 90 cents. A wide range of exhibits showing the history of telecommunications, from

Morse Code to Satellites, and a large collection of radios.

Western Australian Fire Brigade Education Centre and Museum: cnr Irwin and Murray Streets, Perth. Phone: 08 9323 9468. Open Monday to Friday 10.00 am to 3.00 pm. Interesting displays of old firefighting equipment and fire safety.

Western Australian Maritime Museum: Cliff Street, Fremantle. Phone: 08 9431 8444. Open daily 10.30 am to 5.00 pm. Boxing and Anzac days 1.00 pm to 5.00 pm. Closed Christmas Day and Good Friday. Admission by donation. This is a world class maritime exhibition, located in a magnificent convict constructed building. The Museum has a wonderful display of marine archaeology, including artefacts from Australia's oldest shipwreck, *The Trial*. Cannons, coins, bottles, plates, anchors and ships' bells salvaged from many 17th and 18th century Dutch ships wrecked off the Western Australian coast may also be seen in The Dutch Wrecks Gallery. Of special interest is the reconstructed stern section of the Dutch ship, *Batavia*, which was wrecked in 1629.

WA Medical Musuem: Harvey House, Barker Road, Subiaco. Phone: 08 9340 1506. Open Wednesday 10.00 am to 4.00 pm, Sunday 2.00 pm to 4.00 pm. Cost: adults $2.00, children 50 cents. Situated in an historic limestone building. Exhibits show how medicine has changed over the last 100 years. See an old Royal Flying Doctor plane, an iron lung and a range of medical paraphernalia.

Western Australian Museum: Francis Street, Perth. Phone: 08 9427 2700. Open Sunday to Friday 10.30 am to 5.00 pm, Saturday, Boxing and Anzac days 1.00 pm to 5.00 pm. Closed Christmas Day and Good Friday. Admission by donation. Perth's largest museum covering a wide range of exhibits ranging from early Aboriginal life to the arrival of the British, including an early settler's cottage and Perth's first gaol, built in 1856. There is also a marine gallery housing a complete Blue Whale skeleton, 24 metres long, and many other examples of marine life. In addition, you can visit galleries displaying birds, butterflies, dinosaurs and vintage cars. There is also an exhibition of meteorites which have been found in the Western Australian outback, the biggest of which weighs 11 tonnes. A Museum Shop and Coffee Shop are on the premises, but for a wider selection of refreshments, Northbridge is nearby.

World of Energy: 12 Parry Street, Fremantle. Phone: 08 9430 5655.Open Monday to Friday 9.00 am to 5.00 pm, Saturday, Sunday and public holidays 1.00 pm to 5.00 pm. Closed Christmas Day and Good Friday. Cost: adults $2.00, children $1.00. This is an up-to-date interactive information centre devoted to the State's energy industry, past, present and future. Students of all ages can learn about energy related matters such as how electricity is generated, what is a Tesla Coil, a Jacob's Ladder, a Van de Graaf Generator and much more.

CHAPTER 7

GALLERIES

Perth is well endowed with art galleries exhibiting a wide range of works by local, Eastern States and overseas artists. There are small, intimate galleries, as well as the large Art Gallery of Western Australia which is centrally situated close to Perth Train Station. Many galleries can be found in suburbs such as Claremont, Subiaco and also in Fremantle. You can reach them all relatively easily by public transport.

The Association of Western Australian Art Galleries publishes a quarterly magazine entitled *Gallery Circuit* which is a guide to the exhibitions in all art galleries in Perth. It is available at the galleries. All galleries have special exhibitions during the Festival of Perth (February/March).

A SELECTION OF GALLERIES FOLLOWS:

Accent Art Gallery: 23 Railway Road, Subiaco. Phone: 08 9381 6177. Open Monday to Friday 9.00 am to 5.30 pm, Saturday 9.00 am to 1.00 am and Sunday 2.00 pm to 5.00 pm. Has exhibitions of contemporary mixed media, generally by local artists, changing every few months.

Art Gallery of Western Australia: Perth Cultural Centre, James Street Mall, Northbridge. Phone: 08 9492 6600. Open daily 10.00 am to 5.00 pm; Anzac Day 1.00 pm to 5.00 pm; closed Christmas Day and Good Friday. Admission is free except for some special exhibitions. Over 1000 works of art are on display including many fine examples of Western Australian, Australian and International art, Aboriginal art, contemporary art and craft and design. Café available for light meals. Art Gallery shop. Free guided tours are available from Tuesday to Friday, and Sunday, at 1.00 pm.

Artplace: Upstairs, Old Theatre Lane, off 52 Bayview Terrace, Claremont. Phone: 08 9384 6964. Open Tuesday to Saturday 10.00 am to 5.00 pm and Sunday 2.00 pm to 5.00 pm. This gallery exhibits contemporary paintings, drawings, sculptures, photographs, jewellery as well as aboriginal works of art. Closed on public holidays.

Artist in Residence, **Aboriginal Art Gallery**: Fraser Avenue, Kings Park. Phone: 08 9481 7082. Open daily 9.00 am to 5.30 pm. This gallery is situated right underneath the Lookout, on Fraser Avenue. It was developed to enable Western Australian Aboriginal artists to work in a studio environment and to exhibit their art. Traditional and innovative art and artefacts are for sale.

Atwell Gallery: cnr North Lake Road and Canning Highway, Alfred Cove. Phone: 08 9330 2800. Open Monday to Friday 10.00 am to 5.00 pm, Saturday and Sunday 1.00 pm to 5.00 pm. Offers art classes for painting, drawing and sculpture. They hold in-house and external exhibitions, changing every two weeks and covering a wide range of media.

Fremantle Arts Centre: 1 Finnerty Street, Fremantle. Phone: 08 9335 8244. Open daily 10.00 am to 5.00 pm. Admission free. This is one of Western Australia's leading arts organisations with a very diverse cultural programme. There are exhibitions of contemporary visual art and craft; creative arts courses; and free music concerts on Sunday afternoons. The Arts Centre is housed in the same historic building as the Fremantle History Museum. There is also a café, bookshop and craft shop.

Gadfly Gallery: 71A Princess Road, Nedlands. Phone: 08 9386 8369. Open Monday to Friday 11.00 am to 5.00 pm, Saturday and Sunday 2.00 pm to 5.00 pm. Closed Tuesday. This gallery exhibits high quality contemporary art from emerging and experienced Australian and international artists.

Gallerie Dusseldorf: 9 Glyde Street,

Mosman Park. Phone: 08 9384 0890. Open Tuesday to Friday 10.00 am to 4.30 pm and Sunday 2.00 pm to 5.00 pm. Changing exhibitions of contemporary works by Western Australian and Eastern States artists are displayed here.

Gallery East: 94 Stirling Highway, North Fremantle. Phone: 08 9336 6231. Open Tuesday to Saturday 10.00 am to 5.00 pm, Sunday 2.30 pm to 5.00 pm. Exhibits contemporary and traditional oriental art.

Goddard de Fiddes: 31 Malcolm Street, West Perth. Phone: 08 9324 2460. Open Wednesday to Friday 12 noon to 6.00 pm and Saturday 2.00 pm to 5.00 pm. Exhibits contemporary Western Australian, Australian and international art. Exhibitions change every month.

Gomboc Gallery Sculpture Park: 50 James Road, Middle Swan. Phone: 08 9274 3996. Open Wednesday to Sunday 10.00 am to 5.00 pm. Situated in the heart of the wine growing district of the Swan Valley, about 30 minutes drive from the city centre. The Gomboc Gallery is the largest privately owned gallery in WA. There is an on-site bronze foundry and a diverse array of fine art, as well as special monthly exhibitions. A large area is devoted to works by both established and emerging Western Australian artists of all genres.

Greenhill Galleries: 37 King Street, Perth. Phone: 08 9321 2369. Open Monday to Friday 10.00 am to 5.00 pm and Sunday 2.00 pm to 5.00 pm. Works covering all styles and genres, mainly by Western

Australian artists, with some interstate and overseas artists represented.

Indigenart (The Mossenson Gallery): 115 Hay Street, Subiaco. Phone: 08 9388 2899. Open Monday to Saturday 10.00 am to 5.00 pm and by appointment. Exhibits by famous Aboriginal artists include works on canvas, paper and bark as well as sculptures, artefacts and crafts. Works from more than 20 Aboriginal communities are represented here.

Japingka Gallery: 47 High Street, Fremantle. Phone: 08 9335 8265. Open every day. This is one of Australia's leading Aboriginal fine art galleries. It exhibits and sells Aboriginal paintings and a large selection of limited edition prints. It also stocks hand-tufted pure wool rugs, with designs by famous Aboriginal artists including Jimmy Pike, and other quality artefacts.

John Curtin Gallery: Curtin University of Technology, Kent Street, Bentley. Phone: 9266 2259. Open Tuesday to Friday 11.00 am to 6.00 pm, Sunday 2.00 pm to 5.00 pm. Has changing exhibitions focusing on contemporary art of all kinds. Artists from Australia and overseas are represented.

Kulcha: upstairs, 13 South Terrace, Fremantle. Phone: 08 9336 4544. Usually open Monday to Friday 10.00 am to 5.00 pm. This is a multicultural arts centre displaying art as well as musical and stage performances from all over the world.

Lawrence Wilson Art Gallery: University of Western Australia. Phone: 08 9380 3707. Open Tuesday to Friday 11.00 am to 6.00 pm,

Sunday 12 noon to 5.00 pm. Closed Christmas Day to 6th January. Situated next to the sunken garden, it has a permanent exhibition of Australian art, including works by Sydney Nolan, Charles Blackman and Arthur Boyd. There are also regular exhibitions of contemporary art by Western Australian artists. A gift shop and café are also on the premises.

Moores Building: 46 Henry Street, Fremantle. Phone: 08 9335 8366. Open 10.00 am to 5.00 pm daily during exhibitions. Built in the 1860s, the Moores Building is a heritage listed building. The gallery exhibits mainly contemporary art by emerging Western Australian artists.

New Collectables Gallery: cnr George and Duke Streets, East Fremantle. Phone: 08 9339 7165. Open Wednesday to Friday 10.30 am to 5.00 pm, Saturday 11.00 am to 5.00 pm, and Sunday 1.00 pm to 5.00 pm. This gallery features the work of local artists and craftspeople and is housed in an historic old pub.

Perth Galleries: 61 Forrest Street, cnr Railway Road, Subiaco. Phone: 08 9380 9595. Open Monday to Friday 10.00 am to 5.00 pm, Sunday 2.00 pm to 5.00 pm. Closed public holidays. Represents Sotheby's in Western Australia. Displays paintings, ceramics and furniture by established and emerging Australian artists.

Perth Institute of Contemporary Art (PICA): Perth Cultural Centre, 51 James Street, Perth. Phone: 08 9227 6144. Open Tuesday to Sunday 11.00 am to 8.00 pm. Admission free. Promotes contemporary and experimental art by holding exhibitions and workshops on non-traditional media. Meet and talk to the artists.

Stafford Studios: 102 Forrest Street, Cottesloe. Phone: 08 9385 1399. Open Tuesday to Friday 10.00 am to 5.00 pm and Sunday 2.00 pm to 5.00 pm. There are changing monthly exhibitions by local and international artists. Paintings, sculptures, ceramics and silver may be viewed here.

The Photography Gallery of Western Australia: Perth Cultural Centre, 53 James Street, Northbridge. Phone: 08 9227 6620. Open Tuesday to Sunday 1.00 pm to 5.00 pm. A small gallery in the city's cultural complex, next door to PICA. Exhibitions of various styles of photography including landscape, portrait, photojournalism and computer manipulated photography are regularly held here.

CHAPTER 8

ATTRACTIONS

This chapter includes information on Perth and Fremantle's historic buildings and churches, as well as Sorrento Quay/Hillarys Boat Harbour, Fremantle's Fishing Boat Harbour, the Old Perth Port/Barrack Street Jetty, Perth Observatory and Scitech (a science discovery centre). There are of course numerous places to visit which fall into other categories and are therefore described elsewhere in this book.

HISTORIC BUILDINGS

Details of many better known, but by no means all of Perth and Fremantle's earliest buildings, are given in this section. Unfortunately, comparatively few of these remain, after a severe case of 'out with the old and in with the new', in the 1960s.

As the buildings are fairly scattered, the simplest way of seeing them all is to phone the WA Heritage Council, on 08 9221 4177, as they provide *Heritage Trail* brochures which can be picked up from 108 Adelaide Terrace, East Perth, for a minimal charge. Or, they will post brochures to you. These Heritage Trail brochures also cover numerous places of historical interest not only in the metropolitan area and Fremantle, but throughout the State.

Alternatively, guided walks of the city which include early colonial buildings and points of historic interest, are conducted by City Walking Tours, phone: 08 9293 3054. Tours leave from the WA Tourist Centre, Forrest Place, Perth, on Tuesday and Thursday at 9.30 am. Cost: $9.00, or $7.00 concession, for a two-hour tour.

Similarly, Fremantle Historic Walking Tours (phone: 08 9336 1906), offers two different one and a half hour tours, describing the early development of Fremantle, by appointment only. Cost: adults $7.50, concession and groups of four or more $6.00 per person.

HISTORIC BUILDINGS TO VISIT INCLUDE:

Barracks Archway: top of St Georges Terrace (in front of Parliament House), Perth. This is all that is left of the army barracks which were built by convicts for the Pensioner Guards of the British Army in 1863. The accommodation wings of the Barracks were demolished in 1966 amidst much public protest.

Fremantle Prison: 1 The Terrace, Fremantle. Phone: 08 9430 7177. Open daily from 10.00 am to 6.00 pm.

Closed Christmas Day and Good Friday. Tours depart every 30 minutes and take an hour and a quarter. Last tour 5.00 pm. Cost: adults $10.00, concession $8.00, children (6–15) $4.00. Candlelight tours can be booked for Wednesday and Friday at 7.30 pm. Cost: adults $12.00, children (6–15) $6.00. Fremantle Prison was a working maximum security prison from 1855 until November 1991. Knowledgeable guides explain what life in the prison was like, and show the tiny, cold damp cells, concrete exercise yards, punishment cells and gallows. For an eerie experience with special effects the candlelight tour is an outing with a difference.

The Old Mill at the southern end of the Narrows Bridge in Mill Point Road, South Perth. Phone: 08 9367 5788. Open daily 10.00 am to 4.00 pm. This was the first working wind-powered flour mill in the Swan River Colony. Its foundation stone was laid by Governor James Stirling in 1835, but the Mill only operated for some 20 years as wind-powered milling proved unprofitable. Today the Old Mill, with its nearby Miller's Cottage, is a museum depicting life as experienced by the early settlers.

Old Perth Boys' School: 139 St Georges Terrace, Perth. Built between 1852 and 1854, this sandstone Gothic-style building, now owned by the National Trust, was Perth's first boys' school. The building has been restored and now serves as a café.

Perth Mint: 310 Hay Street cnr Hill Street, East Perth. Phone: 08 9421 7277 or 08 9421 7425 (Mint Shop). Easy walking distance from the City centre. Open Monday to Friday 9.00 am to 4.00 pm, Saturday and Sunday 9.00 am to 1.00 pm. Entry is free, however there is a fee to enter the gallery and minting area from where you can watch the gold pouring. Cost: adults $5.00, children $3.00. Established in 1899, Perth Mint is Australia's longest operating Mint and still uses its original 'melting house'. A visit offers many things to see and do, including watching a gold bar being poured, or gold, silver and platinum coins being minted. You can mint your own medallion, and attempt to pick up a 12kg gold bar. There is a reconstructed gold prospector's camp and a comprehensive display of nuggets, coins and gold bars. The Perth Mint Gold Shop sells a wide range of gold jewellery, coins, nuggets and souvenirs, as well as Argyle Diamonds and Broome Pearls.

Roundhouse: 10 Arthur Head, Fremantle. Open daily 9.00 am to 6.00 pm. This is Western Australia's oldest public building, dating back to 1831 when it was the Swan River Colony's first gaol. Aboriginals were also held here prior to transportation to the prison on Rottnest Island. The outer wall has twelve sides and there is a central courtyard. In 1837, the Whalers' Tunnel was constructed underneath the Roundhouse to link High Street to the ocean. At 1.00 pm everyday a gun similar to the famous noon gun in Hong Kong is fired by volunteer guides.

Tranby House: Johnson Road, Maylands. Phone: 08 9272 2630.

Opening times in summer: Tuesday to Saturday 2.00 pm to 5.00 pm, Sunday 11.00 am to 5.00 pm; and winter: Wednesday to Saturday 2.00 pm to 5.00 pm, Sunday 11.00 am to 5.00 pm. Closed for the month of June. Cost: adults $3.00, concessions $2.00, children $1.50. Picturesquely situated on the banks of the Swan River, this is one of the oldest houses in the State. Built for the Hardey family in 1839, it was the first farmhouse built on the Swan River. The furniture is from the period 1830 to 1850, and some of the pieces, such as the brass bed, were brought out from England by the Hardey family. This is a National Trust property and there is a gift shop and tea rooms. Tranby House is frequently visited by river cruises.

Woodbridge House: Ford Street, West Midland. Phone: 08 9274 2432. Open Monday to Saturday (excluding Wednesday) 1.00 pm to 4.00 pm, Sunday and public holidays 11.00 am to 5.00 pm. Not open for the month of July. Cost: adults $3.50, children and concessions $1.50, and family passes (2 adults and up to 4 children under 16) $8.00. This double storey Victorian mansion was built in 1885 and is furnished to reflect the lifestyle of the wealthy at that time. It is owned and maintained by the National Trust and overlooks the Swan River. Cruises to the vineyards frequently call in here.

OTHER COLONIAL BUILDINGS

PERTH: The Old Court House, The Cloisters, The Deanery, Perth Town Hall, Government House, the facade of the Palace Hotel and the Central Government Buildings. His Majesty's Theatre is a magnificent Edwardian theatre and is home to the WA Opera and Ballet.

FREMANTLE: The Esplanade Hotel, Fremantle Fire Station, Old Customs House, Lionel Samson Building and the Fremantle Town Hall. The Fremantle History Museum, The Western Australian Maritime Museum and Samson House are all historic buildings which are described in Chapter 6: Museums, page 39.

OLD CHURCHES/CEMETERIES

All Saints Church: Henry Street, Henley Brook. This is Western Australia's oldest church built in 1841 overlooking the Swan River in the Upper Swan Valley.

Guildford Grammar School Chapel: Terrace Road, Guildford. Phone: 08 9377 9222. You can visit this beautiful chapel, built of Donnybrook stone and consecrated in 1914, on weekdays between 8.00 am and 5.00 pm.

St Georges Cathedral: cnr St Georges Terrace and Cathedral Avenue, Perth. Open weekdays 9.00 am to 5.00 pm. Anglican Cathedral built between 1879 and 1888.

St Marys Cathedral: Centre of Victoria Square, Perth. Open all hours. Roman Catholic Cathedral built by Roman Catholic monks around 1863. Extensions were added to the church in the late 1920s.

St Johns Anglican Church: Kings Square, Adelaide Street, Fremantle. Built between 1879 and 1882.

St Patricks Catholic Church: cnr Adelaide and Parry Streets, Fremantle. First services were held here in 1900 but it has since been extended.

Wesley Church: cnr Hay and William Streets, Perth. Open weekdays 9.00 am to 4.30 pm, Sunday 8.30 am to 12.00 noon and 5.00 pm to 6.00 pm. Built between 1867 and 1870.

Trinity Church Group: 72 St Georges Terrace, Perth. Open weekdays 9.00 am to 5.00 pm. There are two churches on this site. The rear and original church was built in 1865, whilst the front and newer church was opened in 1894.

Pioneer Cemetery: cnr Bronte and Plain Streets, East Perth. As the name suggests, many of the original settlers and colonial pioneers are buried here, including the Colony's first Surveyor General, John Septimus Roe. The first burial took place in 1830, a Gothic-style mortuary chapel was built in 1871 and the last known burial occurred in 1899. On Sunday afternoons from 2.00 pm onwards volunteers from the National Trust are available to take guided tours around the graves and chapel.

OTHER ATTRACTIONS

Fishing Boat Harbour Fremantle: Mews Road, Fremantle. This bustling fishing boat harbour is an ideal place to visit as there are pleasant boardwalks with restaurants overlooking the harbour and ocean. The wide range of food styles available range from McDonalds, pasta, or fish and chips, to a top class Japanese restaurant. Freshly caught seafood is readily available. The Maritime Museum is an easy stroll from here and a number of souvenir shops are close by. See Chapter 6: Museums, page 39.

Old Perth Port/Barrack Street Jetty: Barrack Square, Barrack Street Jetty. Old Perth Port consists of several boatsheds on the Barrack Street Jetty on the Swan River. It is accessible by foot, tram or free bus service from the city centre. You will find restaurants (typical Australian fare and Chinese), kiosks, souvenir shops and booking points for river and Rottnest Island Cruises, which depart from the Jetty.

Other facilities offered from the Barrack Street Jetty include:

The Activity Booking Centre: Phone: 08 9221 1828. This centre is situated on the Jetty, is an excellent source of information and a booking point for a multitude of fun activities covering water, land and air. They also hire bicycles, tandems and pedal cars and can arrange a picnic basket so you can choose your own picnic spot along the river. You can hire snorkelling gear, fishing rods and buy bait, and can book your bikes for Rottnest.

Next to the Old Port is a unique golf driving range. You hit the golf ball from land to a large pontoon in the River. A hole in one will win you a wonderful prize. (See under Golf with a Difference, page 121.)

Travel from the jetty to any riverfront restaurant in a water taxi which you can hire by phoning 08 9221 9191 or 015 478 608, or go to Kiosk No 3. Prices start at $30 for a return trip.

Perth Observatory: Walnut Road, Bickley. Phone: 08 9293 8255. Information Line: 08 9293 8109. Situated 25 kilometres east of the city. Tours run every Sunday at 3.00 pm and last approximately an hour and a half. Cost: adults $6.00, children $4.00. This is Australia's only remaining operational State Observatory and its importance is enhanced by the fact that the Milky Way (the centre of our Galaxy) passes almost directly overhead. There are four major telescopes, but the public viewing area has several more. During summer months, evening viewing sessions of approximately an hour and a half, are held during the first quarter of the moon, roughly two weeks a month, to view the wonders of the southern skies through the telescopes. Cost: adults $12.00, children $8.00 week nights, and adults $15.00 and children $10.00 Friday and Saturday nights. Prior booking for night viewing is essential as these sessions are very popular. There is also a museum on site.

Scitech: City West Centre, cnr Railway Parade and Sutherland Street, West Perth. Phone: 08 9481 5789. Open every day except Christmas Day 10.00 am to 5.00 pm. Cost: adults $11.00, children (three to 15 years) $7.00, family passes $30.00 (two adults, two children), family year membership pass $78.00. This is an award winning hands on science discovery centre, with over 160 interactive displays particularly aimed at children. There are both permanent and changing special exhibitions which explain: how electricity is generated; how parts of the body, like the eyes, heart and lungs function; or how lasers and 3-D imaging work. Discoverland is a special exhibition for children aged three to seven. There is a cafeteria and well-stocked souvenir shop.

Sorrento Quay/Hillarys Boat Harbour West Coast Drive, Hillarys. Phone: 08 9246 3545. This is an appealing marine style village built on boardwalks over the Indian Ocean. On the Quay, there are numerous restaurants and cafés, gift and souvenir shops. Ocean-based activities offered include deep sea fishing, yacht hire, scuba diving, whale watching and a ferry service to Rottnest Island. There are also protected swimming beaches and a leisure park with water slides (see also The Great Escape in Water Parks/Playgrounds in Chapter 15: Activities on the Water, page 107, mini golf, motorcycle tours and sports car hire. Underwater World is located on the western side of Sorrento Quay. See Underwater World in Chapter 14: Wildlife, page 95, for more details. You could easily spend a full day at this diverse and leisurely complex.

CHAPTER 9

SHOPPING AND SOUVENIRS

The main shopping centres, markets and places to buy souvenirs are described in this chapter. Unique Western Australian items for sale include Aboriginal art; opals and pearls; local arts and crafts; bushman-type clothing and hats; as well as T-shirts and stuffed koalas and kangaroos. International travellers can take advantage of the duty free shops both in Perth and Fremantle which sell a wide variety of merchandise.

Shopping hours in Perth and suburbs vary, depending on the area and the kind of shopping. Opening hours generally are:

■ weekdays 9.00 am to 5.30 pm, with late night shopping in the city on Fridays, and in the suburbs on Thursdays, until 9.00 pm;
■ Saturdays 8.30 am to 5.00 pm;
■ Sunday, markets and central city shops are open but hours vary.

Smaller food shops and delicatessens can stay open seven days a week, 12 hours a day, or more if they wish. There are a few 24-hour convenience stores. See Chapter 20: General Information, Shopping hours, page 157.

Central Perth has a large number of shopping malls, some on three levels, as well as three major Department Stores: Myer, Aherns and Target. Perth City's Malls and Arcades map is on page 55.

Suburban shopping centres range from local village type shopping streets to huge air-conditioned shopping complexes.

Market-style shopping is popular, with the Fremantle Markets and the 'Subi' Markets being the best known. However, most of the markets are only open on Fridays and at weekends so check opening hours if you wish to visit one.

In both Perth and Fremantle you can buy duty free goods in the city as well as at the airport. International travellers can take advantage of this facility.

SHOPPING SUGGESTIONS
ABORIGINAL ART
Artist in Residence, Aboriginal Art Gallery: Fraser Avenue, Kings Park, West Perth. Phone: 08 9481 7082. Open daily, 9.00 am to 5.30 pm. This

gallery/shop is situated underneath the Lookout on Fraser Avenue. It sells and exhibits authentic Aboriginal fine art and artefacts and you can often see artists at work.

Bellamy's Aboriginal Art Gallery: 43 High Street, Fremantle. Phone: 08 9430 7439. Open weekdays 10.00 am to 5.30 pm, Saturday 10.00 am to 4.30 pm, Sunday 11.00 am to 4.30 pm. A wide range of arts and artefacts, including paintings, boomerangs and didgeridoos.

Boodja Aboriginal Art and Craft: Fremantle Markets. Phone: 08 9430 4061. Also at E Shed Markets. Phone: 08 9335 6945. For market hours, see more details in the Markets section later in this chapter. Sells paintings, prints, didgeridoos, boomerangs, music sticks, baskets and so on.

Creative Native:
■ 32 King Street, Perth City. Phone: 08 9322 3398.
■ 65 High Street, Fremantle. Phone: 08 9335 6995.
Both showrooms are open daily. Sells quality Aboriginal art and artefacts including didgeridoos, boomerangs, carved emu eggs, pottery, jewellery, T-shirts, hats and scarves.

Gananda:
■ 71 Barrack Street, Perth. Phone: 08 9325 1190.
■ Shop 7 and 8 King Street Art Centre, King Street, Perth. Phone: 08 9226 1221.
A wide range of original aboriginal artefacts, including boomerangs, carved emu eggs, didgeridoos, fabrics and garments.

Indigenart (The Mossenson Gallery): 115 Hay Street, Subiaco, Perth. Phone: 08 9388 2899. Original Aboriginal art works on canvas, paper and bark as well as sculptures, artefacts and crafts.

Japingka Gallery: 47 High Street, Fremantle. Phone: 08 9335 8265. This is one of Australia's leading Aboriginal fine art galleries, with paintings, limited edition prints, and hand-tufted pure wool rugs designed by famous Aboriginal artists.

DUTY FREE SHOPPING

Although Duty Free shopping is available at Perth Airport, there are also Duty Free shops in Perth, Fremantle and Mandurah. At some jewellers, hi-fi and camera shops you may be able to negotiate a tax or duty free purchase on presentation of your airline ticket and passport. International travellers in possession of a valid plane ticket and passport can purchase duty free alcohol and cigarettes two days prior to departure, but bigger items such as cameras and stereos can be bought up to 30 days in advance. However, all duty free items must leave the country. Cigarettes, alcohol and perfume may also be purchased duty free on arrival at Perth International Airport.

Listed below are the main specialist duty free shops:

City International Duty Free:
■ 772 Hay Street, Perth. Phone: 08 9321 7248.
■ 705–707 Hay Street Mall, Perth. Phone: 08 9322 1277.
■ Shop 53, 172 Murray Street, Forrest

Chase, Perth. Phone: 08 9325 2300.

Compass Duty Free: downstairs, 237 Murray Street Mall, Perth. Phone: 08 9321 1433.

Downtown Duty Free:
- 709 Hay Street Mall, Perth. Phone: 08 9321 7882.
- 22 Queen Street, Fremantle. Phone: 08 9335 1382.
- Perth International Airport. Phone: 08 9477 1888.

Gateway Duty Free: Shop: H1/H3 City Arcade, Perth. Phone: 08 9321 4586.

Portside Duty Free: 26A Queen Street, Fremantle. Phone: 08 9335 7538.

JEWELLERY

Allgem Jewellers:
- 653 Hay Street Mall, Perth.
- Shop 28–30 London Court, Perth. Phone: 08 9325 2255.
A large selection of opals, pearls, jewellery and watches.

Artisans of the Sea: The Bank, Corner Marine Terrace and Collie Street, Fremantle. Phone: 08 9336 3633. Displays aspects of the pearling industry, and sells Broome pearls, gifts and pearl jewellery.

Circle of Jewels: Shop 62, Hillarys Boat Harbour, Sorrento Quay, Hillarys. Phone: 08 9246 3880. Specialises in Australian jade (chrysoprase), gemstone watches, and semi-precious gemstones set in sterling silver or solid gold.

Exclusive Gold: Plaza Arcade, off Hay Street Mall, Perth. Phone: 08 9325 8296. Quality Australian and international gold jewellery.

Flora Metallica: Shop 9, Claremont Court, 44 Gugeri Street, Claremont. Phone: 08 9384 9939. Australian native flora encased in gold and fashioned into jewellery.

Gemtec: 39 Barrack Street, Perth. Phone: 08 9325 7144. This company not only mines, cuts and polishes opals, but has its own workshops and produces hand-made designer jewellery. They are closed on Saturdays.

Linneys: 37 Rokeby Road, Subiaco. Phone: 08 9382 4077. An award winning jeweller, specialising in Argyle Diamonds, Broome Pearls and Kalgoorlie gold. The jewellery is designed and crafted on the premises.

Motts: Shop 5/4 Cantonment Street, Fremantle. Phone: 08 9335 1209. Opals and a wide variety of souvenirs.

The Nugget Shop: Shop 6 Atwell Arcade, High Street, Fremantle. Phone: 08 9430 8994. Gold nuggets, iron ore, gemstone jewellery, freshwater pearls and costume jewellery.

Opal Creations: 129 William Street, Perth. Phone: 08 9322 2475. As the name suggests, they specialise in Australian opals and opal jewellery.

Opal Exploration Co: 616 Hay Street, Perth. Phone: 08 9325 2907. A good selection of well priced opal jewellery.

Opal Strike Perth: Shop 22, Carillon Arcade, Murray Street level, Perth. Phone: 08 9324 2882. An extensive range of quality opal jewellery.

Perth Mint: 310 Hay Street, cnr Hill Street, Perth. Phone: 08 9421 7277. As well as being a working Mint and museum, there is also a shop which sells gold in a wide variety of forms,

PERTH CITY'S MALLS AND ARCADES

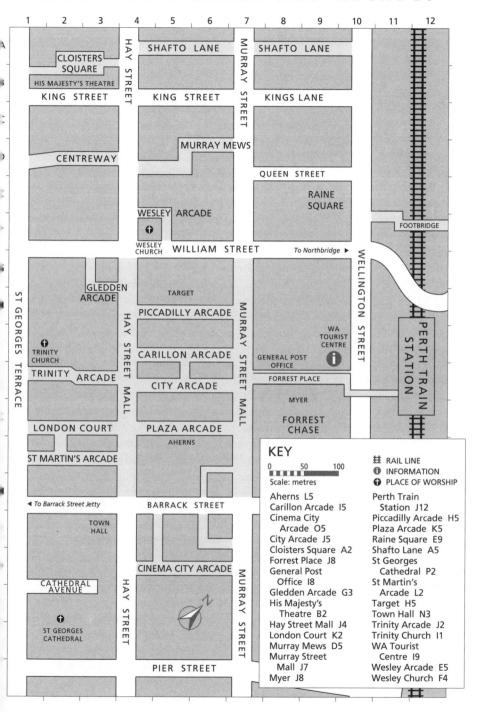

KEY

0   50   100
Scale: metres

⌗ RAIL LINE
ⓘ INFORMATION
✚ PLACE OF WORSHIP

Aherns L5
Carillon Arcade I5
Cinema City
   Arcade O5
City Arcade J5
Cloisters Square A2
Forrest Place J8
General Post
   Office I8
Gledden Arcade G3
His Majesty's
   Theatre B2
Hay Street Mall J4
London Court K2
Murray Mews D5
Murray Street
   Mall J7
Myer J8

Perth Train
   Station J12
Piccadilly Arcade H5
Plaza Arcade K5
Raine Square E9
Shafto Lane A5
St Georges
   Cathedral P2
St Martin's
   Arcade L2
Target H5
Town Hall N3
Trinity Arcade J2
Trinity Church I1
WA Tourist
   Centre I9
Wesley Arcade E5
Wesley Church F4

from nuggets and bars to coins and beautiful jewellery.

Perth Opals and Nuggets: Plaza Arcade, Central Perth. Phone: 08 9325 7086. A large range of Australian opals set in solid gold, or loose stones; Australian and international gold coins; and a selection of platinum and gold jewellery and nuggets.

Quilpie Opals and Gems: City Arcade, off Murray Street Mall, Perth. Phone: 08 9321 8687. A wide range of opals including black and boulder opals as well as diamonds, pearls and gold nuggets.

Rosendorff's Diamond Jewellers: 673 Hay Street Mall, Perth. Phone: 08 9321 4015. Agents for Argyle Diamonds, this jeweller carries an enormous range of loose diamonds of all shapes, sizes and colours, including pink, champagne and cognac. They also have a good selection of Broome Pearls and Australian opals. All come with an international certificate of authenticity.

Swan Diamonds: Shop 4, London Court, Perth. Phone: 08 9325 8166. As the name suggests, this shop specialises in diamond sales, particularly of pink Argyle diamonds and white and champagne diamonds.

MARKETS

Canning Vale Markets: 80 Bannister Road, Canning Vale. Phone: 08 9455 1389. One of Western Australia's largest flea markets, with several hundred stalls. Open Sunday from 7.00 am to 2.00 pm. During the week Canning Vale is Perth's wholesale fruit and vegetable, meat, fish and flower market.

E Shed Markets: Victoria Quay, Fremantle. Phone: 9430 6393. Open Friday, Saturday and Sunday and public holidays. There are over 100 speciality stalls in a restored warehouse, selling gifts, souvenirs, and local arts and crafts. An international food hall serves a variety of Asian and European foods, and at times there is live entertainment.

Fremantle Markets: cnr South Terrace and Henderson Street, Fremantle. Phone: 08 9335 2515. Open Fridays 9.00am to 9.00 pm, Saturdays 9.00 am to 5.00 pm, Sunday and public holidays (when they fall on Monday) 10.00 am to 5.00 pm. Established in 1897, this grand old National Trust classified Victorian building still operates as a bustling weekend market. Over 170 stalls offer just about everything from fruit, vegetables and a wide range of foods, to clothes, shoes, jewellery, Australiana, antiques and much more. There are buskers, and a bar.

Galleria Art and Craft Markets: Art Gallery and Museum Concourse, Perth Cultural Centre, Northbridge. Phone: 08 9310 2159. Open weekends 9.00 am to 5.00 pm. Numerous stalls selling art and craft, souvenirs and clothes in the heart of Perth.

Gosnells Railway Markets: cnr Albany Highway and Fremantle Road, Gosnells. Phone: 08 9398 5399. Open Thursday to Sunday and public holidays from 10.00 am. Easily accessed from the city by train. The markets are in a Victorian style railway station and consist of numerous stalls selling craft and fresh produce. There is also an international food hall which is open until 9.00 pm.

Midland Military Markets: 3 Clayton Street, Bellevue. Phone: 08 9250 2998. Open Fridays and Saturdays 9.00 am to 6.00 pm, Sunday and public holidays 8.00 am to 6.00 pm. This is a general market with over 200 variety stalls and food stalls. Free rides for kids.

Midland Sunday Market: The Crescent, Midland. Phone: 08 9370 5599. Open Sunday 8.00 am to 4.00 pm. This market sells a wide range of goods including food, arts and crafts.

Scarborough Fair Markets: West Coast Highway, Scarborough (opposite Rendezvous Observation City). Phone: 08 9245 1670. Open weekends 9.00 am to 5.30 pm and public holidays 10.00 am to 5.00 pm. Accessible by Bus No.400 from the City. As well as a licensed international food hall, there are more than 40 stalls selling antiques, curios, collectables, jewellery, pottery and fashion. There are also speciality services available, including tattooing, body piercing, reflexology and tarot readings.

Station Street Markets: Station Street, Subiaco. Phone: 08 9382 2832. Open weekends and Monday public holidays 9.00 am to 5.00 pm. Situated a stone's throw from Subiaco Railway Station and across the road from Subiaco Pavilion Markets. About 100 stalls with a wide selection of goods, including souvenirs, food and confectionery. There is also live entertainment and free merry-go-round rides for kids.

Stock Road Markets: cnr Stock Road and Spearwood Avenue, Bibra Lake. Phone: 08 9418 5356. Open weekends and Monday public holidays 9.00 am to 5.00 pm. Air-conditioned undercover markets with an international food hall, cheap fresh fruit and vegetables, fresh bread and over 60 variety stalls.

Subiaco Pavilion Markets: 2 Rokeby Road, Subiaco. Phone: 08 9382 2498. Open Thursday and Friday 10.00 am to 9.00 pm, weekends 10.00 am to 5.00 pm. Over fifty speciality stalls selling jewellery, giftware, pottery, leatherware, books and clothes in a converted warehouse. There is also an international food hall with live entertainment in the evenings and on Sunday afternoons.

Wanneroo Weekend Mega Market: 33 Prindiville Drive, Wangara. Phone: 08 9409 8397. Open Saturday, Sunday and public holidays on Monday 9.00 am to 5.30 pm. This is the State's biggest market with over 140 stalls offering an enormous variety of goods, including fresh produce, clothing and souvenirs. Fully under cover and air cooled, there are two eating areas serving a variety of international cuisine.

MEAT AND SEAFOOD FOR EXPORT

Kailis Bros: 100 Roe Street, Northbridge. Phone: 08 9227 7747. This is one of Perth's best known seafood suppliers, who provide top quality Australian seafood specially packed in airline approved thermal bags.

G and A Terranova and Son Butchers: 113 Aberdeen Street, Northbridge. Phone: 08 9328 7244. This award winning butcher can supply vacuum packed and sealed premium quality meat products of your choice suitable for export.

Torre and Sons: 41 Lake Street, Northbridge. Phone: 08 9328 8317. This butcher specialises in a wide variety of premium grade meat and poultry and will vacuum pack for export.

SHOPPING CENTRES

Major shopping centres in the Perth Metropolitan area usually provide a large number of shops all under one roof, with undercover parking. As they are air-conditioned, this can be a pleasant way of escaping the summer heat. There are usually department stores, supermarkets, speciality food shops, cafés, restaurants, banks, travel agents as well as clothing, shoe, electrical and a myriad of other shops. In fact, a major shopping centre provides a one stop shopping experience, and in some cases, there is a major cinema complex attached to the centre.

MAJOR SHOPPING CENTRES INCLUDE:

Belmont Forum: cnr Belmont Avenue and Abernethy Road, Cloverdale. Phone: 08 9277 6325.

Garden City Shopping Centre: 125 Riseley Street, Booragoon. Phone: 08 9364 7911.

Innaloo City Centre: cnr Scarborough Beach Road and Oswald Street, Innaloo. Phone: 08 9446 5244.

Karrinyup Shopping Centre: Karrinyup Road, Karrinyup. Phone: 08 9445 1122.

Lakeside Joondalup Shopping City: Joondalup Drive, Joondalup. Phone: 08 9300 3888.

Midland Gate Shopping Centre: Brockman Road, Midland. Phone: 08 9250 3688.

Warwick Grove Shopping Centre: cnr Beach and Erindale Roads, Warwick. Phone: 08 9447 4800.

Westfield Carousel: 1382 Albany Highway, Cannington. Phone: 08 9458 6344.

Westfield Galleria: cnr Collier and Walter Roads, Morley. Phone: 08 9375 3228.

Whitford City Shopping Centre: cnr Whitfords and Marmion Avenue, Hillarys. Phone: 08 9401 4599.

As well as the shopping centres listed above, some streets are well known for their village style atmosphere and quality shopping. These include:

- Napoleon Street, Cottesloe.
- St Quentins Avenue and Bay View Terrace, Claremont.
- Rokeby Road and Hay Street, Subiaco.
- King Street, Perth
- Beaufort Street, Mount Lawley.
- Oxford Street, Leederville.

SOUVENIR SHOPS/AUSTRALIANA

Australian Geographic Shop: 13 Forrest Chase, Murray Street, Perth. Phone: 08 9421 1781. There are also branches in Booragoon and Morley. Educationally and environmentally aware people would enjoy shopping here. There is a wide range of bush walking equipment, clothing, jewellery, posters, puzzles, games, toys mainly with a geographic theme.

Australian Reflections:
- 100 William Street, Perth. Phone: 08 9321 0772.
- Shop 5, Cinema City, Hay Street, Perth. Phone: 08 9221 7721. Australiana T-shirts, sweatshirts, towels and souvenirs.

Australian Reflections of the Sea: 616 Hay Street Mall, Perth. Phone: 08 9421 1774. Souvenirs with an underwater theme centred around whales, dolphins, penguins as well as a good selection of Australiana clothing.

Bannister Street Craft Works: 8–12 Bannister Street, Fremantle. Phone: 08 9336 2035. Open Tuesday to Saturday 10.00 am to 5.00 pm, Sunday and public holidays 12.30 pm to 5.00 pm. Well-known Western Australian craftsmen produce and sell their products including pottery, glassware, wooden items and jewellery.

Bindoon Cottage Craft: Shop 8, South Terrace Piazza, Fremantle. Phone: 08 9335 7466. There is also an outlet at the Fremantle Markets. This shop has an enormous selection of Australian sheepskin products including ugg boots, sheepskin coats, caps and rugs.

Craftwest: King Street Arts Centre, 357–365 Murray Street, Perth. Phone: 08 9325 2799. Open Monday to Saturday 10.00 am to 5.00 pm and Sunday 12.00 noon to 5.00 pm for special exhibitions. A gallery and retail outlet for contemporary craft

such as wood turning, ceramics, jewellery, metalcraft, textiles and multimedia.

Desert Designs: 114 High Street, Fremantle. Phone: 08 9430 4101. Fashion items in cotton, silk and linen with authentic aboriginal art patterns and designs.

Done Art and Design: Shop 16, Forrest Chase, Perth. Phone: 08 9221 4432. Ken Done is a well known Australian artist whose designs capture the spirit and feel of Australia and are reproduced on a huge variety of items, including resort and swimwear, linen and souvenirs.

Everything Outback: Shop 25, Plaza Arcade, Perth. Phone: 08 9221 2773. Western Australian made outdoor clothing, hats, didgeridoos and other souvenirs.

Fremantle Arts Centre: 1 Finnerty Street, Fremantle. Phone: 08 9335 8244. See also page 44 in Chapter 7: Galleries. The craft shop sells high quality Western Australian handmade products and there is also a bookshop which has an excellent range of Australian literature.

Gumnut Factory: 30 Prindiville Drive, Wangara (600 metres off Wanneroo Road). Phone: 08 9409 6699. Open daily 9.30 am to 4.00 pm. The factory tour shows how many nuts and seedpods, collected from Australian native trees and shrubs, can be turned into all sorts of novelty items, such as gumnut animals and nut-men. There is a craft shop full of gumnut creations, wooden products, mallee clocks, souvenirs and wildflowers. There is also a nine-hole garden mini-golf course, a gumnut model village railway, timber display, and tearooms. Admission to factory tour, gumnut land and museums: adults $3.00, concessions $2.50, children $2.00. Minigolf: adults $3.00, concessions $2.50, children $2.00.

Koala Bear Shop: Shops 7 and 8 London Court, Perth. Phone: 08 9325 2297. This shop sells a wide range of soft toys such as kangaroos, koalas and wombats, as well as the usual range of souvenirs such as keyrings and placemats.

La Maiolica: 20 Norfolk Street, Fremantle. Phone: 08 9335 3630. For a souvenir with a difference, this shop sells hand crafted and painted Mediterranean style pottery. The functional pieces include brightly coloured dinnerware, platters, vases and planters whilst wall plates and tiles are amongst the decorative pieces.

Mineral Kingdom: Shop M113, City Arcade, Perth. Phone: 08 9321 9730. A variety of gemstones, iron ore, opals and Western Australian timber products and jewellery.

Mount Lawley Craft Centre and Art Gallery: 676a Beaufort Street, Mt Lawley. Phone: 08 9271 2023. This craft centre offers a wide range of Western Australian paintings and craft works including wooden products, pottery, hand-knitted jumpers and numerous other gift items.

Nature's Gemhouse (also known as the Shell Museum): 5 Beach Street, Fremantle. Phone: 08 9336 1588. Part of this shop is a museum with a large display of shells, but they also sell shells, rocks, fossils and souvenirs.

Numbats Gifts and Souvenirs: 60 Market Street, Fremantle. Phone: 08 9430 8838. This shop specialises in boomerangs and a wide range of high quality souvenirs.

Purely Australian Clothing Co:
- 731 Hay Street, Perth. Phone: 08 9321 4697.
- South Terrace Piazza, South Terrace, Fremantle. Phone: 08 9430 4401.

There are two other branches in the city, and one at Sorrento Quay and the International Airport. These shops sell a wide range of Australian-style clothing, some based on work wear like Drizabones, Akubra hats and moleskin trousers. They also have high quality Coogi knitwear, Hi Sport knitwear, Canterbury clothing, Aboriginal designed clothing and the usual souvenir T-shirts with pictures of Perth, kangaroos, koalas and so on.

R.M. Williams Bushman's Outfitters: 38 Carillon Arcade, Perth. Phone: 08 9321 7786. The clothing sold in this shop is not cheap but is of very high quality. They are well known for their wide range of leather boots, moleskin trousers, shirts and ladies' skirts, oilskin jackets and a multitude of other country clothing.

Seashores: Shop 29, Plaza Arcade, Perth. Phone: 08 9325 2595. This shop specialises in gifts with a marine theme (centred around dolphins, fish, shells and the beach) such as ornaments, clocks and toys.

Spinback Boomerang: Phone: 08 9398 1681. Situated in the Fremantle Markets, selling different types of boomerangs.

Kings Park offers several excellent vantage points to admire the views over Perth City and the vast expanse of the Swan River.

The Esplanade Hotel in Fremantle is a fine example of colonial architecture. Along with many other buildings in Fremantle, it was refurbished prior to Fremantle hosting the America's Cup in 1987.

The 'Cappuccino Strip' in South Terrace, Fremantle, is a place to enjoy a light meal or cup of coffee whilst soaking up Fremantle's Mediterranean atmosphere.

The Sail and Anchor Pub is one of Fremantle's most attractive heritage buildings. It has its own brewery producing a variety of boutique beers.

Fremantle Markets were established in 1897 and still operate as a bustling weekend market. They are one of Fremantle's most popular tourist attractions.

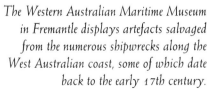

The Roundhouse in Fremantle was built in 1831 and served as the Swan River colony's first gaol.

The Western Australian Maritime Museum in Fremantle displays artefacts salvaged from the numerous shipwrecks along the West Australian coast, some of which date back to the early 17th century.

The red and green kangaroo paw is the floral emblem of Western Australia and is one of the many wildflowers found in Kings Park.

The black swan is native to Western Australia and may be seen on the Swan River and many of the inland lakes in the metropolitan area.

St Marys Cathedral was constructed by Roman Catholic monks in the 1860s. It is built in the English gothic style and is situated in Victoria Square, Perth.

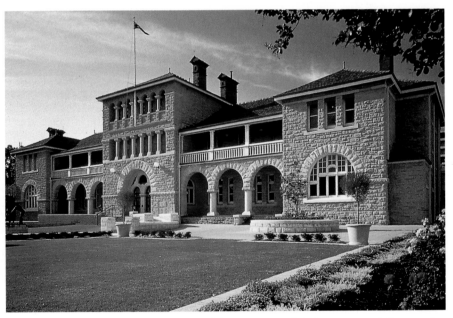

The Perth Mint was established in 1899. Today it is a popular place to see medallions and coins being produced and gold being poured.

London Court is a mock Tudor shopping arcade running between the Hay Street Mall and St Georges Terrace in central Perth. It is a great place for tourists to shop for souvenirs.

Burswood International Resort and Casino is situated on the banks of the Swan River within a few minutes drive from the centre of Perth.

The Western Australian Cricket Association Ground (the WACA) hosts the Sheffield Shield, One Day and Test cricket matches.

Cycling is a popular activity on Rottnest Island. As the island is only 11 kilometres long, it may easily be cycled in one day.

The quokka is one of Rottnest Island's unique attractions. Early Dutch seafarers mistook them for large rats and named the island 'Rotte-nest' (rat's nest) after them.

Bathurst Lighthouse is a well-known Rottnest Island landmark. Sandy beaches and clear blue water make Rottnest a wonderful tourist destination.

Staircase Gallery: 57 High Street, Fremantle. Phone: 08 9430 6447. Open Monday to Saturday 10.00 am to 5.00 pm and Sunday 11.00 am to 5.00 pm. This shop and gallery specialises in the sale of exquisitely crafted pieces in jarrah, which is a timber unique to Western Australia. There are other high quality works of art for sale.

Star Surf Shop: 332 Murray Street, Perth. Phone: 08 9321 6230. Sells a wide variety of surfing gear, including board shorts, bathers, T-shirts and shoes. Well-known labels include Quicksilver, Billabong, Rusty, Rip Curl and Mambo.

Walkabout Souvenirs Australia: 11/12 Forrest Chase, opposite the General Post Office. Phone: 08 9325 2190.

Also has a branch at London Court. Sells a wide range of Australian souvenirs including boomerangs, T-shirts and soft toys.

Waves Surfwear: Shop LM2, City Arcade, Perth. Phone: 08 9322 6996. This shop sells Australian surf clothing and accessories, including items from Mambo, Billabong, Hot Tuna and Rip Curl.

Wildflower Factory: Unit 2, 5 Beach Road, Fremantle. Phone: 08 9430 6016. This shop sells a selection of dried Western Australian wildflowers (tourist-packs a speciality).

Wombat Lodge: 75 and 77 Barrack Street, Perth. Phone: 08 9325 4220. Quality souvenirs, T-shirts, soft toys, Australian clothing, for example, Drizabones and Akubra hats.

SPORT TO WATCH

Watching others play sport is a popular Australian pastime. Perth has world class sporting facilities in the Challenge Stadium (swimming and diving), the WACA (cricket), Perth Hockey Stadium (hockey) and the Vines Resort (golf). The famous Australian game of 'Aussie Rules' football is played every weekend in winter and Western Australia has two teams in the national competition. Other sport to watch includes tennis, basketball, soccer, horse racing and trotting.

Tickets for most major sporting events can be bought from Red Tickets. Phone: 08 9484 1222.

BASEBALL
Perth Heat is the local team in the Australian Baseball League. Phone: 08 9279 8473. They play at the Swan Districts Football Club, Bassendean, from October to February, mostly at weekends, but telephone for fixtures. Tickets cost: adults $11.00, children/concession $8.00. The Baseball Development Foundation runs local matches. Phone: 08 9383 7735.

BASKETBALL
The Perth Wildcats (men) and the Perth Breakers (women) play at the Perth Entertainment Centre in Wellington Street, Perth. The season runs from October to April. For details of match times and dates phone 08 9388 3511. Basketball WA Administration organises

state league matches. Phone: 08 9386 5525.

CRICKET
The WA Cricket Association Ground (known as the WACA Ground) in Nelson Crescent, East Perth, hosts Sheffield Shield, One-day and Test Matches. Phone: 08 9265 7222 for details of forthcoming matches. Season runs from beginning of October to mid-March. Tickets cost: adults $6.00 for Sheffield Shield and $8.00 adult for Mercantile Mutual games and up to $45.00 per day for internationals.

FOOTBALL
Australian Football League (AFL) games are held most weekends over winter at either Subiaco Oval, Roberts Road, Subiaco; or the WACA Ground, Nelson Crescent, East Perth. The two local teams, the West Coast Eagles and the Fremantle Dockers normally play on

alternate weekends at home. Contact West Coast Eagles on 08 9381 1111, or Fremantle Dockers on 08 9430 8975 for details of matches. The season is from March to the end of September. Club members are allocated the best seats, but the public can buy standing room for $13.50 (adults) or a seat if you can get one, for $17.50 (budget) to $32.50 (premium). This is a uniquely Australian sport and many matches are a sell-out. Westar Rules, the local league, plays matches every weekend during the season. For details of venues and times phone 08 9381 5599.

GOLF

The Heineken Classic is held annually in late January/early February, at the Novotel Vines Resort Golf Course, Verdelho Drive, The Vines, Upper Swan Valley. Phone: 08 9297 0222. This Australian PGA Tour event attracts world class Australian and international players and is Australia's richest golf tournament.

GREYHOUNDS

Cannington Greyhounds: Station Street, cnr Albany Highway, Cannington. Phone: 08 9458 4600. Dogs race every Thursday and Saturday evening. There is a café, bar, restaurant and a creche. Cost: adults $4.00, concession $1.00, children free.

Mandurah Greyhounds: Gordon Road, Mandurah. Phone: 08 9581 7188. Greyhound racing is every Tuesday and Friday evening. There is a café, bar and restaurants but no creche. Cost: adults $4.00, concession $1.00, children free.

HOCKEY

Western Australian Hockey Association Inc: Phone: 08 9451 3688. Matches are played on astro-turf at the Perth Hockey Stadium, Hayman Road, Bentley. International matches are held intermittently. The Classic League (local teams) competes from March to September at a variety of venues.

HORSE RACING/TROTTING

Ascot Race Course: 38 Grandstand Road, Ascot. Race meetings held between October and May. Cost: adults $6.00, aged concession $3.00, free for children under 18. Carnival dates, e.g. Perth Cup, cost more. There are various restaurants and child care is available (children must be toilet trained).

Belmont Park Race Course: Goodwood Parade, Rivervale. Race meetings held between May and October. Cost: adults $6.00, aged concession $3.00, free for children under 18. Carnival dates cost more. There are various restaurants and child care is available although children must be toilet trained. Telephone enquiries to WA Turf Club: 08 9277 0777.

Gloucester Park (WA Trotting Association): Nelson Crescent, East Perth. Phone: 08 9323 3555. Trotting every Friday night. Gates open 5.00 pm. First race is 6.45 pm. Admission: adults $5.00, pensioners and concessions $3.00, free for children accompanied by adults. Food and refreshments are available from hot dog stands through to the up-market Beau Rivage room, where bookings are essential. Phone: 08 9325 7553. A creche operates from 6.30 pm until 10.30 pm; cost: $5.00 per child (ages three to 14). Activities include basketball, sega games and videos.

RUGBY LEAGUE

At the time of writing, there is no local representative team in the national league. For details of local rugby league matches phone Western Australian Rugby League Inc on 08 9277 3055.

RUGBY UNION

Rugby Union WA Inc:
Phone: 08 9383 7714. Phone for details of forthcoming major matches, and details of venues and times of local matches.

SOCCER

The local team which plays in the national league is Perth Glory. For details of matches phone 08 9383 9911, or for local games and venues, phone Soccer Administration of WA Inc, on 08 9383 7878.

SPEEDWAY

Claremont Speedway: Claremont Showgrounds, Ashton Avenue, Claremont. Phone: 08 9383 1155 or 08 9383 1825. Speedway is held every Friday evening in summer (mid-October to end March). Cost: adults $16.00, children $8.00.

TENNIS

The only international tennis played on a regular basis in Perth is the Hopman Cup which is played at the Burswood Dome, Burswood Casino and Resort, Great Eastern Highway every January. Book tickets through BOCS, phone 08 9484 1133.

The WA Open is normally played at the State Tennis Centre, Bolton Avenue, Burswood every December. Contact Tennis West (WA Lawn Tennis Association). Phone: 08 9361 1112.

CHAPTER 11

ROTTNEST ISLAND

Rottnest Island is renowned for its picturesque sandy beaches, secluded bays and incredibly clear blue water. It is situated 18 kilometres west of Fremantle, about half an hour by ferry. Its close proximity to the mainland makes it an ideal destination for both day trippers and those who desire a longer stay.

This small flat island is composed largely of limestone and sand dunes and there are five salt lakes inland. It is about 11 kilometres long, 4.5 kilometres wide and has approximately 40 kilometres of coastline. The maximum elevation is 45 metres above sea level. Climatically similar to Perth, with mainly winter rainfall (annual rainfall 720 mm) and hot dry summers, it is slightly cooler than the mainland. The average maximum daily temperature in January is 27°C, and 17°C in July.

The warm Leeuwin Current flows around the Island allowing divers to view coral and sub-tropical fish, normally only found in tropical regions much further north. There are numerous reefs around the Island, causing more than a dozen sailing ships to have been wrecked on them over the years. Their remains provide interesting dive sites for snorkellers and scuba divers.

Rottnest was named in 1696 by Dutch explorer, Willem de Vlamingh, who mistakenly thought that the local small marsupial (the quokka) was a large rat, and named the island Rotte-nest (rat's nest).

Mr Robert Thomson (Thomson Bay is named after him) and his family were the first settlers on the Island, shortly after the founding of the Swan River Colony in 1829. They collected salt, cured fish and farmed until the Government decided to land Aboriginal prisoners there in 1838, when land leases were revoked.

Since then Rottnest Island has been used as an Aboriginal penal settlement, 1838 to 1903, and an internment camp for Austrian and German dissidents during the First World War. Between 1848 and 1919, Governors of Western Australia had a holiday residence on the Island. In 1917, Rottnest was declared an A Class Public Reserve. In 1919 the first ordinary holidaymakers arrived, staying in campsites, huts and flats which resulted from the conversion of the Governor's Holiday Residence. The Oliver Hill Gun Battery, built in the late 1930's, was part of the coastal defence system to protect vessels in Fremantle

Harbour during the Second World War. The Rottnest Hotel was built in 1953, and Rottnest quickly grew in popularity as a holiday destination for people from all walks of life. Now, ferry services are both frequent and efficient, currently transporting approximately 400,000 people to visit the Island each year.

Rottnest Island is managed by the Rottnest Island Authority. Under its auspices is the Visitor and Information Centre (phone: 08 9372 9752) which is situated at the end of the main jetty at Thomson Bay. Here you can purchase souvenirs, obtain information, maps and brochures on everything to see and do on the Island and staff can confirm bookings for bus and train tours. You can also rent lockers to store any belongings which you do not want to cart around the Island.

Accommodation on the Island ranges from tents to quality hotel accommodation. The Rottnest Island Authority, phone: 08 9432 9111, offers 270 self-catering holiday homes in four locations, and the Accommodation Office at the end of the main jetty can provide information about these. There are two hotels on the Island, which you must contact directly for bookings or information. See Accommodation at the end of this chapter, page 74 for details on all options, and how to book.

GETTING TO ROTTNEST BY BOAT:
Boat Torque 2000:
Phone: 1300 368 686. Ferries to Rottnest depart from:
- Pier 4, Barrack Street Jetty, Perth. Phone: 08 9221 5844. Journey takes approximately one and a half hours.

- Rous Head Harbour, North Fremantle. Phone: 08 9430 5844. Journey takes approximately 25 minutes.
- Hillarys Boat Harbour, Sorrento Quay. Phone: 08 9246 1039. Journey takes approximately 45 minutes.
Prices of day return tickets vary depending on the time of year, departure point and vessel used. The Super Flyte is the most expensive. Cost: adults $50.00, concession $45.00, children $15.00 for a return fare from Perth. However, prices for adults can be as low as $30.00 from Perth or $27.00 from Fremantle, return. Extended stays are slightly more expensive. There are seasonal differences in departure times so phone for up to date information. Enquire about courtesy transport from your hotel or Fremantle Railway station when booking.

Boat Torque 2000 also offers a Fremantle shopover package, a Friday Night Rottnest Adventure Cruise, and several TLC Packages which may include lunch at the Rottnest Lodge, bike hire, coach tour of the island, or an Underwater Explorer cruise.

Oceanic Cruises:
Ferries to Rottnest depart from:
- Pier 2, Barrack Street Jetty, Perth. Phone: 08 9325 1191. Cost: adults $40.00 same day return, children (four to 12) $14.00. The trip takes approximately one and a half hours.
- East Street Jetty, East Fremantle. Phone: 08 9430 5127. Cost: adults $27.00 same day return, children (four to 12) $10.00. The trip takes approximately half an hour.

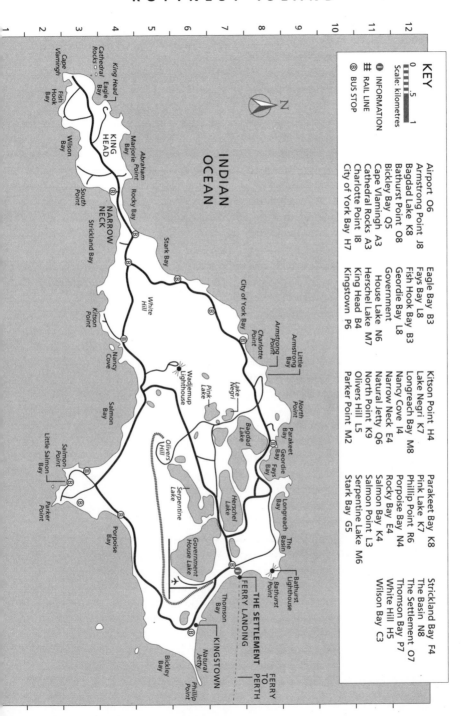

ROTTNEST ISLAND

KEY

Scale: kilometres
0 .5 1

- INFORMATION
- ♯ RAIL LINE
- Ⓑ BUS STOP

Airport O6
Armstrong Point J8
Bagdad Lake K8
Bathurst Point O8
Bickley Bay Q5
Cape Vlamingh A3
Cathedral Rocks A3
Charlotte Point I8
City of York Bay H7

Eagle Bay B3
Fays Bay L8
Fish Hook Bay B3
Geordie Bay L8
Government
House Lake N6
Herschel Lake M7
King Head Bay B4
Kingstown P6

Kitson Point H4
Lake Negri K7
Longreach Bay M8
Nancy Cove I4
Narrow Neck E4
Natural Jetty Q6
North Point K9
Olivers Hill L5
Parker Point M2

Parakeet Bay K8
Pink Lake K7
Phillip Point R6
Porpoise Bay N4
Rocky Bay E4
Salmon Bay K4
Salmon Point L3
Serpentine Lake M6
Stark Bay G5

Strickland Bay F4
The Basin N8
The Settlement O7
Thomson Bay P7
White Hill H5
Wilson Bay C3

INDIAN OCEAN

Cape Vlamingh
Fish Hook Bay
Wilson Bay
Eagle Bay
Cathedral Rocks
King Head
KING HEAD
Marjorie Point
South Point
Abraham Point
NARROW NECK
Rocky Bay
Strickland Bay
Stark Bay
White Hill
Kitson Point
Nancy Cove
Salmon Bay
Salmon Point
Little Salmon Bay
Parker Point
Porpoise Bay
Serpentine Lake
Olivers Hill
Wadjemup Lighthouse
Pink Lake
Lake Negri
Bagdad Lake
Herschel Lake
Government House Lake
City of York Bay
Charlotte Point
Armstrong Point
Little Armstrong Bay
North Point
Parakeet Bay
Geordie Bay
Fays Bay
Longreach Basin
The Basin
Bathurst Point
Bathurst Lighthouse
FERRY LANDING
THE SETTLEMENT
Thomson Bay
KINGSTOWN
Natural Jetty
Phillip Point
Bickley Bay
FERRY TO PERTH

6 7

Oceanic Cruises offers a $5.00 discount to pensioners, students, VIP and YHA card holders. All costs are slightly higher for extended stays. A Rottnest Package Tour which includes the return ferry fare, buffet lunch and a two-hour bus tour or train tour costs $70.00 from Perth and $57.00 from Fremantle. During the low season, there are often special reduced fares. They offer a free pick-up service from City hotels and Fremantle Railway Station. Enquire about this when checking current ferry departure times and making bookings.

Rottnest Express:
Ferries to Rottnest depart from:
- C Shed, Victoria Quay, Fremantle (behind Fremantle Railway Station). Phone: 08 9335 6406. Cost: adults $32.00, seniors $27.00, high school students $24.00, children $10.00 for same day returns. Fares slightly increased for extended stays. The trip takes about half an hour.

GETTING TO ROTTNEST BY PLANE:

Rottnest Air Taxi: Phone: 1800 500 006. Return fare for the hire of the whole four-seater plane is $150.00 (plus Government Charges). The plane can carry three adults or two adults and two children. The cost includes courtesy car pick up.

Skyworx Aviation: Phone: 1800 244 833. A whistlestop trip from Jandakot Airport to Rottnest, including a scenic flight over Perth City and a two-hour stopover at the Island. Costs $120.00 per person (minimum of two people); $75.00 per person for five people. Longer stays on the island available.

TRANSPORT ON THE ISLAND

All of Rottnest is easily accessible by well-maintained roads which run around the edge, and criss-cross the Island. Most of the Island is comparatively flat, but as there are some hills a reasonable level of fitness is required, especially in summer temperatures. It is advisable to carry water as the Island is arid and other than at Thomson and Geordie/Longreach Bays, there are few facilities.

BICYCLES

There are no private cars on the Island. The only vehicles allowed belong to the Rottnest Island Authority. Bus, bicycle or foot are the only means of transport. By far the quickest method of getting around is on a bicycle. The *Rottnest Island Bicycle Guide* can be bought cheaply from the Visitor and Information Centre. It has lots of extra information about the Island's flora and fauna. The Island is small enough to ride around in about three and a half hours.

Most people hire bikes on arrival at Thomson Bay, but you can take your own bike (for $5.00 return) or hire one prior to departure, for example from Boat Torque Cruises. They charge $15.00 per day, but it is cheaper to hire bikes for longer periods, for example, seven days costs $45.00. You can also book a bike ahead through the Activity Centre on Barrack Street Jetty. Phone: 08 9221 1828. Cost: $18.00 per day (for a geared bike) up to $52.00 for six or seven days. Your bike will be brought to you when you disembark on the jetty at Rottnest Island. However, if you are prepared for a short stroll towards the

Rottnest Hotel, Rottnest Island Bike Hire, phone: 08 9292 5105, next door will charge $18.00 a day ($52.00 per week) for a geared bike or $13.00 a day ($40.00 per week) for a single speed bike. Hourly rates available. All these companies charge a $20.00 refundable deposit per bike and the cost includes the use of a lock and a helmet (non-wearing of helmets may result in an on the spot fine). Most bike hire companies have a good selection of children's bikes, including those with training wheels, and also bikes with baby seats. Use of bike locks is advisable, particularly in more remote areas.

BUSES

A free shuttle bus runs between the main jetty, Geordie Bay, Kingstown Barracks and the Airport departing from the main jetty every half hour (sometimes hourly). Timetables are available at the Visitor and Information Centre at Thomson Bay.

Rottnest Island Bus Tours: Phone: 08 9372 9752.

The Bayseeker Bus is ideal for day trippers who don't want to hire bikes. It drives around the island taking approximately 45 minutes. You can get on and off at whichever secluded bay or landmark you please. Cost for a day: adults $5.00, children $2.00. The bus leaves regularly (hourly in the summer) from the main bus stop opposite Rottnest Lodge. Timetables are available at the Visitor and Information Centre.

The Island Bus Tour travels from one end of the Island to the other and is a two-hour fully guided tour, giving information about history, environment and wildlife. Leaves from the main bus stop opposite Rottnest Lodge. Details are available at the Visitor and Information Centre. Cost: adults $12.00, pensioners and students $9.00, children $6.00.

ON FOOT

Free guided walking tours are run by the Rottnest Island Voluntary Guides all year round. Enquire at the Visitor and Information Centre for details of tours and departure times. Examples of tours are the Historical Walking Tour of the Settlement (about an hour), and Bird Tours which are run during the holidays. There are also tours of the guns and tunnels at Oliver Hill, which include a 20-minute bike ride and 45-minute walk. Cost: adults $2.00, children 50 cents.

TRAIN

Rottnest Island Railway Trust: Phone: 08 9372 9752.

The Oliver Hill Train departs Settlement Station for guided tours of the gun emplacement and tunnels. Trains depart at 10.30 am, 11.30 am, 12.30 pm and 1.30 pm, with extra tours in summer. Cost for train ride and tour: adults $9.00, concession $6.00, children $4.50.

EATING ON ROTTNEST

Food is available for purchase or consumption from the following places:
Dome Café: Henderson Street, Rottnest. Phone: 08 9292 5026. The first restaurant you will see after arriving by

ferry. It offers al fresco dining overlooking Thomson Bay. Breakfasts, lunches and dinners are served. It is noted for its high quality coffee, and also serves cakes and snacks.

Geordie Bay General Store: Phone: 08 9292 5017. Sells a multitude of general groceries, fishing requirements, magazines, pharmaceuticals, beer and wine, T-shirts and souvenirs.

Red Rooster: opposite the bakery. Phone: 08 9292 5087. Sells BBQ chicken and chips to takeaway.

Rottnest Bakery:The Settlement, Thomson Bay, Rottnest. Phone: 08 9292 5023. Sells good quality pies, pizzas, bread, buns and cakes and also cool drinks. There are numerous tables and chairs between the Bakery and Red Rooster where you can sit to eat.

Rottnest General Store: The Settlement, Thomson Bay, Rottnest. Phone: 08 9292 5017. This well-stocked shop sells general groceries, magazines and books as well as ice creams, bread and drinks (alcoholic and non-alcoholic).

Rottnest Hotel: Phone: 08 9292 5011. Renowned for its Quokka Arms pub and beer garden. For casual a la carte dining, breakfast, morning and afternoon tea, lunch and dinner are served at Brolly's Restaurant and Cocktail Bar. There is a $16.00 all you can eat buffet lunch. This restaurant has ocean views. Hamptons Sports Bar and Char-Grill has a large screen video for sports viewing.

Rottnest Lodge: Phone: 08 9292 5161. Has a first class restaurant and cocktail bars at which non-residents

are welcome. There is a pleasant al fresco dining area around the pool, which offers buffet breakfasts in the morning and light meals throughout the day.

Rottnest Tea Rooms: Phone: 08 9292 5171. Open daily from 7.00 am to 9.00 pm. Serves a wide range of food from sandwiches and burgers to more substantial meals. Licensed to serve alcohol with meals. Casual family dining overlooking Thomson Bay, with views over the moorings. Linked by a boardwalk to the Rottnest Hotel, the Dome Café, and Visitor and Information Centre.

WATER ACTIVITIES
FISHING

The Visitor and Information Centre on the Island sells waterproof *Fish Guides* with pictures of all the fish found around the Island.

The general stores at both Thomson and Geordie Bays sell hand lines, bait and fishing tackle. Fishing, for example for herring, can be carried out from any jetty, such as those at Thomson Bay and Geordie Bay. Rods are necessary for fishing from the beaches, for example, at Ricey Beach you might catch: herring, tailor and sand whiting. Another good fishing spot is Natural Jetty, near Kingstown Barracks. Ask the locals for more information or enquire at the Visitor and Information Centre.

Herring are the most common fish caught in the waters around Rottnest, but the many other varieties include tailor, skipjack, mackerel and salmon.

Crayfish are plentiful on the reefs around Rottnest, however licences are required to catch them. Contact the Visitor and Information Centre about these. The use of spear guns and gidgies is prohibited. The following company hires fishing equipment:

Malibu Diving: Thomson Bay. Phone: 08 9292 5111. Hires fishing gear. Cost: $15.00 for 24 hours, with a $10.00 refundable deposit.

SNORKELLING AND SCUBA DIVING

With water temperatures in the 20s all year round, and great water visibility, Rottnest provides some of the best diving in Western Australia. There are limestone caverns and formations under the sea, along with coral, sponges and sub-tropical fish.

There are also numerous old shipwrecks on the reefs around the island, most of which now have marker plaques next to them naming the ships and describing how and when they sank. The Visitor and Information Centre sells maps with details of 15 dive sites (snorkel trails), including descriptions of how to access two wrecks from the beach. The map costs $8.00. Waterproof cards, with pictures of fish found around Rottnest, are available to help you identify fish whilst under water.

These companies offer snorkelling and diving tours off Rottnest Island or hire out diving/snorkelling equipment:

Malibu Diving: Thomson Bay. Phone: 08 9292 5111. Hires masks, snorkels, fins and carry bags, and offers advice on various dive sites. Cost: $15.00 for hire of all equipment.

Diving Ventures: Phone (Fremantle): 08 9430 5130. Phone (Perth):

08 9421 1052. A variety of diving trips to Rottnest, including early morning budget dives (Saturday and Sunday mornings only) and day trips. A day trip with all gear and lunch supplied costs $120.00, but if you provide your own diving gear, it could cost as low as $60.00. Bookings are essential. Day trips on the Sea Trek, a 60 foot state-of-the-art dive vessel, leave from Fremantle Fishing Boat Harbour at 9.00 am, returning at 4.00 pm.

Perth Diving Academy:
- Hillarys Boat Harbour. Phone: 08 9344 1562.
- Rous Head, Fremantle. Phone: 08 9430 6300.

All equipment available for hire. Budget dives Saturday and Sunday early morning from $15.00 (gear excluded), or a day trip with two dives costs from $55.00.

Rottnest Island Aquatic Adventures: Phone: 0419 863 602, or phone/fax: 08 9434 2737. Departs Fremantle daily from October to May. Cost: adults $105.00, students, YHA, VIP cardholders $95.00, children (six to 14 years) $90.00. Includes snorkel gear, wetsuits, use of fishing tackle, BBQ food and refreshments and all transport (a courtesy bus from Perth City to Fremantle and back). Tour consists of: snorkel diving in several locations (including on historic shipwrecks), BBQ lunch and viewing dolphins, sea lions and humpback whales (in season). They also offer scuba diving. Phone for costs.

Snuba tours of Rottnest Island: Phone: 08 9292 5919 or 019 683 343. Snuba operates from November to April only. Snuba is a simple diving system connecting you to an inflatable raft that supports your air supply. Even with no prior experience, after a 20-minute orientation on land, you can dive to a depth of five to six metres. Skilled snuba guides will accompany you. Dives cost $45.00 per person (age eight and up) or $35.00 per person for a group of four or more. Dives last about 40 minutes, and the whole experience, including tuition, approximately one and a half hours.

Underwater Explorer: Rottnest Island. Phone: 08 9221 5844. Operated by Boat Torque Cruises, it offers snorkelling tours lasting up to one and a half hours, in the crystal clear turquoise blue waters of Rottnest Island. Explore shipwrecks, coral reefs and see tropical and salt water fish. All tours are supervised by a qualified divemaster and are perfect for beginners. Cost: adults $18.00, concession $15.00, children $10.00. There is a charge of $5.00 per person for equipment hire. The tour runs from 12.00 noon until 1.30 pm daily in summer, and is subject to good weather conditions.

For those who wish to see under the ocean without getting wet, the Underwater Explorer is a semi-submersible boat with glass windows. The Reef and Wreck Tour allows viewing of coral reef formations and 100 year old shipwrecks plus a huge variety of marine life and fish, some of which wait eagerly to be fed by hand. This tour lasts 45 minutes. Cost: adults $16.00, concession $13.00, children $9.00, family passes

$40.00. Up to five tours daily in summer, but check with Boat Torque Cruises on 08 9221 5844 or enquire at the Visitor and Information Centre on the Island. There is also a Twilight Cruise during which you can watch a fish feeding session by flood lights. A light BBQ supper is included in the cost: adults $12.00, concession $10.00, children $8.00. The cruise lasts two hours and leaves at 6.30 pm.

West Australia Dive Centre: 1st Floor, 37 Barrack Street, Perth. Phone: 08 9421 1883. Offer one day dive trips to Rottnest Island at a cost of adults $150.00 and children under 11 years of age $130.00 on Monday, Wednesday and Friday. Operates between October and May. Costs include transport from your hotel, boat fees, a guided dive, gear hire and lunch. They also offer a two-day dive holiday to Rottnest Island for $300.00, which includes dormitory accommodation at Rottnest, four boat or beach dives, all meals and equipment and guide. Dive sites include Crystal Cave, Roe Reef, Kingston Reef and Little Armstrong Bay.

SURFING AND BOOGIE BOARDING

Rottnest provides some excellent surfing spots, including Cathedral Rocks and Strickland Bay. Because some of the breaks are situated on reefs some distance off shore, care should be taken by beginners or weak swimmers. The following company hires surfboards and bodyboards:

Malibu Diving at Thomson Bay. Phone: 08 9292 5111. Hires out bodyboards and surfboards and can advise on good places to surf.

SWIMMING

Rottnest Island is endowed with many secluded bays, sandy beaches and crystal clear water. The Leeuwin Current which flows past the island ensures that the water is pleasantly warm all year round. Relatively close to The Settlement, Thomson, Porpoise, Fays, Geordie and Parakeet Bays, and The Basin, are particularly safe for family swimming because of the outer reefs that surround the island. Many other beaches further afield are equally suitable for safe swimming. There are toilet and changing facilities at The Basin, Kingstown and Thomson Bay and toilets behind the store at Geordie Bay.

WINDSURFING

If you take your own equipment, the strong, early sea breeze usually makes for good windsurfing or wave-sailing conditions. Mary Cove is as good as any place to try.

LAND ACTIVITIES

BOWLS

You can bowl at the Country Club but check opening hours.
Phone: 08 9292 5144.

GOLF

The Rottnest Island Country Club: Phone: 08 9292 5144. There is a nine-hole golf course. It is a bit arid in the summer and at its best from May to November. Usually open Monday to Saturday from 8.00 am, Sunday 9.00 am, but it is advisable to phone to check. Opening hours may vary with the seasons. Nine holes costs $8.00 and clubs are available for hire.

LIGHT PLANE FLIGHTS

Rottnest Air Taxi: Phone: 041 126 4547. Offers scenic flights commencing at $18.00 per person for a circuit of the Island (minimum of two people). An hour's flight taking in Perth, Fremantle and Rottnest costs $80.00 per person.

MINI-GOLF, TRAMPOLINE, POOL TABLE, AMUSEMENT ARCADE

Brett Heady Family Fun Park.: Phone: 08 9292 5156. Opposite the Rottnest Lodge. Open 9.00 am to 9.00 pm in summer; 8.00 am to 4.00 pm in winter. Play mini-golf, pool, jump on the trampoline, or amuse yourself with a wealth of electronic games. Cost: family pass $18.00.

OLIVER HILL GUN BATTERY

This was built in the late 1930s and formed part of the Australian coastal defences during the Second World War. The guns have never had a shot fired in anger. Regular guided tours of the guns and associated tunnel systems are conducted by the Rottnest Voluntary Guides. The fit can access Oliver Hill by foot or bike. In hot weather, others may prefer to take the train as the terrain is steep and tiring. It departs from the Settlement Station several times a day in season, and a timetable is available at the Visitor and Information Centre. The cost of the train ride and tour of Oliver Hill is adults $9.00, concession $6.00, children $4.50.

ROTTNEST ISLAND MUSEUM

Phone: 08 9372 9753.
Built by Aboriginal prisoners in 1857, this building was originally a hay shed

and a granary. Today it houses displays covering the history of the Island, its shipwrecks and its natural history. Located behind the Settlement shops, the Museum is open daily from 11.00 am to 4.00 pm. Cost: adults $2.00, concessions $1.00, children 50 cents.

TENNIS

There are well-maintained synthetic tennis courts at Bathurst and Geordie Bay. To book a court or hire racquets and balls, contact the Visitor and Information Centre, phone: 08 9372 9752, or for Geordie Bay Courts, see Geordie Bay Store.

WALKING

If you don't wish to take one of the guided walks organised by the Rottnest Island Voluntary Guides, the Visitor and Information Centre and the Museum have details of self-guided walk trails, including visits to colonial and convict-built buildings and war-time installations.

The Visitor and Information Centre will also supply you with a walking guide to the salt lakes, to better your viewing of the abundant bird life. The five salt lakes on the Island are home to a great variety of birds, including avocets, turnstones, banded stilts (known as the Rottnest snipe), caspian terns, plovers, herons and black swans. There are at least a dozen pairs of osprey or sea eagles nesting on the Island. Many other birds inhabit the woodlands, beaches and cliffs. In total, over 100 varieties of birds may be found on the Island. Pamplets and books from $2.00 are available from the Visitor and Information Centre to help with identification.

Rottnest Island's most famous inhabitant is undoubtedly the quokka, a small marsupial which was initially mistaken for a large rat by Willem de Vlamingh in 1696. The quokka is actually a small wallaby and you would be unlikely to visit Rottnest Island without encountering any. As they are nocturnal, during the day they are to be found in shady areas underneath bushes and small trees. In the evenings, around the Settlement, quokkas are plentiful and care has to be taken not to run them over with your bicycle.

Please do not feed the birds or quokkas as the birds become aggressive and quokkas can die. Fines may be imposed.

ACCOMMODATION

Apart from the Rottnest Lodge, Rottnest Hotel and the Youth Hostel at Kingstown Barracks, bookings for all accommodation on the Island must be made through the Rottnest Island Authority, phone: 08 9432 9111. As detailed below, they have a wide range of self-catering accommodation on the Island. The Authority's vehicles meet each incoming ferry and provide a complimentary drop-off and pick-up service for luggage, as long as it is well labelled. They also provide a hire service for crockery, cutlery, linen, TV sets, heaters and toasters.

HOTELS

At non-peak times, both the Rottnest Hotel and the Lodge frequently offer special packages which are well worth enquiring about.

Rottnest Hotel: Phone: 08 9292 5011. Located on the beach at Thomson

Bay, this was once the summer residence of the Governor of Western Australia. It is affectionately known by locals as the Quokka Arms. Costs vary according to room and time of year, but double room rates are between $90.00 and $175.00, including a continental breakfast for each guest. The hotel has two restaurants, bars and a beer garden.

Rottnest Lodge: Phone: 08 9292 5161. Situated on the banks of Garden Lake on the outskirts of Thomson Bay. The Lodge offers three styles of accommodation, from top quality holiday apartments to budget priced rooms or family suites. The maximum cost for a double room is $200.00 per night (peak season) or for a family apartment (three bedrooms, sleeping up to 10 people) $295.00. The Lodge has a restaurant, bars and a pool.

SELF-CATERING ACCOMMODATION

The Rottnest Island Authority: Phone: 08 9432 9111. Holiday accommodation in Thomson Bay, Geordie, Longreach and Fays Bay. There are several categories of accommodation from four-bed units or cottages to villas with eight beds. Most have ocean views.
Prices vary depending on size, location and proximity to the sea.

For school holiday periods (excluding the second term holidays,in July, when bookings can be made up to 12 months in advance) allocation of accommodation is by ballot. For information on how to apply, refer to the *West Australian* classifieds section under holiday accommodation on the following days:
- last Wednesday in June, for the January holidays
- last Wednesday in November, for Easter and first term holidays
- last Wednesday in March, for third term holidays.

There are also tent sites and cabins available for hire. A six-bed cabin will cost $263.00 for a week during the peak season. The above booking procedures apply for cabins during the school holidays. Camping costs $5.00 per adult, $2.50 per child, for one night.

Kingstown Barracks: Phone: 08 9372 9780. A 50-bed YHA hostel and also dormitory style and self-contained chalet accommodation. A bed in a dormitory costs $19.00 per night for non-members, $16.00 for members of the Youth Hostel Association. The chalets are for groups, usually school or club groups. As a guideline, the cost of the nine-bed chalet is $153.00 per night.

CHAPTER 12

Wineries and Breweries

Vines grow very well in the alluvial soils and Mediterranean climate of this region. The Swan Valley, half an hour's drive from the city and 15 minutes from the airport, is one of Perth's best-known wine growing areas and is an ideal destination for either a day or half-day trip. It is home to over 20 wineries ranging in size from small family concerns to large well-established wineries which have won international awards. It is possible to taste the wines, usually free of charge, prior to purchasing any you like. Several of the wineries have restaurants, cafés or places to picnic.

English settlers are credited with bringing the first rooted vine cuttings by sailing ship from Cape Town in South Africa to Western Australia. In 1829, cuttings were planted at Olive Farm in South Guildford. This was the beginning of the thriving wine industry of today.

The Mediterranean climate, with its abundant sunshine and ample winter rain, and the rich alluvial soils of the Swan Valley, are ideally suited to the production of premium wines. This was recognised by the southern European migrants of the 1920s and 1930s, who were quick to start producing their own wines using traditional methods their families had used for generations. Many of these small family vineyards are still operating today. Frequently wine-tastings are served by the owner/wine-maker himself. Wine-making techniques have improved greatly over the years, leading to a very high standard of premium wine production.

VISITING THE VALLEY

Visit the Swan Valley wineries by boat (see River Cruises, page 134), by coach (see Coach Tours, page 130), by chauffeur driven luxury car (see page 130) or drive yourself, but be aware of the 0.05 blood alcohol limit! The Swan Valley Tourist Drive (Route No. 203) is clearly signposted and most of the vineyards described below are on the route or a short distance from it.

Several vineyards have cafés or

restaurants offering lunches and light meals, however if you drive further afield, there is a charming restaurant, The Farmhouse, at 955 Chittering Road, Lower Chittering. Phone: 08 9571 8227. This is open for lunch Friday, Saturday and Sunday and dinner on Friday and Saturday nights. The restaurant serves delicious hot and cold meals using local produce and you can bring your own wine from your visits to the wineries.

Sandalfords and Houghtons are the best known of the Swan Valley vineyards described below, and the most frequently visited by organised tour groups. However, some of the smaller wineries, for example Little River Winery, Lamonts and Jane Brook, sell quality wines and provide rustic al fresco dining.

WINERIES

Banara Winery: Benara Road, Caversham. Phone: 08 9279 2169. Open 10.00 am to 6.00 pm daily. This traditional family winery goes back many generations. It specialises in vintage and liqueur ports and Muscat liqueurs.

Baskerville Wines: 247 Haddrill Road, Baskerville. Phone: 08 9296 1348. In a picturesque setting at the foot of the Darling Range, this winery produces Shiraz, Grenache, Chardonnay and a sweet wine called Oscar's Gold. Open for tastings Thursday to Monday 10.00 am to 4.00 pm. A restaurant serves lunch, Thursday to Monday, and dinner Friday, Saturday and Sunday.

Baxter-Stokes Wines: 65 Memorial Avenue, Baskerville. Phone:

08 9296 4831. Open weekends and public holidays from 9.30 am to 5.00 pm, or by appointment. One of the newer vineyards in the Valley, it produces Chardonnay, Verdelho, Shiraz, Pinot and Shiraz Cabernet.

Cobanov Winery: 31 Stock Road, Herne Hill. Phone: 08 9296 4210. Open 10.00 am to 5.00 pm daily. This winery, established in 1937 by a migrant from Yugoslavia, sells table wines, including Chardonnay, Chenin Blanc and fortified wines, especially ports. Bulk wine sales are available.

Garbin Estate Wines: 209 Toodyay Road, Middle Swan. Phone 08 9274 1747. Open Monday to Saturday 8.30 am to 5.30 pm, Sunday 10.30 am to 5.30 pm. This winery deals mainly in cellar door sales of Chardonnay, Chenin Blanc, Merlot, Shiraz and fortified wines. The huge entry doors to the winery are made from 600 to 700 year-old jarrah.

Henley Park Wines: cnr West Swan Road and Swan Street, Henley Brook. Phone: 08 9296 4328. Open daily 10.00 am to 5.00 pm except Monday. White and red wines, ports, liqueurs and sparkling wines can be sampled here. There is a $2.00 fee to taste the wines, but this is deducted from the cost of purchases. Light lunches are available 12.00 noon to 3.00 pm Friday, Saturday, Sunday and public holidays. There is a picnic area and kids' playground.

Houghton Winery: Dale Road, Middle Swan. Phone: 08 9274 5100. Open 10.00 am to 5.00 pm every day of the year except Christmas Day and Good Friday. An imposing driveway leads to this beautifully presented winery, which is a must see on any trip to the Swan Valley. Vast, well-manicured lawns, with large shady trees, are ideal for picnics and family relaxation. This is a well-established winery, dating back to 1836, with an historic 1863 homestead and a lovely old cellar, wine museum and art gallery. The Jacaranda Café serves coffee or lunch al fresco style on a vine covered terrace. Houghtons is Western Australia's best known winery, particularly renowned for its White Burgundy, which is one of the top selling white wines in Australia. Besides using grapes grown in the Swan Valley, Houghtons purchase fruit produced elsewhere in the State. They make a wide range of award-winning table wines, including Verdelho, Chenin Blanc, Chardonnay and Cabernet Sauvignon. They also sell the Wildflower Ridge and Moondah Brook range of wines. A Moondah Brook Chenin Blanc has won an award at the London International Wine Show.

Jane Brook Estate Wines: 229 Toodyay Road, Middle Swan. Phone: 08 9274 1432. Open daily 12 noon to 5.00 pm. A large well-presented cellar, with a wide range of high quality, award-winning wines, such as Chardonnay, Chenin Blanc, Sauvignon Blanc, Cabernet Merlot, Shiraz and Ports. There is a $2.00 tasting fee. Have a vineyard platter lunch in the vine covered courtyard, on the jarrah decking overlooking the Jane Brook or, in winter, in front of the fire in the Barrel Room. A band

plays over the Easter weekend and also at weekends in September/October. Bookings are advisable at this popular lunch venue.

Lamont Winery, Restaurant and Gallery: Bisdee Street, Millendon. Phone: 08 9296 4485. Open Wednesday to Sunday for lunch, 10.00 am to 5.00 pm, and the first Saturday of every month, for dinner at its well-known restaurant, overlooking the vineyard. Lamont's restaurant is famous for its innovative cuisine and the speciality of the house is home-grown marron (fresh water crayfish). Booking at this restaurant is essential. For more casual al fresco dining, there are a large number of tables outdoors and you can enjoy a variety of excellent light meals from the café, washed down by a bottle of table wine from the Lamont cellar. Wines sold from the cellar include Chenin Blanc, Chardonnay and a dry white blend White Burgundy. They also sell Rose, Cabernet, a Methode Champenoise Cabernet and a flor fino Sherry. The gallery and gift shop is particularly well presented and stocked with a wide range of high quality merchandise. Lamonts also sell gourmet food and wine hampers and gift boxes.

Little River Winery and Restaurant: cnr West Swan and Forest roads, West Swan. Phone: 08 9296 4462. Open daily (except Thursdays) 10.00 am to 5.30 pm. This boutique winery, owned by a French Count and his wife, reflects the French style of wines, and the ambience of a provincial French café in their

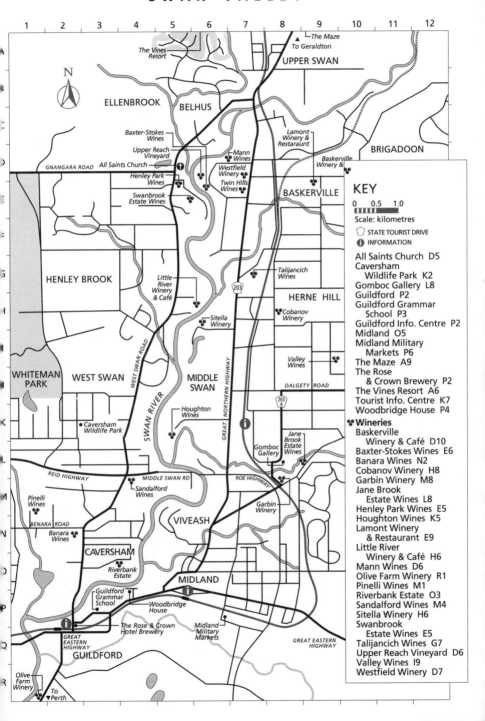

SWAN VALLEY

KEY

0   0.5   1.0
Scale: kilometres

◯ STATE TOURIST DRIVE
ⓘ INFORMATION

All Saints Church D5
Caversham
   Wildlife Park K2
Gomboc Gallery L8
Guildford P2
Guildford Grammar
   School P3
Guildford Info. Centre P2
Midland O5
Midland Military
   Markets P6
The Maze A9
The Rose
   & Crown Brewery P2
The Vines Resort A6
Tourist Info. Centre K7
Woodbridge House P4

🍷**Wineries**
Baskerville
   Winery & Café D10
Baxter-Stokes Wines E6
Banara Wines N2
Cobanov Winery H8
Garbin Winery M8
Jane Brook
   Estate Wines L8
Henley Park Wines E5
Houghton Wines K5
Lamont Winery
   & Restaurant E9
Little River
   Winery & Café H6
Mann Wines D6
Olive Farm Winery R1
Pinelli Wines M1
Riverbank Estate O3
Sandalford Wines M4
Sitella Winery H6
Swanbrook
   Estate Wines E5
Talijancich Wines G7
Upper Reach Vineyard D6
Valley Wines I9
Westfield Winery D7

outdoor café which serves delicious light lunches. Wines are sold exclusively at the cellar door, and you can order by phone. Excellent tasting notes are provided at the winery and the owners thoroughly enjoy promoting their fine quality wines, which include a particularly good Chenin Blanc as well as Chardonnay, Shiraz, Cabernet Sauvignon and a lighter red Beaujolais style Grenache/Shiraz. Also included is Vin Doux and a Noble Classic, both made from late picked Muscat.

Mann Wines: Memorial Avenue, Baskerville. Phone: 08 9296 4348. Open weekends 10.00 am to 5.00 pm, and most weekdays 9.00 am to 5.00 pm. This winery is owned by Dorham Mann, whose famous father, Jack, was a pioneer of the wine-making industry in the Swan Valley. Jack was employed by Houghtons for 51 years and was responsible for improving the quality of wines here, to such an extent that his 1971 Cabernet Sauvignon was judged in London as one of the top 11 wines in the world from a field of over 700 entries. Dorham was Senior Winemaker at Sandalfords for 14 years before setting up his own winery where he produces exclusively Mann Methode Champenoise, made from Cabernet grapes to a closely guarded secret family recipe.

Olive Farm Wines: 77 Great Eastern Highway, South Guildford. Phone: 08 9277 2989. This is the closest winery to the airport. Its cellar and café are open weekdays 10.00 am to 5.30 pm, weekends and public

holidays 11.00 am to 3.00 pm. Closed Wednesday. This was Western Australia's first winery, established in 1829 with vine cuttings and rooted grape vines brought from Cape Province in South Africa. The cellar, which is still used today, dates back to the early 1830's. The main white table wines are a full bodied Chenin Blanc, Chardonnay (their biggest seller) and Chablis, whilst a Cabernet Sauvignon and a Cabernet Shiraz Merlot blend are the most popular reds. They also make a Methode Champenoise.

Pinelli Wines: 30 Bennett Street, Caversham. Phone: 08 9279 6818. Open daily 9.00 am to 5.30 pm. This traditional family winery concentrates on cellar door sales of moderately priced wines with particular emphasis on bulk wine sales. Their Chardonnay and Chenin Blanc have both won awards, whilst their reds, in particular Cabernet Sauvignon and Shiraz, represent very good value for money.

Riverbank Estate: 126 Hamersley Road, Caversham. Phone: 08 9377 1805. Open weekends and public holidays 10.00 am to 5.00 pm. Table wines include Cabernet Shiraz, Pinot Noir, Semillon (award winning), Verdelho, Chenin and Chardonnay. A café serves light lunches.

Sandalford Wines: 3210 West Swan Road, Caversham. Phone: 08 9374 9374. Caversham Estate cellar sales daily: 10.00 am to 5.00 pm, closed Good Friday and Christmas Day. Wine has been produced at this winery for well over a hundred years and it is one of the best known of the Swan Valley vineyards. Wines are made from grapes grown at both the Caversham and Margaret River Vineyards and are available for tasting. Amongst their better known wines are a 1995 Shiraz (an award winner at the London Wine Show), their Premium Chardonnay and a Margaret River Verdelho. Sandalera, a fortified dessert wine, has won over 20 medals. You can purchase a Vineyard or Mediterranean platter to enjoy under the delightful vine covered pergola. Morning and afternoon teas are also available. There is an excellent gift shop, selling a multitude of wine accessories, clothing and high quality locally produced arts, crafts and preserves.

Sitella Winery and Café: 100 Barrett Road, Herne Hill. Phone: 08 9296 2600. Open for tasting and light lunches on weekends and public holidays from 11.00 am to 4.00 pm. This new winery is in a wonderful position overlooking landscaped gardens and the vineyard. It produces a variety of wines including Chenin Blanc, Verdelho, Shiraz and Port.

Swanbrook Estate Wines: Swan Street, Henley Brook. Phone: 08 9296 3100. Open daily 10.30 am to 4.00 pm. This winery, formerly owned by Evans and Tate, who have moved their whole operation to their Margaret River vineyard, is set in a beautiful garden surrounded by vines. It offers premium wines such as Verdelho, Shiraz and Chardonnay, for tasting. Gourmet food in its tearooms complements the wine. There is a gift and art shop which is well stocked with high quality merchandise.

Talijancich Wines: 26 Hyem Road, Herne Hill. Phone: 08 9296 4289. Open Sunday to Friday 11.00 am to 5.00 pm. Closed Saturday. The first vines were planted here in 1932 and some of the original vines are still providing grapes for the Shiraz. They produce two white wines: a Semillon/Chardonnay/Chenin Blanc blend (called Voices) and a Verdelho. The red wines produced are a Grenache and a big gutsy Shiraz. A Ruby Port and two liqueurs are also available.

Twin Hill Wines: 1093 Great Northern Highway, Baskerville. Phone: 08 9296 4272. Open daily 10.00 am to 5.00 pm. A family winery, established in 1937, best known for its Port, Sherry and its Verdelho and Chenin Blanc. Bulk wines are available.

Upper Reach Vineyard: 77 Memorial Avenue, Baskerville. Phone: 08 9296 0078. Picturesquely situated on the upper reaches of the Swan River, hence its name. This is a new vineyard. Tasting and cellar sales are available on weekends or by appointment. They produce an oaked and an unoaked Chardonnay, Shiraz and a Cabernet Sauvignon.

Valley Wines: 352 Lennard Street, Herne Hill. Phone: 08 9296 4416. Open Sunday 10.00 am to 5.00 pm, or by appointment. This winery produces table and fortified wines, and sales of bulk wine are available. They also sell aged wine vinegar and cold pressed olive oil.

Westfield Winery: 180, Memorial Avenue, Baskerville. Phone: 08 9296 4356. Open Monday to

Saturday 10.00 am to 5.00 pm, Sunday 11.00 am to 4.00 pm. This is an attractive owner-operated winery with shady parking under vine covered pergolas. In the pleasantly cool underground cellar you can chat to the owner's wife while tasting Cabernet, Shiraz, Merlot, Chardonnay, Chenin and Verdelho wines made from grapes grown in Westfield's Swan Valley and their cooler Pemberton vineyards. The liqueur Muscat, sold only at the cellar door, is particularly worthy of mention.

OTHER WINERIES (NEAR PERTH, BUT NOT IN THE SWAN VALLEY) INCLUDE:

Baldivis Estate: Lot 165 River Road, Serpentine. Phone: 08 9525 2066. Open 10.00 am to 4.00 pm weekdays and 11.00 am to 5.00 pm weekends. This winery produces Cabernet Merlot, both wooded and unwooded Chardonnay, a Sauvignon Blanc/ Semillon blend and a Pinot Cabernet. There are under-cover gas BBQ's and a function area. Light lunches are served at weekends.

Carabooda Estate Wines: 297 Carabooda Road, Carabooda (just off Wanneroo Road). Phone: 08 9407 5283. Open daily 10.00 am to 6.00 pm for cellar sales. Specialises in red wines, including Shiraz and Cabernet Sauvignon. Whites include Sauvignon Blanc and Chardonnay. A picnic area is provided.

Carosa Vineyard: 310 Houston Street, Mt Helena. Phone: 08 9572 1603. Cellar sales: 11.00 am to 5.00 pm Saturday and Sunday and public holidays. Offers two dry red wines, a

Cabernet Merlot and a Pinot Noir. Their white wines include Chardonnay and Classic Dry White. They also make a sparkling white wine. Local artists' work is on display, and light lunches, for example gourmet platters and open sandwiches, are available.

Conti: 529 Wanneroo Road, Woodvale. Phone: 08 9409 9160. Open Monday to Saturday 9.30 am to 5.00 pm, Sunday by appointment. Red wines sold include Pinot, Cabernet, Grenache and Shiraz, for which they are best known. White wines produced are Chenin and Chardonnay and there is also a Late Harvest Muscat. This is a small, attractive family-run winery, and you may well come across the owner himself behind the bar in the wine cellar. Park beside the original orchard. The restaurant, which is in the original family homestead, is open for lunch Tuesday to Friday, and dinner Tuesday to Saturday.

Darlington Estate: 39 Nelson Road, Darlington. Phone: 08 9299 6268. Open Thursday to Sunday 12.00 noon to 5.00 pm for cellar door sales and café-style lunches, and Friday and Saturday nights for dinner. This winery is situated in a very attractive bushland setting overlooking the vineyard. In spring, when wildflowers are in bloom, there are lovely bush walks close by. In winter there is a blazing log fire. The three white wines produced here are Chardonnay, Semillon and Sauvignon Blanc. Reds include a Shiraz, Cabernet Sauvignon and a lighter Beaujolais style. There is also a red and a white Port.

Jadran Wines: 456 Reservoir Road, Orange Grove. Phone: 08 9459 1110. Open Monday to Saturday 9.30 am to 8.30 pm, and Sunday 11.00 am to 5.30 pm. This winery was established in 1927 by immigrants from the Adriatic coast of Yugoslavia. Their fortified wines include Sherries, white and red Ports. They also produce bottled premium wines such as a Burgundy and soft Rose, Chardonnay and Cabernet Sauvignon. The wines are available in bottles, flagons and, unusually for a Western Australian winery, in casks. Wines are only sold through the cellar door.

Peel Estate: Fletcher Road, off Stakehill Road, Baldivis (about 45 minutes south of Perth). Phone: 08 9524 1221. Open seven days 10.00 am to 5.00 pm. Picnic facilities. Wines can be bought and sampled in the grounds. These include Verdelho, Chenin, Chardonnay, Shiraz, Cabernet and Zinfandel (Californian red). A vintage Port is also produced.

Piesse Brook Wines: 226 Aldersyde Road, Bickley. Phone: 08 9293 3309. Open on Saturday 1.00 pm to 5.00 pm, Sunday 10.00 am to 5.00 pm. Closed during vintage. This is one of Western Australia's smallest vineyards, which mainly concentrates on full-bodied, dry red wines like Cabernet,

Shiraz and Merlot. They also produce Cabernova which is a lighter-style red to be drunk chilled in summer.

BREWERIES

Swan Brewery: 25 Baile Road, Canning Vale. Phone: 08 9350 0222. Offers group tours for 12 or more people but prior appointment essential. Day and evening tours available. Cost: $7.00. Includes informative tour and sampling of beers and bar snacks. Gift shop.

The Sail and Anchor Pub Brewery: 64 South Terrace, Fremantle. Phone: 08 9335 8433. Allows visits to their boutique brewery, and organises beer tasting by prior appointment. Cost is dependent on number attending.

Inchant Brewing Company: behind the Rose and Crown Hotel, 105 Swan Street, Guildford. Phone: 08 9379 3884. This micro brewery specialises in small batch, hand-crafted, old-style and traditional ales and lagers. No preservatives are used. Visitors may tour this brewery during working hours, or after hours and at weekends by appointment only. The ales and lagers may be sampled at the Rose and Crown Hotel in front of the brewery. There are a number of other boutique breweries (e.g. Matilda Bay Brewery) which do not encourage visits from the public.

CHAPTER 13

PARKS AND GARDENS

Perth's best-known park is Kings Park, which is the city's most frequently visited attraction and a must-see for any tourist. As well as being a magnificent park, the views of Perth City are breathtaking, both during the day and at night. Other major parks and gardens found around Perth and Fremantle are also described in this chapter, many with BBQs, benches and play equipment for children.

Some of the parks listed below are large national parks up to an hour's drive from the centre of Perth. You need a day trip to visit one. Others are smaller, inner city parks, ideal for a quiet rest from shopping or exploring.

Allan Green Plant Conservatory: The Esplanade, Perth. Open 10.00 am to 4.00 pm Monday to Saturday, Sunday and public holidays 12.00 noon to 4.00 pm. Admission is free. This pyramid-shaped glasshouse houses many tropical and semi-tropical plants.

Araluen Botanic Park: 523 Croydon Road, Roleystone. Phone: 08 9496 1171. Thirty kilometres south-east of Perth. Open every day of the year 9.00 am to 6.00 pm. Cost: adults $3.00, children $1.00. A lovely park to picnic or BBQ in. There are walk trails through the jarrah forest and beautiful old established gardens, through which a creek flows all year. The park is famous for the tulips and other spring bulbs which flower from

August to October. At this time, entry to the park is slightly more expensive. There is a kiosk and a licensed restaurant.

Bold Park: Oceanic Drive, Floreat (opposite Bold Park Drive). This park is covered by coastal woodlands and scrub, and has many different types of plant species. There are paths, walkways and bridle trails throughout the park. The highest point is Reabold Hill which is 85 metres high and offers 360 degree views of the city and the ocean. A scenic drive takes you to the top of the hill and wildflowers may be seen in spring. The park lies adjacent to Perry Lakes and both could be included in the same outing.

Botanic Golf Gardens (see also Mini-golf, page 120): 25 Drovers Place, Wanneroo (25 kms north of Perth). Phone: 08 9405 1475. Open Tuesday to Sunday 10.00 am to 4.30 pm. Closed Mondays except school and public holidays. This exceptional 18-

hole mini-golf course is nestled amongst five acres of botanical gardens, with manicured lawns, lakes and exotic flower displays. Towering trees provide plenty of shade for players and spectators and there are many seats if you wish to relax and appreciate the gardens. Paths meander through the lush greenery, past waterfalls, and frequently cross small streams. This well-kept facility is one of Perth's premier gardens. Something to see and do for all ages. Kiosk, café and BBQ facilities.

Burswood Park: Resort Drive (off Great Eastern Highway), Burswood. Phone: 08 9361 4475. Just a stone's throw from the city, Burswood Park has won several tourism awards. Situated on the banks of the Swan River, this grassy park offers walking, cycling and jogging trails. There is also a heritage trail punctuated by bronze sculptures of figures from Western Australia's history. Free guided walks along the heritage trail are held daily at 11.30 am. Ample parking, free electric BBQ's, play areas for children and shady picnic spots make this an ideal area to visit. Over 40 varieties of bird life and waterfowl may be seen here. See Chapter 14: Wildlife, page 90 for more information.

Hyde Park: Vincent Street, Highgate. This park consists of an ornamental lake surrounded by delightful green lawns and garden beds. Many giant Moreton Bay Fig trees make it a cool and shady place in summer. There are many water birds, including swans and ducks. Facilities include a walking trail, children's playground, BBQ's and seating. The park is close to Northbridge and the City.

John Forrest National Park: Great Eastern Highway, Glen Forrest. Phone: 08 9298 8344 (ranger). Cost: $5.00 per car. Situated at the crest of the Darling Range escarpment, about 26 kilometres from the centre of Perth. A half-hour drive takes you to this popular A-Class Reserve, which covers some 1580 hectares of mainly natural jarrah forest. Wildflowers may be seen in spring and there is abundant wildlife, including many species of birds, kangaroos, brush wallabies, echidnas and some reptiles. There are pretty walking trails to pools and waterfalls on Jane Brook. A natural swimming pool has change facilities provided. There are also horse trails and a scenic drive with panoramic views over the Darling Scarp to Perth and the coastal plain. In addition, there are cultivated native gardens, tearooms and restaurant, BBQ facilities and extensive picnic areas.

Kings Park: Kings Park Road, Perth. Phone: 08 9480 3600. Originally called Perth Park, but renamed Kings Park in 1901, in honour of King Edward VII, this is Western Australia's most heavily visited tourist attraction. It is situated just a few minutes from the centre of Perth and covers about 400 hectares, much of which is natural bush land. The park is set high above the Swan River with spectacular views over Swan River, Perth city, towards the Darling Range in the east, and the coast in the west.

From the city you can walk, go by bus, or tram. See Chapter 2:

Getting Around; Trams, page 13. There are several roads through the park and extensive walking and cycling tracks. A great way to see the park is by bike and these can be hired (see Bike Hire, page 12).

The Information Office in Fraser Avenue has an extensive selection of brochures detailing both guided and self-guided walking tours of the park and the flora and fauna you will see. These include over 450 species of flowering plants. See Walks in Chapter 17: Activities on the Land; page 126. There are over 70 bird species and many reptiles and mammals.

In spring, the bush comes alive with wildflowers, including kangaroo paws and mass displays of everlastings. The Wildflower Festival is held in the Botanic Garden in September and offers a chance to see every conceivable type of wildflower en masse, some under cover. Thousands attend this Festival every year.

The State War Memorial is in the Park and there are avenues of trees within the park which commemorate soldiers killed in action. The main entrance (Fraser Avenue) is lined with tall gum trees each with a plaque in honour of prominent citizens of Perth in its first 100 years of settlement (1829–1929).

In summer there is often live theatre staged in the park, as well as outdoor films (Sunset Cinema). The latest addition to the park's attractions is Artist in Residence: an Aboriginal Art Gallery, situated under the Lookout on Fraser Avenue. See Chapter 7: Galleries, page 43.

There are several picnic, BBQ and playground areas within the park and many grassed areas. The Lotteries Family Area consists of: the Ivey Watson Playground for children under six; a playground for children under 12; the Stickybeaks Café; and the Hale Oval which is a dual cycle path weaving around grassy picnic spots, BBQs and gazebos.

Lake Leschenaultia: Rosedale Road, Chidlow. Phone: 08 9572 4248. Cost: $5.00 per car. Fifty kilometres from the centre of Perth. This is a large freshwater lake with sandy beaches surrounded by tall shady trees. You can hire canoes, swim in the lake, fish for trout, walk or cycle along numerous trails. A miniature railway runs through the bush past signposted trees and plants. In spring, wildflowers are found in abundance. There are excellent BBQ and picnic facilities, a kiosk and tearooms. This is a very popular place for family days out.

Linga Longa Park: 157 Fletcher Road, Baldivis/Karnup. Phone: 08 9524 1656. Open Sunday to Thursday and public holidays 10.00 am to 5.00 pm. Closed Christmas Day and Good Friday. Cost: adults $6.50, pensioners $5.50, children $4.50. One of the main attractions is a hands-on Science Discovery Centre. Suitable for families with young children. There is a playground, free mini train, maze, and shady lawns for picnics and BBQs. Children will enjoy the many farmyard animals (goats, sheep, cows, pigs and rabbits), some of which can be bottle fed. There are trout and

KINGS PARK

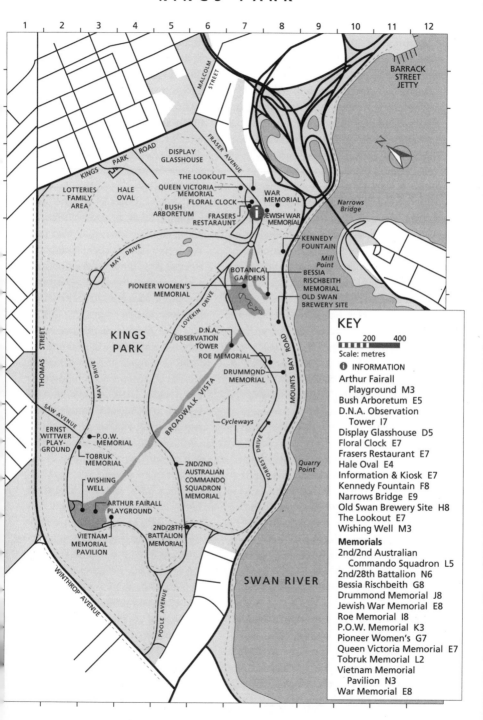

KEY

0   200   400
Scale: metres

🛈 INFORMATION
Arthur Fairall
  Playground M3
Bush Arboretum E5
D.N.A. Observation
  Tower I7
Display Glasshouse D5
Floral Clock E7
Frasers Restaurant E7
Hale Oval E4
Information & Kiosk E7
Kennedy Fountain F8
Narrows Bridge E9
Old Swan Brewery Site H8
The Lookout E7
Wishing Well M3

Memorials
2nd/2nd Australian
  Commando Squadron L5
2nd/28th Battalion N6
Bessia Rischbeith G8
Drummond Memorial J8
Jewish War Memorial E8
Roe Memorial I8
P.O.W. Memorial K3
Pioneer Women's G7
Queen Victoria Memorial E7
Tobruk Memorial L2
Vietnam Memorial
  Pavilion N3
War Memorial E8

marron ponds. A kiosk sells ice creams, drinks and snacks.

Mundaring Weir: Mundaring Weir Road, Mundaring. Situated 40 kilometres East of Perth. Mundaring Weir dams the Helena River and has supplied water to Kalgoorlie and the Goldfields since 1903 by way of CY O'Connor's famous pipeline. Apart from a walk along the top of the dam wall to admire the huge expanse of water, there are formal gardens with BBQ and picnic areas. Below the wall is the O'Connor Museum, housed in the original pumping station. See The O'Connor Museum, Chapter 6: Museums, page 41.

Perry Lakes: entry from Meagher Drive off Underwood Avenue, or Perry Lakes Drive, Floreat Park. A large expanse of bushland with enjoyable bush walks, cycle tracks, playgrounds and BBQ facilities. There are two lakes, with many varieties of water birds, including wild ducks and swans. The large grassy well-shaded picnic areas are popular with families. Pedal cars can be hired on weekends for a ride around the park.

Queens Gardens: cnr Hay and Plain Streets, Perth. See a replica of Peter Pan's statue (as in Kensington Gardens, London) in this small, leafy and tranquil English style park near the centre of the city. Has swans and ducks on its lakes.

Supreme Court Gardens: cnr Riverside Drive and Barrack Street, Perth. The Supreme Court buildings are situated in these gardens, which provide an attractive and peaceful place for city workers to eat their lunches.

Walyunga National Park: Walyunga Road, Upper Swan. Phone: 08 9571 1371 (ranger). Forty kilometres north east of Perth off the Great Northern Highway, is 1800 hectares of unspoilt bush, through which the Swan River winds its way down to Perth. The many varieties of gums and other vegetation provide a home for colonies of kangaroos, wallabies and numerous water and bushland birds. Lizards, skinks, geckos and goannas may also be seen, along with snakes such as dugites and tiger snakes. During the winter season after heavy rains, there are often rapids for canoeists to tackle. On the first weekend in August, a white water race, the Avon Descent, passes through the park. Many different kinds of watercraft such as kayaks, canoes and motorised dinghies participate. There are beautiful bush walks too, especially enjoyable in spring when wildflowers abound. BBQ facilities and picnic areas are available and camping is allowable with the Ranger's permission.

Whiteman Park: 30 mins drive from City. Entrance off Lord Street via Marshall Road, West Swan. Phone: 08 9249 2446. Open every day from 9.00 am to 6.00 pm; with the main attractions from Wednesday to Sunday and public holidays, between 11.00 am and 4.00 pm. This park consists of 2500 hectares of Australian bushland setting. There is a land transport theme with a vintage electric tram and steam train rides. Also a Motor museum displays 120 vintage cars and other historic vehicles. Visitors can see sheep shearing, visit craft shops, hire bikes and utilise the walking trails through the bush. At weekends there are sometimes camel and pony rides. There are many BBQ and picnic areas, the most popular of which is Mussel Pool, named after the freshwater mussels which were found in it.

Wireless Hill Park: Entry from Aldmondbury Road or McCallum Crescent, Ardross (approx. 10 kilometres south west of Perth city). This is a 40 hectare reserve which was originally the site of one of Australia's earliest telecommunications stations. The original Overseas Telecommunications Commission building now houses the Wireless Hill Telecommunications Museum. See also Chapter 6: Museums, page 41. The Wireless Hill Park Heritage Trail retraces the history of the telecommunications station and its development into a nature reserve. The trail is a 750-metre walk through natural bushland, noted for its beautiful native flora, particularly during the months of September and October. More than 26 species of birds can be seen, including cockatoos, parrots, thornbills and kookaburras. Within the park there is a grassed picnic area, playground and

viewing towers providing panoramic views of the Swan River, city skyline and the Darling Range.

Yanchep National Park: Wanneroo Road, Yanchep. Phone: 08 9561 1004. Situated 50 kilometres from Perth City. Cost: $8.00 per car for up to eight people. Visitors' guides to the park are available as you enter the gates to the park. This huge park, some 2800 hectares, includes vast lawned areas, some sloping down to Loch McNess. The lawns provide an attractive area for family BBQs and picnics. Yanchep is home to the largest colony of koalas in Western Australia which are the main tourist attraction of the park. There are some wonderful walking trails through banksia, tuart woodlands and wetlands enabling viewing of kangaroos, emus and birds. Information on the various trails is available at the visitor centre. There is also the Gloucester Lodge Museum (which describes the park's history), rowing boat hire on Loch McNess and a nine-hole golf course (BYO clubs). Tours of the spectacular limestone Crystal Cave are also available. Yanchep Inn is situated within the park. Yanchep National Park is an ideal place for a day out with visitors from overseas.

CHAPTER 14

WILDLIFE

For lovers of wildlife, Perth has much to offer. Most first time visitors to Australia are keen to see koalas and kangaroos and also less well-known Australian animals such as the wombat, echidna and platypus. As well as the Perth Zoo, there are several wildlife parks where you can see kangaroos and koalas and in many you can hand feed the kangaroos. At one park you can have your photograph taken cuddling a koala!

You can see quokkas on Rottnest Island, swim with the dolphins near Rockingham and go whale watching from September to November when the humpback whales migrate down the Western Australian coast. At Underwater World you can see sharks and stingrays at close quarters, and in the hills outside Perth you can trek with llamas! The black swan, symbol of Western Australia, is prolific at Lake Monger, and some parks are noted for their wide variety of water birds.

Following are places to visit, if you wish to see Australian animals, birds, reptiles or marine life:

Armadale Reptile Centre: Lot 55 South Western Highway, Wungong. Phone: 08 9399 6927. Open daily 10.00 am to 4.00 pm. Cost: adults $6.00, children $4.00. An opportunity to see more than 200 reptiles, including snakes, lizards, goannas, skinks, turtles and frogs, all in natural settings. Some of these reptiles, including a python,

skinks and turtles may be handled if you wish. There is a kiosk serving drinks and ice cream.

Burswood Park: Resort Drive, Burswood. Phone: 08 9361 4475 or 08 9470 2060. This land on the banks of the Swan River has been transformed from a suburban rubbish dump to a park which now calls itself home to over 30 varieties of bird life and water fowl, including many varieties of ducks, grebes, stilts, herons, black swans and spoonbills. A series of bird life interpretation plaques are placed throughout the park to help visitors identify species of birds. This park is conveniently situated close to the city and has many attractions. See page 85 in Chapter 13: Parks and Gardens.

Caversham Wildlife Park: cnr Arthur Street and Cranleigh Road, West Swan. Phone: 08 9274 2202. Open daily 9.00 am to 5.00 pm. Cost: adults $8.00, concession $7.00, children

$3.00. There is a wide range of Australian native wildlife at this park, including koalas, Tasmanian devils, wombats, emus, birds, possums and dingos. You can hand feed kangaroos, wallabies and deer and there are also farmyard animals and buffalo. Facilities include BBQs, picnic areas, a kiosk serving light refreshments and souvenirs.

Cohunu Koala Park: Lot 287a Mills Road, Gosnells (35 minutes by car from the City centre). Phone: 08 9390 6090. Open daily 10.00 am to 5.00 pm. This park, on a 40-acre site has over 300 kangaroos and more than 20 koalas living in natural surroundings. You can have your photo taken holding a koala any time between 10.00 am and 4.30 pm, a very popular activity with overseas tourists. Apart from the koalas and kangaroos, there are emus, talking parrots, a walk-through aviary, wombat tunnel, lakes and water birds. Buy food at 40 cents per bag to hand feed the kangaroos and emus. On site is the Koalas View revolving family restaurant, with Australian cuisine (emu, crocodile, kangaroo and seafood) and views of Perth city lights at night (Friday and Saturday night only).

Dizzy Lamb Park and Koala Gardens: cnr Karaborup Road and Wanneroo Road, Carabooda. Phone: 08 9407 5388. Open to the public Sunday, school and public holidays, and for group bookings, any day of the year between 10.00 am and 5.00 pm. Cost of entry to both sections of this large complex: $10.00 adults,

$8.00 aged pensioners, $7.00 children (four to 14 years, under four free). Rides cost extra: from 50 cents to $3.00. At the Koala Gardens and Wildlife Park, you can take close up photographs of many of the animals, including wombats, quokkas, wallabies, emus, cockatoos, parrots, koalas and kangaroos (including a rare white kangaroo). Kangaroos and emus may be handfed. The koalas sometimes snooze on the handrails of the walkway round their enclosure, so you can stroke them if you are lucky. Next to the wildlife section, Dizzy Lamb Park has rides for younger children. There are picnic areas, gas BBQs, mini water playground, refreshment kiosk, a gift shop, a Vintage Car Museum and a WA Military Museum, with a good collection of Anzac memorabilia.

Herdsman Lake Wildlife Centre: cnr Flynn and Selby streets, Wembley. Phone: 08 9387 6079. Open weekdays 8.15 am to 4.30 pm and weekends 1.00 pm to 4.30 pm. Cost: adults $2.00, children and pensioners $1.00. This is a significant wetland, providing a wildlife sanctuary and breeding ground for many species of water bird. About 85 species may be seen here during the year, the most common of which are: coots, swamp hens, moorhens, varieties of grebes and ducks, pelicans, egrets, spoonbills, ibis and heron. In spring and summer, migratory waders from Siberia can be seen. Many of the birds may be observed from the five metre high mezzanine viewing area in the Information and Display Centre, run by The Western Australian Gould League. Here there are changing educational displays, not only related to birds but also other wetland creatures including live lizards, frogs and baby turtles in aquariums. The Gould League runs early morning guided bird walks on the third Saturday of each month. The lake's recreational facilities include grassed parklands, walking and cycling tracks and a children's playground.

Lake Monger: Lake Monger Drive, Leederville. This large park covers 146 hectares, of which the lake occupies 97 hectares. A 3.5 kilometre multi-purpose path runs around the lake, which is surrounded by shady trees and green lawns. Lake Monger is renowned for its wide variety of bird life and, as it never dries out, it provides a refuge for aquatic birds during the summer months. The most famous of these are the black swans, but there are also coots, grebes, swamp hens, pelicans and many varieties of wild duck. The birds are used to being hand fed and may greet you a little over enthusiastically at times. There is a small children's playground and picnic tables, but you may have to share your picnic with the wildlife! The multi-purpose path is very popular with the locals for walking, jogging and bike riding.

Llama Encounter: Shadowlands, 414 Chittering Road, Chittering. Phone: 08 9576 1187. The llamas carry a picnic for you through farmland and bush to a scenic picnic spot. Morning and afternoon teas, champagne breakfasts, lunch or sundowners are catered for if arranged in advance. Sturdy walking shoes are essential.

Llama Leisure/Southglen Estate: Hardey Road, Glen Forrest (35 minutes east of Perth city centre). Phone: 08 9298 8617. This is home to 20 South American house-trained llamas which wander in and out of the house at will. Visitors can spend the night and have a trek through the hills for breakfast or a moonlight supper with the provisions transported by the llamas.

Marapana Wildlife World: 157 Paganoni Road, Karnup (less than an hour's drive south of Perth, and 10 minutes from Mandurah). Phone: 08 9537 1404. Open 9.00 am to 5.00 pm every day except Christmas Day. Cost: adults $8.00, children (4 to 15) $5.00. A 2.5 kilometre drive allows you to closely view and hand feed free-ranging kangaroos and deer. There is also a koala enclosure, emus, wombats, camels, water buffalo and birds. Facilities include BBQs, a kiosk serving light meals, a water playground for children and a golf driving range with club and ball hire.

Parrots of Bellawood Park: 64 Furnissdale Road, Mandurah (about an hour's drive south of Perth). Phone: 08 9535 6732. Open Monday, Thursday, Friday, Saturday, Sunday, public holidays and school holidays, 10.00 am to 4.00 pm. There are over 500 birds, including 50 of Australia's 55 species of parrot, housed in a large walk-in aviary. The parrots may be hand fed. The landscaped gardens blended with natural bushland, provide a pleasant parkland for picnics and BBQs. A kiosk sells teas, ice-creams and drinks.

Penguins and Seals can be seen on Penguin Island which lies about one kilometre offshore from Safety Bay. It is home to a large breeding colony of fairy penguins. You may see them in their natural habitat, but as they spend a lot of time at sea, CALM (Department of Conservation and Land Management) runs the Penguin Experience Discovery Centre. Here you can watch the penguins swimming around in their pool and being fed.

Seal Island lies very close to Penguin Island. It is home to sea lions. Bird Island is somewhat further away, and is home to numerous birds.

Penguin and Seal Island Cruises depart from Mersey Point Jetty, Shoalwater (45 minutes south of Perth). Phone: 08 9528 2004. They run trips to these islands, either individually or as combined tours, which can include snorkelling. Phone for more information about other tours. A trip to Penguin Island only costs: adults $7.50, concession $6.50, children $4.50. These prices include entry to the Penguin Experience Discovery Centre mentioned above.

Perth Zoological Gardens: 20 Labouchere Road, South Perth. Phone: 08 9367 7988; 24 hour recorded Infoline: 08 9474 3551. Open every day of the year 9.00 am to 5.00 pm. Cost: adults $10.00, concessions $7.00, children $5.00, mini-group (two adults, two children) $27.50. A pleasant way to get to the Zoo from the city is to catch a ferry from Barrack Street Jetty to Mends Street Jetty and stroll up Mends Street to the Zoo in Labouchere Road. The ferries leave approximately every half-hour (though they are more frequent in the rush hour) and the journey takes approximately 10 minutes and costs 90 cents. Phone: 08 9221 2722 for exact ferry information. Perth Zoo is Australia's most popular zoo per capita, with over 600,000 visitors a year. Over 1600 animals representing 280 species are presented in surroundings which recreate their natural habitat, especially in the Australian Bushwalk (koalas, kangaroos, emus and wombats), African Savannah and Nocturnal House. You can see all the popular zoo animals: elephants, giraffe, bears, primates, big cats, reptiles, otters, meerkats and a white rhinoceros, to name but a few. There is a walk-through aviary and a tropical butterfly house. The Zoo is attractively laid out and compact enough to enable you to see all the animals in a day's visit. There are a number of regular keeper talks and animal feed times scheduled throughout the day, and you can pick up the information sheet and timetable from the Information Centre near the entrance. There is a café, playground and lovely picnic and BBQ areas. The paths linking exhibits meander through delightful well-established gardens, but if you get tired of walking, there is a motorised tram which leaves every 45 minutes, for a 20 minute ride through the Zoo. Cost: $3.00 per person and you can get on and off all day. There is a very good shop and an Education Centre. Check Infoline for special Twilight programme in summer.

Rottnest Island is home to the quokka, a small marsupial, originally mistaken by early explorers for a large rat. The animals are very numerous on the island and it would be hard to visit Rottnest without coming across a few, even in the Settlement. See Chapter 11: Rottnest Island, page 65.

Shetland Barn: 2 Sounness Drive, Bullsbrook (just off Great Northern Highway). Phone: 08 9571 1549. Open daily from 9.30 am to 4.30 pm. Cost: $8.00 per car or $2.00 per bus passenger. Set on 50 acres, this property has paddocks and gardens with walking trails, that have been developed to attract native birds. Picnics and games can be enjoyed on the extensive grassed areas. There are two shady holding areas of Shetland ponies to pat. Optional pony drawn wagon rides at $2.00 per person provide an ideal way to see Shetland ponies roaming free, as well as the rest of the farm. A saddle-making workshop can be found in the barn, which is also used for dancing, such as bootscooting and clogging. There is a souvenir shop and an air-conditioned restaurant.

The Maze: Sequoia Park, Neaves Road, Bullsbrook (on Highway 86). Phone: 08 9571 1375. Open Tuesday to Sunday 9.30 am to 5.30 pm and all public and school holidays. Cost: adults $9.00, children $6.00. Family passes available. No dogs allowed. There are six koalas as well as kangaroos, emus, birds and some farm animals. Occasionally there are camel rides during busy periods. Extensive manicured lawns with plenty of shady trees to sit under provide a pleasant setting for picnics and BBQs. There are two small mazes for toddlers, and three that even an adult could get lost in. Choose your maze from wood, hedge or pine plantation. Mini-golf and a playground provide extra amusement for children. There is a small souvenir shop, and a café serving snacks and Devonshire teas.

Tumbulgum Farm: South West Highway, Mundijong (40 minutes from Perth). Phone: 08 9525 5888. Open daily 9.30 am to 5.00 pm. This farm won a 1997 Western Australian Tourism Award. Entertainment includes:

Farm Shows: 10.00 am, 1.00 pm and 3.15 pm. You can see a typical Australian farm in action including sheep mustering, shearing, sheepdogs in action and enjoy billy tea and damper.

Aboriginal Culture Shows: Monday, Wednesday, Thursday and Friday 11.00 am and 2.30 pm and Saturday at 2.30 pm. You can see traditional dances of the Noongah tribe, performed by the Abodijeri Australia Dance Troup, and listen to the haunting sounds of the didgeridoo and the clapping sticks. The kiosk is open for snacks, Devonshire teas, burgers and ice-creams, while the Leonda Function Centre offers BBQ lunches with traditional Australian choices including kangaroo, emu, yabbies, crocodile, snapper, chicken, beef or lamb.

Underwater World (at Sorrento Quay): 91 Southside Drive, Hillarys Boat Harbour. Phone: 08 9447 7500. Open every day except Christmas Day, 9.00 am to 5.00 pm. Cost: adults $16.50, children $9.00, family pass $42.00. This is an oceanarium with a difference. Visitors travel on a moving walkway through a transparent tunnel, on a journey under the sea, and come face to face with thousands of marine creatures including sharks, rays and schools of fish, which are hand fed at 11.00 am and 2.00 pm. You can also see displays of dangerous marine creatures, for example, sea snakes and stone fish. In the touch pool, have a hands-on encounter with seastars, turtles and sharks. Feeding times are 12 noon and 3.00 pm. Marine films are screened throughout the day in the theatre. Outside in the Dolphin Sanctuary, three bottlenose dolphins can be seen in their harbour sea-pen. There is an educational presentation and display of natural dolphin behaviours. Feeding times are at 10.30 am, 1.30 pm and 4.00 pm. All feeding times may be subject to change. Please check. There is a café and licensed bar. Qualified scuba divers can dive with the sharks and other fish in the underwater enclosure. Bookings and your own equipment essential. Cost $75.00. Underwater World experts run whale watching safaris in season. See Whale Watching section below.

Western Rosella Bird Park: Lot 10, Old Pinjarra Road, Mandurah (one hour's drive from Perth). Phone: 08 9535 2104. Open every day except Good Friday and Christmas Day, from 8.00 am to 5.30 pm. Cost: adults $6.00, children and pensioners $4.00. Set on the banks of the Serpentine River with waterways, lakes and picnic areas. There is a large selection of Australian birds (30 to 35 varieties) and a giant walk-in aviary, where you can hand feed rainbow lorikeets. You can also feed the kangaroos, emus and farm animals. Facilities include BBQs and a café selling BBQ packs, snacks and Devonshire teas. There is also a children's playground, with free mini-golf and miniature train rides.

Wild Kingdom Wildlife Park and Zoo: Two Rocks Road, Yanchep. Phone: 08 9561 1399. Open 10.30 am to 5.00 pm every day except Christmas Day. Cost: adults $4.00, children $2.00. This park has a large range of Australian wildlife, such as kangaroos, emus, dingos, wombats as well as a camel, miniature horses and birds. You can buy special food to hand feed the animals. BBQs and picnic areas are available.

Yanchep National Park: Wanneroo Road, Yanchep. Phone: 08 9561 1004. Open 7 days. Cost: $8.00 per car. Has the largest colony of koalas (more than 30) in Western Australia and the walk-through enclosures are designed so visitors can get within a few metres of the animals. You can meet the koalas at 2.15 pm on weekends and public holidays. There are also enclosures with kangaroos and emus and, on the lawns around the lake, many wetland birds can be seen (and might like to share your lunch!). Native parrots are frequently seen in abundance. White-tailed Black Cockatoos sometimes congregate in the trees in such numbers that the sound can be deafening and visitors may feel they are trapped inside an aviary. Yanchep is an ideal destination for a day's outing to see native Australian animals and enjoy a picnic lunch in a scenic setting. See page 89 in Chapter 13: Parks and Gardens, for more information about the park and its many facilities.

WHALE WATCHING

Humpback whales migrate down the Western Australian coastline from September to December and may often be seen off the coast of Perth. Several companies offer whale watching trips but cannot guarantee sightings. Below is a sample of companies offering whale watching trips. See also under Boat Hire or Charter in Chapter 15: Activities on the Water, page 98.

Boat Torque Cruises: Pier 4, Barrack Street Jetty, Perth. Phone: 08 9221 5844. Various whale watching trips and cruises, some combined with other sightseeing. Boats depart from Barrack Street Jetty (Perth), Hillarys Boat Harbour (Sorrento Quay), and Northport (Rous Head, Fremantle). From Perth, a four-hour round trip including courtesy coach pick-ups from city hotels, costs: adults $37.00, students/seniors/backpackers $28.00, children $20.00. This includes whale watching and a trip up and down the

river. Alternatively from Fremantle, a two-hour whale watching cruise costs: adults $20.00, students, seniors and backpackers $14.00, children $9.00, including coach pick-up from Fremantle Railway Station. Phone for more details.

Fishing Charters of WA: 47 Mews Road, Fremantle. Phone: 08 9430 6001 or 015 990 884 or freecall 1800 656 616. Whale watching charter boats are available in October and November. Prices depend on number of people and size of vessel. Humpback and southern right whales are usually be seen during the four-hour cruises.

Mills Charters: Shop 46, Sorrento Quay, Hillarys Boat Harbour. Phone: 08 9246 5334, a/h 08 9401 0833. Three-hour whale watching trips from September to early December. Cost: $25.00.

Oceanic Cruises: East Street Jetty, East Fremantle. Phone: 08 9430 5127. Whale watching cruises in season (end August to October) either on the Rottnest ferry Sea Cat or on a schooner accommodating about 60 people. Phone for more details. Cost: Sea Cat $15.00; schooner $25.00.

Underwater World: 91 Southside Drive, Hillarys Boat Harbour. Phone: 08 9447 7500. Whale watching safaris are run on three or four Sundays in October/November. A marine mammal specialist is on board the 54-foot yacht and a light lunch is provided during the four-hour safari. Cost: $55.00.

CHAPTER 15

ACTIVITIES ON THE WATER

The coastline of Western Australia runs from north to south for hundreds of kilometres and provides a continuous strip of white sandy beaches fronting the clear, unpolluted waters of the Indian Ocean. This, combined with the broad expanses of the Swan and Canning rivers, provides a mecca for those who enjoy water sports of any description.

Due to the coast's north/south aspect and the sun setting in the west over the Indian Ocean, there are frequently very spectacular sunsets. This has led to the coast north of Cottesloe being known as The Sunset Coast.

The sea breeze tends to come in early in the afternoon so choose your sport accordingly. It is advisable to apply a high factor sunscreen at regular intervals during the day.

BEACHES

River beaches on the shores of both the Swan and Canning Rivers are safe and popular, for example, Matilda Bay and Peppermint Grove on the North side of the river and Como Beach, Applecross foreshore and Point Walter on the South side. Many of these beaches have wide grassy picnic areas with good shady trees to sit under as well as a narrow strip of sand sloping gently down to the river.

Ocean beaches north of Fremantle provide safe swimming in most places, with some being better known for surfing and windsurfing. Many beaches are patrolled by surf life-saving clubs from the beginning of October to the end of March, mainly at weekends and public holidays. Some beaches are susceptible to currents and undertows or rips, therefore it is advisable to swim on patrolled beaches and stay between the red and yellow flags, which the life-savers put out to indicate a safe place to swim.

To the south of Fremantle the beaches, along the shores of Cockburn Sound as far as Safety Bay, are protected by Garden Island and all offer safe swimming, but little surf. Some of these are South Fremantle, Coogee Beach,

Naval Base, Kwinana, Rockingham Beach, Shoalwater Bay and Safety Bay.

THE MAIN NORTHERN BEACHES ARE:

Port Beach: The nearest beach to Fremantle and popular with families. There is a restaurant and kiosk on the beach, which is patrolled by surf life-savers on weekends.

Leighton Beach: Popular with surfers and windsurfers as well as swimmers. Life-savers are present on weekends.

Cottesloe Beach: One of Perth's favourite family beaches. It is a safe swimming beach and is patrolled by surf life-savers. It is also popular for surfing, and watching the sun set over the Indian Ocean. Behind the wide sandy beach there is a lovely grassed area, with huge Norfolk Island pine trees providing plenty of shade. There are several restaurants, cafés and kiosks.

North Cottesloe Beach: Popular with all age groups, and especially with bodysurfers. Beware of undertows which can develop in choppy conditions. There are several cafés and restaurants and a very active surf life-saving club.

Swanbourne Beach: Southern Swanbourne beach is a popular surfing beach, whilst further north, in an area sheltered by sand dunes, lies Perth's only nudist beach. There is a surf life-saving club at the southern end of the beach.

City Beach: Patrolled by surf life-savers, it is safe for swimming but beware of shore dumps.

Floreat Beach: Safe and clean, this beach recently won an award. It is also prone to shore dumps. Surf life-savers are on duty.

Scarborough Beach: Popular surfing, sailboarding and boogie boarding beach. It can be dangerous and is not very suitable for young children. It is extremely important to swim between the flags and read and obey the warning signs. The beach is patrolled by surf life-savers. There are beachside cafés, a hotel and grassed areas.

Trigg Beach: Also a very popular beach for surfers, but it can be dangerous when rough and it is prone to rips, especially near the Bluehole. Once again, obey the warning signs and swim between the flags.

Most of the bays to the north of here are good family beaches, for example, Watermans Bay, North Beach, Mettams Pool (lots of shallow rock pools), Whitfords, Mullaloo (Surf Life-Saving Club and large grassed area next to the beach with playground and electric BBQs) and Burns Beach. The beach by Hillarys Marina is particularly good for small children. This is part of the Hillarys Boat Harbour/Sorrento Quay complex (see pages 51 and 107 for more information). Sorrento Beach, just south of Hillarys Boat Harbour, can get rough but is patrolled by a Surf Life-Saving Club. Still further to the north, the Yanchep Lagoon provides a sheltered swimming spot.

BOAT HIRE OR CHARTER:

Bayside Boat Charter and Cruise Consultants: Phone: 089 221 9191 or 015 478 608. A wide range of modern

BEACHES

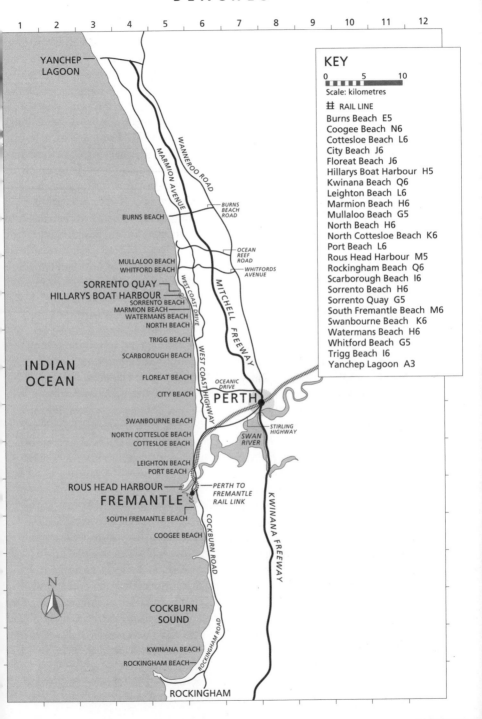

KEY

0   5   10
Scale: kilometres

♯ RAIL LINE

Burns Beach E5
Coogee Beach N6
Cottesloe Beach L6
City Beach J6
Floreat Beach J6
Hillarys Boat Harbour H5
Kwinana Beach Q6
Leighton Beach L6
Marmion Beach H6
Mullaloo Beach G5
North Beach H6
North Cottesloe Beach K6
Port Beach L6
Rous Head Harbour M5
Rockingham Beach Q6
Scarborough Beach I6
Sorrento Beach H6
Sorrento Quay G5
South Fremantle Beach M6
Swanbourne Beach K6
Watermans Beach H6
Whitford Beach G5
Trigg Beach I6
Yanchep Lagoon A3

purpose-built vessels are available for deep-sea fishing, exclusive charters, Rottnest day trips, whale watching in season, Swan River public cruises and yachting on the river or ocean.

Dreamtime Yacht Charters: Phone: 08 9305 5583 or 0419 908 338. This 60-foot yacht departs Hillarys Marina for whale watching from August to December and is then available for charter cruises on the Swan River and the Ocean to Rottnest. They also have three party boats available for charter on the Swan River. Catering is available if required.

Fishing Charters of WA: Fremantle. Phone: 1800 656 616. Fishing Charters of WA represent 18 companies and 25 vessels and can arrange deep-sea or game fishing trips, Swan River or Ocean cruises or whale watching trips (in season) to suit your requirements. For example, they can take up to 25 passengers deep-sea fishing, west of Rottnest, out to the edge of the continental shelf. Cost: from $80.00 per person for a day (6.00 am to approximately 3.00 pm). Take your own food and drink, or catering can be organised for groups of more than 10 people. You might expect to catch dhufish, snapper, trevally and school sharks.

Fremantle Yacht Charters: 7/8 Mews Road, Fremantle. Phone: 08 9335 3844 or 0418 939 117. Various sizes of sailing yachts and motor sailers are available for day, or overnight fully crewed or self-sail charters. They offer twilight sailing on the river with champagne and also ocean cruises, for example to Rottnest Island.

Mills Charters: Ground Floor, Department of Transport Building, Hillarys Boat Harbour. Phone: 08 9246 5334 or a/h 08 9401 0833. Luxury charter vessels are available for deep-sea fishing up to 30 miles off the coast. Gear and bait are supplied, but bring your own lunch and drinks. Fishing trips cost from $75.00 per day mid-week, and $85.00 per day at weekends and public holidays. Whale watching and dolphin and seal excursions can also be arranged.

Sliver: Phone: 08 9337 9498 or 0412 283 988. Sail on a modern 15-metre yacht (with skipper). They operate from November to the end of March, normally at weekends only. Day trips to Rottnest Island cost $85.00 per person, including lunch in a beautiful bay and a visit to the main settlement at Thomson Bay.

Westcoast Bareboat Charters: Phone: 08 9445 9448, or 0411 651 367, or 0419 924 791. Forty-two-foot luxury launches which can be skippered by you, or a crew can be provided. Sleeps up to 12 people.

CANOES AND KAYAKS

About Bike Hire: No 4 Car Park: Riverside Drive, Perth. Phone: 08 9221 2665. Hire out kayaks to explore the Swan River, as well as bicycle hire. Cost: for half an hour $8.00 to $12.00; one hour $12.00 to $20.00; daily $45.00 to $70.00 (depending on size of kayak). Rental includes paddle and life jackets (compulsory).

Acacia Canoes: 9 Mead Street, Warnbro. Phone: 0412 386 469.

Will dropoff kayaks to anywhere on the Swan River as requested or you can arrange to collect kayaks from a pre-arranged point in the city. Cost: $20.00 for half a day or $30.00 for a full day. For four or more people an escorted two- or three-hour kayak tour of a scenic spot on the Swan River, such as Matilda Bay, can be arranged for about $30.00 per person. They also run two- or three-day kayak adventure tours, white water kayaking on the Collie River in summer and the Avon River in winter.

Kayaksports: Phone: 0411 112 742. Hire out canoes at Bassendean, No. 4 Car Park, Riverside Drive, Perth and also at Mandurah. Can organise kayak tours for groups of 10 or more. Phone for costs.

Pedal 'n' Paddle: Phone: 08 9401 9027, or 0417 184 929. There are two different full day pedal 'n' paddle tours involving canoeing on either the Swan or Moore Rivers, followed by pedalling a mountain bike either through the John Forrest or Yanchep National Parks. Full day trips include learning to throw a boomerang, seeing native animals and birds, morning tea and BBQ lunch. Pick-up and return to the city in an air-conditioned mini-bus is included in the cost of $65.00. You must be able to swim and ride a bike. Phone for more details.

Rivergods: 5 Ziera Place, Parkwood. Phone: 08 9259 0749. This company offers canoe and kayak hire, with both singles and doubles available. Day, weekend and weekly rates may be negotiated. Roof racks are available.

They also offer kayaking, swimming, fishing and camping tours much further afield, for example at Monkey Mia in the north of the State. Their Seal Island Day Trip includes transport from Perth to the Shoalwater Islands Marine Park (40 minutes from Perth), use of kayaks and all equipment, picnic lunch and penguin feeding. Highlights of the day include swimming with the sea lions and hopefully viewing dolphins. Cost: $95.00. Booking essential. In winter, Rivergods organise white water rafting on the Avon and Murray rivers. (See White water rafting on page 109)

DIVING AND SNORKELLING

Barrakuda Dive: 1 Cantonment Street, Fremantle. Phone: 08 9335 8292. This company runs diving courses as well as offering day trips (9.00 am to 3.30 pm approximately) to locations such as Rottnest Island. Cost: $110.00 per person includes two dives per day and all equipment. You will dive through limestone caves and see a wide variety of fish.

Diving Ventures: 37 Barrack Street, Perth; or 384 South Terrace, South Fremantle. Phone: 08 9430 5130 (Fremantle); 08 9421 1052 (Perth); Sea-Trek Mobile: 014 884 733. Dive off the Sea Trek, a 60-foot long dive boat using Scuba Pro equipment and computers. Dives cost from $60.00 with gear supplied. Choose from one-day dives or two-day live-on-board trips, for example, to Rottnest Island, where you can explore limestone caverns, shipwrecks and see crayfish, sponge and coral. The company uses over 100 dive sites regularly. Ring for more information. Trips to Exmouth and Ningaloo during the whale shark season (March to June) can also be arranged.

Perth Diving Academy: 8 Rous Head Road, North Fremantle. Phone: 08 9430 6300; and 283 Wanneroo Road, Balcatta. Phone: 08 9344 1562. As well as running scuba diving courses, Perth Diving Academy have dive charter vessels, and run day trips to Rottnest Island, Marmion Marine Park and elsewhere. Prices start from as little as $15.00 per person for a single dive.

Penguin and Seal Island Cruises: (depart from) Mersey Point Jetty, Shoalwater. Phone: 08 9528 2004. Three Island Tour (Penguin, Seal and Bird Islands) during the summer season, leaves at 9.00 am. The glass bottom boat snorkel cruise includes swimming in the bay of Seal Island, visiting Alladins Cave at Bird Island and then on to Penguin Island, where you can stay as long as you like before catching the regular ferry back to shore. You should see sea lions, penguins, dolphins and rare birds. Cost: adults $40.00, pensioners $30.00, children $20.00.

Underwater World: 91 Southside Drive, Hillarys Boat Harbour. Phone: 08 9447 7500. Qualified divers with their own equipment can dive in the Underwater Journey section of Underwater World for $75.00. Booking essential. Come face to face with sharks, rays and schools of fish.

West Australia Travel and Dive Centre: 1st Floor, 37 Barrack Street, Perth. Phone: 08 9421 1883. This company

offers diving courses (training dives can be held in the Burswood swimming pool). Beach dives are conducted off Rockingham Beach, where four different wrecks can be explored, or you can dive at Crystal Cave and off Roe and Kingston Reefs at Rottnest Island. The company offers diving trips to numerous renowned diving spots such as Exmouth, Ningaloo Reef, Coral Bay and the Abrohlos Islands. You can enjoy a one-day Ocean Safari diving off either Carnac Island or Rottnest Island. The cost for adults is $150.00 and includes transport from your hotel, boat fees, dive guide, gear hire and lunch. See Chapter 11: Rottnest Island, page 71, for snorkelling and scuba tours of Rottnest Island.

FISHING

Fishing is a popular recreational activity for both locals and tourists. Along the Canning and Swan Rivers are many jetties from which people fish. Fishing off the beach is also popular. The Fisheries Department of Western Australia (phone: 08 9482 7333) provides a brochure of fish you can catch, and details of bag limits and legal sizes. It is essential to have a recreational licence from the Fisheries Department for abalone, rock lobster, marron, net fishing and south-west freshwater angling. Fishing areas and associations include:

The Swan-Canning River prawning season lasts from 1st November to 31st July. There are laws on legal ways of catching prawns and crabs, a daily bag limit per person or per boat, and a minimum size for crabs. Contact the Fisheries Department for details, otherwise you may inadvertently be breaking the law.

Recfishwest: Phone: 08 9387 7864. This is an association representing local anglers.

DEEP-SEA FISHING

To arrange a deep-sea fishing trip, see under Boat Hire or Charter, earlier in this chapter. Alternatively, arrange a beach fishing trip with:

Gone Fishing Beach Safaris: 14 Beaumont Way, Greenwood. Phone: 08 9342 1056 or 017 853 697. Cost: $65.00. Be driven in an air-conditioned four-wheel-drive vehicle to a secluded beach to fish or swim and relax. Afternoon tea and evening BBQ meal are provided, also fishing gear and bait. Fishing guidance is given so no experience is necessary. Free pick-up and drop off. Trip departs 1.00 pm and returns 10.00 pm approximately. You can tailor a fishing safari to suit yourself.

JET SKI HIRE SERVICES

Kwinana Beach West Coast Jet Ski Hire: Kwinana Beach. Phone: 08 9592 1256. Season lasts approximately October to April, dependent on weather conditions. The cost is $20.00 for a 15-minute ride, including use of life jackets, and instruction.

Coogee Beach Jet Ski Hire: Cockburn Road, Coogee Beach. Phone: 0418 556 589. Twenty minutes from Perth. Open daily during summer, weather permitting. Have an exhilarating ride at a cost of $30.00 for

15 minutes, or $100.00 per hour. Up to three people per craft. Life vests supplied. Anyone under 17 years must be accompanied by an adult.

■ Note: Jet skiing is allowed in a couple of designated areas on the Swan River, however there are no commercial operators hiring out jet skis for use on the river.

PARASAILING

Fremantle Parasailing: Cicerello's Wharf, Fishing Boat Harbour, Fremantle. Phone: 0417 188 502. Parasail over the Indian Ocean at a cost of $50.00 per ride. Tandem rides cost $90.00.

Mills Charter Sorrento: Ground Floor, Department of Transport Building, Hillarys Boat Harbour Phone: 08 9246 5334; a/h 08 9401 0833. Parasail over the Indian Ocean behind a 28-foot speedboat. Cost: $55.00 for a flight lasting 10 minutes.

PMFM Parasailing: The Narrows, Mill Point Road exit, South Perth. Phone: 08 9313 3897 or 0411 842 775. Parasailing over the Swan River at the Narrows Bridge, very close to central Perth. One hundred percent safety record. Cost: $50.00 for a flight lasting 10 minutes.

■ Note: Parasailing is usually better in the mornings before the sea breeze comes in.

RIVER CRUISES

Several companies offer scenic cruises of varying lengths both up and down the Swan River. There is comprehensive list of River Cruises in Chapter 18: Organised Tours, page 133.

SAILING

If you do not wish to charter a yacht, but would like to sail, try contacting the Sailing Administrator at one of the Yacht Clubs listed in the *Yellow Pages*. Skippers are sometimes looking for experienced crew, and would welcome an extra pair of hands. A sail might be arranged by speaking to the Sailing Administrator at:

Royal Perth Yacht Club: Australia II Drive, Crawley. Phone: 08 9389 1555. The club holds races every Wednesday afternoon and also on Saturdays from October to April. White clothing must be worn.

Fremantle Sailing Club: Success Harbour, Marine Terrace, Fremantle. Phone: 08 9335 8800. They race on Saturday afternoons and twilight sail on Wednesday evenings. White clothing is preferable.

SURFCATS

Funcat Hire: Coode Street Jetty, South Perth. Mobile: 018 926 003. Open 9.00 am to 7.00 pm. Closed end May to September. Cost: $20.00 per hour for a maximum of three people. Sail a catamaran on the safe and scenic Swan River and admire the city skyline from the water. Free tuition is available if necessary.

SURFING

The best-known surf in Western Australia is found in the Margaret River region, 277 kilometres south of Perth. However, reasonable surfing breaks may be found in the metropolitan beaches of Perth, including Trigg, Swanbourne,

Cottesloe and Leighton. In 1999 a boomerang-shaped artificial surfing reef was built at Cable Beach (Mosman Park) which dramatically increased the number of good surfing days. For those who wish to hire surfboards or learn to surf, see below:

Broadway Surf and Sail: 155 Broadway, Nedlands. Phone: 08 9386 7876. Has surfboards and wave-skis for hire.

Surfing WA: Phone: 08 9448 0004. Surf schools at Trigg Beach. $100.00 for four lessons over four weekends. Private coaching $40.00 per hour. Also special school holiday programmes of coaching for two hours per day over four days, for $80.00. All equipment provided.

SWIMMING POOLS: PUBLIC

Most public pools sell books of concession tickets which reduce the cost of pool entry for frequent users. Phone for details of entrance fees; most range between $1.50 and $3.00. A variety of public swimming pools are listed below:

Aquamotion: Civic Drive, Wanneroo (behind Wanneroo Shopping Centre). Phone: 08 9306 2882. Twenty-five-metre heated indoor pool, toddlers pool, gym, spa, sauna, café.

Armadale Aquatic Centre: Champion Drive, Armadale. Phone: 08 9399 6966. Fifty-metre and 25-metre pools, shallow 40-metre kidney shaped boat pool for kids. Seventy-metre imitation river for children to paddle in. Sandpits, play gym and BBQ facilities. Also has three aquatubes which are open on weekends and school holidays 11.00 am to 5.00 pm and cost $9.00 extra (for the day). Closed for winter.

Arnolds Swim Centre: 32 Balgonie Avenue, Girrawheen. Phone: 08 9247 2470. 25-metre heated indoor pool and a teaching pool.

Balga Aquatic Centre: Princess Road, Balga. Phone: 08 9342 5495. Closed for winter.

Bayswater Waves: Broun Avenue, Morley. Phone: 08 9276 6538. This recently renovated complex boasts a 50-metre pool plus a wave pool (both under cover) as well as a lazy river, whirlpool, child care centre and gym.

Beatty Park Aquatic and Gym Centre: 220 Vincent Street, North Perth. Phone: 08 9273 6080. Twenty-five-metre, 30-metre and 50-metre pools. Also a freeform children's play pool area with a whale, slides and bubbles.

Belmont Oasis Leisure Centre: cnr Abernethy and Alexander Roads, Belmont. Phone: 08 9277 1622. Two heated indoor pools, one of which is a children's pool. Open all year. More pools outside.

Bilgoman Olympic Swimming Pool: Great Eastern Highway, Darlington. Phone: 08 9299 6597. Fifty-metre heated outdoor pool. Closed winter.

Bold Park Pool: The Boulevard, Floreat. Phone: 08 9385 8767. Heated outdoor olympic pool and toddlers pool. For winter swimming phone and check.

Canning Aquatic Centre: cnr Baldock and Queens Streets, Bentley. Phone: 08 9231 0701. Fifty-metre pool (heated), 25-metre pool, diving pool and two splash pools for children. Closed in winter.

Challenge Stadium: Stephenson Avenue, Mount Claremont. Phone: 08 9441 8222. Three 50-metre pools and diving pool, all heated. Swim all year. Huge sporting complex also offering fitness centre, gymnastics centre, basket ball court, physiotherapy, cafeteria.

City of Gosnells Leisure World: Culross Avenue, Thornlie. Phone: 08 9493 4399. Twenty-five-metre indoor heated pools, spa, sauna, creche.

Claremont Swimming Pool: Davies Road, Claremont. Phone: 08 9384 1682. Outdoor 50-metre pool with diving pool, 25-metre pool and baby pool. Closed in winter. Aged and invalid pensioners free.

Craigie Leisure Centre: Whitfords Avenue, Craigie. Phone: 08 9307 4566. Huge indoor and outdoor swimming complex with special areas for young children. Gym, spa, sauna and café.

Fremantle Leisure Centre: 10 Shuffrey Street, Fremantle. Phone: 08 9335 6233. Fifty-metre pool, 25-metre pool, shallow kids pool with small slides, whirlpool and spa bath.

Inglewood Aquatic Centre: Alexander Drive, Inglewood. Phone: 08 9276 3216. Diving pool, learners pool (waist deep), 50-metre Olympic pool and covered toddlers' pool. Open year round (pools heated to 27 degrees in winter).

Kelmscott Swimming Centre: Rushton Park, Orlando Street, Kelmscott. Phone: 08 9390 5614. One 33-metre five-lane pool and two small wading pools. Closed in winter.

Melville Aquatic Centre: Marmion Street, Booragoon. Phone: 08 9316 1867. Twenty-five-metre heated 1-metre deep pool (open all year). Outdoor 50-metre pool and shaded toddler pool. Playground and sandpit.

Rockingham Aquatic Centre: cnr Benjamin Way, Rockingham. Phone: 08 9527 2592. Twenty-five-metre shallow pool and 50m Olympic pool, toddlers pool. Closed in winter.

Somerset Pool: Somerset Street, East Victoria Park. Phone: 08 9361 3312. Fifty-metre heated Olympic pool. Open every day except Christmas Day and Good Friday.

South Lake Leisure Centre: South Lake Drive, South Lake. Phone: 08 9417 3003. Indoors: heated 25-metre pool, also slide pool with beach area. Open all year. Outdoors: baby pool, two slide pools and a whirlpool attached to a 15 metre by 12 metre pool. Closed in winter.

Swan Park Leisure Centre: Gray Drive, Midvale. Phone: 08 9250 2120. Two indoor 25 metre heated pools open all year round. Also outside pools for children with slides and playgrounds. Closed in winter. Gymnasium, sauna and spa also available.

SWIM WITH DOLPHINS

Rockingham Dolphins: 76 Harrison Street, Rockingham. Phone: 0418 958 678. Swim with dolphins in clear shallow water near Garden Island. The proprietor has been swimming with this group of wild dolphins for the last nine years and has built up a good rapport with them. The tour leaves from the Cruising Yacht Club Departure Jetty, Palm Beach, Rockingham or there is a courtesy bus from Perth to the jetty. The cost of $120.00 per person includes the use of wet suits and snorkelling equipment, return transport from Perth if required, and a light lunch and refreshments. Booking is essential.

TUBE RIDES, KNEE-BOARDING AND WAKE-BOARDING

This group of water sports is similar to water-skiing in as much as you are being towed behind a speedboat whilst riding on a variety of different equipment. A tube ride probably calls for the least skill, and involves sitting in a rubber ring (like the inner tube of a truck tyre); a knee-board is like a small surf-board which you kneel on; and a wake-board is like a surf-board but it has fixtures to place your feet in so that it is possible to stand up on the board and jump or do tricks in the wake of the preceding boat. The following companies offer this group of water sports:

Mills Charter: Ground Floor, Department of Transport Building, Hillarys Boat Harbour. Phone: 08 9246 5334; a/h 08 9401 0833. A 28-foot speedboat can take you tube riding or knee-boarding on the ocean at a cost of $75.00 for half an hour. Telephone to book.

Narrows Water Sports: Mill Point Road (under Narrows Bridge), South Perth. Phone: 0419 853 941. Enjoy magnificent views of the city of Perth as·you are towed behind a speedboat. They operate every day except Sunday from about 9.00 am until 4.30

pm all year, weather permitting. Cost: $10.00 for a 10-minute tube ride or $15.00 for wake-boarding or knee-boarding. They also offer water-skiing for $15.00.

PMFM Fun Tubes: Mill Point Road (under Narrows Bridge), South Perth. Phone: 0412 644 621. Situated under a large umbrella. Offer tube rides, wake-boarding and knee-boarding for $10.00 per ride. They also offer water-skiing.

Skicraze Water-ski Hire: Belmont Ski Area, Swan River (look for the white marquee). Phone: 08 9448 8129. They operate most days from October until about the end of April. Cost: Wake-boarding, knee-boarding and tubing is $10.00 for 10 minutes. Water-skiing is also available.

WATER PARKS AND PLAYGROUNDS

Adventure World: 179 Progress Drive, Bibra Lake. Phone: 08 9417 9666. Information Service: 1900 997 399. Open summer (end September to end April) every day except Christmas Day and Good Friday 10.00 am to 5.00 pm. Occasional evening opening. Phone for information. Cost: adults $25.00, concessions $22.50, children (5 to 14) $20.00, family passes (two adults, two children) $80.00. There is enough to do here to keep the family occupied for the whole day. Adventure World consists of a series of pools, with water slides and tubes, paddle or bumper boats and an enormous swimming pool. It also has a Grand Prix raceway, a monorail, train, toboggans down Alpine Mountain, and many rides

including the famous Bounty's Revenge and a roller coaster. Entry fee covers all entertainment. Take your own picnic to eat on the grassy lawns, otherwise there is a restaurant and kiosk.

Ascot Water Playground: 97 Mathieson Road, Redcliffe. Phone: 08 9277 8550. Open daily 10.00 am to 6.00 pm. Cost: adults $1.50, children and pensioners $1.00, family of four (two adults and two children) $4.00. Closed end April to end September. This playground is mainly aimed at children under 12. There are seven pools, the deepest of which is 70 cm, a toddlers' slide and splash pools, BBQs, picnic areas, playground with swings, slides, bikes and mini-golf.

Cables Water-ski Park: 8 Troode Street, Spearwood. Phone: 08 9418 6888. A fun park, with a variety of attractions, makes it a great day out for all the family. For more information and detailed costs of the attractions, see under heading Water-skiing below. Apart from water-skiing and skurfing, there are swimming pools, water slides, a sling shot (reverse bungee jump) and mini-golf.

Hillarys The Great Escape: Hillarys Boat Harbour, 22 Southside Drive (off West Coast Highway), Sorrento. Phone: 08 9448 0800. Open 10.00 am to 6.00 pm. This new leisure playground has three different types of heated water slides, 18 holes of miniature garden golf and the Oasis café. Entry cost: $14.00 and includes unlimited use of the three water slides and one round of mini-golf. Water slides are closed from end April to

September. Beach parties are held on Friday and Saturday nights from 6.30 pm to 10.30 pm, cost $12.00. They are aimed at young people from 12 upwards and the cost includes unlimited use of water slides, mini-golf, trampolines and a disc jockey. Youngsters are fully supervised so parents are free to enjoy the rest of Hillarys Boat Harbour, or a meal at the Oasis café, which serves a wide range of light meals and enjoys harbour views.

Kalamunda Wet and Wild: cnr Canning and Collins Road, Kalamunda. Phone: 08 9293 4432 or 08 9293 4011 (recorded info). This is a water park with an eight-lane Olympic pool and several other pools including kiddies' slide and splash pools, a high speed slide, two tube slides and a four-lane slide. Phone for opening times, but it is generally open at 9.00 am and closes either at 5.00 pm or 7.00 pm depending on circumstances. The park is closed in winter. Full day entry with use of all facilities costs: adults $15.00, students and concessions $14.00, children (under 14) $13.00, family pass $42.00. For use of pools only (excluding slides) adults $3.00, children $2.00, seniors $1.50. There are extensive shady lawns to picnic and BBQ on and there is a kiosk.

Maylands Waterland: Clarkson Road, Maylands. Phone: 08 9272 4456. Entry by donation. Closed in winter. This playground consists of four small pools suitable for young children. The deepest is 0.75 metres, the shallowest ankle deep. There is also a stream, play equipment and BBQs.

WATER-SKIING
Bonney's WA Water-ski Park: St. Albans Rd, Baldivis. Phone: 08 9524 1401. This park consists of five man-made lakes, and is only 30 minutes from Perth. It is open daily 9.00 am to 6.00 pm. Booking is advisable particularly at weekends. Costs: lessons $27.00 for 15 minutes or three lessons for $69.00; or you can hire a boat, driver and skis for $80.00 per hour. Biscuiting or tubing (sitting in a rubber tube) behind a boat costs $120.00 per hour. Alternatively, combine skiing and tubing for $100.00 per hour. There are lakeside chalets for hire, BBQs and a café.

Cables Water-ski Park: 8 Troode Street (off Rockingham Road), Spearwood. Phone: 08 9418 6888. Open every day except Christmas Day. The water slides and pools close for winter at the end of April. Hours: November to April 9.45 am till 8.00 pm; May to October 11.45 am till 7.00 pm. This is a great place for a family day out with not only water-skiing to suit all ages and abilities, but a wide range of other attractions. For water-skiers, a unique overhead cable system tows you around clean man-made lakes at speeds to suit your ability. Single, double or trick skis, or knee-boards or skurfing are also available. Knee-boarding is kneeling on a small surf-board and skurfing is standing on a surf-board while being towed. Costs: Entry to park and use of swimming pools and BBQ facilities $2.00 per person. Cable water-skiing: $15.00 per hour. Wet suit hire: $5.00 per hour. Use of water slides $5.00 per hour or $15.00 all day. Sling-shot ride (reverse bungee jump) $20.00 per person. Mini-golf $4.00 per round for 18 holes.

Mills Charters: Hillarys Boat Harbour. Phone: 08 9246 5334. Water-ski on the ocean behind a 28-foot speed boat for $75.00 per half hour, including equipment. Tube-riding and knee-boarding are also available by arrangement.

Narrows Water Sports: Mill Point Road (under Narrows Bridge), South Perth. Phone: 0419 853 941. Here you can water-ski on the Swan River right in front of the city of Perth. Operate every day except Sunday from approximately 9.00 am to 4.30 pm. Cost: $15.00 for a 10- to 15-minute water-ski. Also offer tube-riding, knee-boarding and wake-boarding.

PMFM Fun Tubes: Mill Point Road (under Narrows Bridge), South Perth. Phone: 0412 644 621. Situated under a large umbrella. Water skiing costs $15.00. They also offer tube rides, wake-boarding and knee-boarding.

Skicraze Water-ski Hire: Belmont Ski Area, Swan River (look for the white marquee). Phone: 08 9448 8129. Open in the summer (October till about end April) from approximately 9.30 am to 4.30 pm most days. Costs: skiing $15.00 for 2 kilometre leg (approximately 10 to 15 minutes). Also offer wake-boarding, tube-riding and knee-boarding.

WHALE WATCHING

See page 96 for companies which organise whale watching trips.

WHITE WATER RAFTING

River Gods organise white water rafting during winter months (June to September) on the Avon River (half day tour costs $75.00) or the Murray River (full day tour costs $130.00). Costs include transport to and from Perth, lunch and use of a wet suit. Phone: 08 9259 0749.

WINDSURFING

Broadway Surf and Sail: 155 Broadway, Nedlands. Phone: 08 9386 7876. This company hires windsurfers at $30.00 per day or $45.00 per day with instruction. They also hire wave-skis, surfboards and boogie boards. A popular spot for windsurfers is the stretch of river in front of the JH Abrahams Reserve just off Hackett Drive in Crawley. On weekend afternoons when the sea breeze is in, it is not uncommon to see literally hundreds of colourful sails.

Pelican Point Windsurfing: 33 Stirling Highway, Nedlands. Phone/Fax: 08 9386 1830. Mobile: 0412 919 176. Learn to windsurf at Pelican Point in Crawley. The beginners course lasts nine hours and costs $125.00. You must be able to swim 25 metres and wear a buoyancy vest. Everything necessary is supplied. Also board and lesson packages are available depending on skill level, at a cost of $25.00 to $40.00 per hour. Personal training with one-on-one private instruction costs $35.00 per hour.

Sails and Windsurfing Centre: Unit 15, 30 Peel Road, O'Connor. Phone: 08 9314 6566. Rental of windsurfers costs from $50.00 to $150.00 per week, depending on the type of board required. They usually do long term rentals which are much cheaper.

Second Wind Sailboards: 526 Canning Highway, Attadale. Phone: 08 9317 2916. This company gives windsurfing tuition at Lucky Bay, Melville Beach Road in Applecross. Weekend courses (four hours Saturday and four hours Sunday) cost $110.00, including all equipment. Courses not available during winter.

Windsurfing Academy of WA. Phone: 08 9384 7492 or 0414 747 071. Beginner to advanced windsurfing courses from the car park on Melville Beach Road, Applecross, on Saturday and Sunday mornings 10.00 am to 1.00 pm. Cost: $120.00 for a three day course. Booking is essential. Everything is provided except towels.

CHAPTER 16

ACTIVITIES IN THE AIR

It is possible to fly directly to most of the major tourist destinations in the State or merely take a scenic flight over the Swan River and cities of Perth and Fremantle. Air charter companies, operating from Perth and Jandakot Airports, offer a variety of flights which may be tailored to suit individual requirements. For the more daring, helicopter flights can be taken over the city but if you wish to go hang-gliding, hot-air ballooning or parachuting, it will be necessary to drive to places out of Perth, such as York, Beverley, Narrogin and Northam.

AIR SAFARIS AND TOURS

Air Australia: 1(a) Eagle Drive, Jandakot Airport, Jandakot. Phone: 08 9332 5011. Day tours/air taxi service to Margaret River, the Pinnacles, Monkey Mia and Wave Rock as well as joy flights and aerobatics. Also operates a Mile High Club (phone: 08 9414 1998) which costs $400.00 per couple, including champagne, chocolates and strawberries. An hour 6000 feet above Perth, to indulge yourself on a double bed behind a security/privacy screen.

Amity Aviation: 9A Eagle Drive, Jandakot Airport, Jandakot. Phone: 08 9417 1190. They charge $125.00 for up to three people, for a 40-minute joy flight over the city or they will arrange charter flights, as requested.

Kookaburra Air: Phone: 08 9354 1158. Air charters and tours can be arranged

to suit your requirements. Joy flights over the city cost $50.00 per person. Night flights over the city cost $65.00 per person. They can also take you to Rottnest Island ($90.00 per person for a return trip), Margaret River, the Pinnacles, Wave Rock where ground tours can be arranged to suit requirements. A quick trip to Monkey Mia to see the dolphins will cost you $550.00 per head.

Royal Aeroclub of WA (Inc): 41 Eagle Drive, Jandakot Airport, Jandakot. Phone: 08 9332 7722. This company offers air charters, private hire and scenic tours, flying both single and twin engine aircraft. The City and Beaches joy flights cost from $90.00 for three people for 30 minutes.

Sky Worx Aviation: Jandakot Airport, Jandakot. Phone: 1800 244 833. This company specialises in air tours, which include a land-based component.

Examples of costs (including meals): Monkey Mia tour $495.00; Wave Rock and Pinnacles Tour (including trip in a four-wheel-drive vehicle at the Pinnacles) $495.00. They also fly to Rottnest, the South West and other destinations. A last-minute phone call might get you a stand-by seat at a reduced price.

Tiger Moth Scenic Flights of WA: 2 Baron Way, Jandakot Airport, Jandakot. Phone: 041 110 6466. Cost: $103.00 for a 30-minute flight; $198.00 for a 60-minute flight. Experience the unique joy of flying in a 1941 vintage biplane over the city, beaches and Rottnest Island. The pilots have in excess of 20 years of experience flying these planes.

GLIDING

Beverley Soaring Society Inc: PO Box 136, Beverley (90 minutes from Perth). Phone: 015 385 361 or 08 9646 1015 (airfield). The airfield is open every Friday, Saturday and Sunday. Trial flights in a twin-seated glider cost $60.00. Learn to fly yourself if you wish, or be taken for a flight.

Narrogin Gliding Club: Phone: 015 088 314 or 08 9881 1795. Offer trial flights and lessons by qualified instructors in two-seater training gliders. Flights cost from $60.00.

HANG-GLIDING AND PARA-GLIDING

Sky Sports Flying School: 71A Leach Highway, Wilson. Phone: 08 9451 9969. This is a Hang Gliding Federation of Australia approved training facility. They provide lessons

in hang-gliding and tandem hang-gliding. A basic introductory course to hang-gliding costs $295.00 for two days. A tandem flight lasting 20 to 30 minutes costs $180.00.

West Australian Para-gliding Academy: 22 Feldman Crescent, Parkerville. Phone: 08 9295 4551 or 0417 776 550. Hang-gliding Federation of Australia certified instructors teach you to para-glide or power para-glide and tandem flights can also be arranged.

West Coast Hang-gliding School: Lot 501, Gibbs Street, Mullaloo. Phone: 08 9307 1816. Instruction from fully qualified Hang-gliding Federation of Australia instructors, or try a tandem flight for $150.00.

HELICOPTER TRIPS

Devereaux Helicopter Charter: based at Channel 10 Studios in Dianella. Phone: 019 683 500 (all hours) or 08 9442 6333. They offer a half hour local city scenic flight over beaches, river and the city at a cost of $350.00 for up to four passengers. Otherwise, they will fly you anywhere you please at basic charter rates.

Preston Helicopters Services: Phone: 08 9414 1000 or 018 952 317. General charter and scenic flights are available. On Saturdays and Sunday, flights leave from the City Helipad at the Causeway between 12.00 noon and 4.00 pm for a five to seven minute flight over the city and river. Cost: $40.00 per person. Alternatively, a 15 to 20 minute flight down the Swan River to Fremantle and return, costs $75.00 per person.

HOT-AIR BALLOONING

Windward Balloon Adventures:
Northam Aerodrome, Northam.
Phone: 08 9622 3000 or contact Perth
agent, Martin International Travel, on
08 9344 5011. Unfortunately not in
the metro area, but after an hour's
drive you could be ballooning over
the Avon Valley. Operates Saturdays
and Sunday from April to November,
weather permitting. Cost: from
$180.00 per person for a 45-minute to
one-hour balloon ride and champagne
brunch. Cost does not include
transport to and from Northam.

SKYDIVING AND PARACHUTING

Skydive Express: 353 Oxford St.
Leederville. Phone: 08 9444 4199 or
1800 355 833. This is one of the
biggest parachuting companies in
Australia and operates from York (just
one hour from Perth) each weekend
and also on weekdays, as long as there
are four or more participants. All
parachutes are fitted with electronic
automatic opening systems. Beginners
may undertake a tandem jump where
the student is harnessed to an
experienced instructor or students may
undertake the Accelerated Free Fall
course leading to an internationally

recognised skydiving licence. A
tandem jump from 8000 feet would
cost $220.00 increasing to $300.00 for
a tandem jump from 12,000 feet.
Videos and photographs can be taken
if you wish. Courtesy bus available.
Facilities here include on-site back-
packer accommodation, swimming
pool and café.

**WA Skydiving Academy P/L Training
Centre**: Ground Floor 9 to 10, 193
William Street, Northbridge, Perth.
Phone: 08 9227 6066. Skydiving takes
place 85 kilometres south of Perth at
Pinjarra. Experience 40 seconds of
falling through the sky at 120 miles
per hour before your parachute opens
to gently bring you back to earth. A
tandem jump from 10 000 feet,
secured to an experienced instructor,
costs $250.00 or $330.00 if you want
a video made of it. You will need 20
minutes of instruction prior to the
leap. Alternatively, after nine hours of
instruction, beginners can undertake
an Accelerated Free Fall with an
instructor on either side to guide
them down. This will cost $425.00.
Last year, 1600 first timers learnt to
skydive with this company's very
experienced instructors.

ACTIVITIES ON THE LAND

There are a large number of both indoor and outdoor land-based activities available in Perth and we have tried to include the most popular. If you are into such things as climbing (rocks or indoor walls), riding (horses or camels), golf, roller-blading, archery, cycling or walking, this chapter should provide you with the information you need. Numerous other activities are also listed alphabetically below.

ABSEILING

Adventure Out Australia: 2/55 Cargill Street, Victoria Park. Phone: 08 9472 3919. This company organises one-day abseiling adventures, which are mainly held at quarries in close proximity to Perth. After a safety brief and introduction to abseiling equipment, participants tackle progressively more challenging cliffs. A day's abseiling costs $65.00. More exhilarating abseils and climbs are available in the State's south-west, for example, a 280-metre abseil on Bluff Knoll. Previous abseiling experience is recommended for these.

Bungee West: Progress Drive, Bibra Lake, Perth. Phone: 08 9417 2500. Not brave enough to bungee jump? Try abseiling down the bungee tower at a cost of $30.00 for one hour, including harness. Two or three days

notice is necessary prior to abseiling here. Instruction is available as necessary.

Rock Adventure. Phone: 08 9388 0057. This company offers adventure days combining rock climbing and abseiling on a 30-metre high natural cliff face, mainly on weekends, from approximately 9.00 am to 4.00 pm. Cost: $75.00 per head, for a group of three or four participants to one instructor; or $98.00 per head for one or two people. There are 30 or 40 different climbs available, suitable for beginners to intermediate climbers. Take your own refreshments. Transport can be arranged at extra cost.

Roping Adventures: Phone: 08 9398 4937 or 0412 773 466. After a safety briefing, you will learn to abseil first down a 23-metre nursery cliff face, gradually progressing to a

50-metre face. Cost: up to five people, $60.00 each, six and over $55.00 each, for a day's adventure (8.30 am to 4.00 pm). This company also runs abseiling and caving weekends at Margaret River and Albany.

AMUSEMENT CENTRES

Fun and Games Family Leisure Centres:
- 88 James Street, Northbridge. Phone: 08 9227 1241.
- 160 James Street, Northbridge. Phone: 08 9328 4404.
- Leghorn Street, Rockingham. Phone: 08 9528 4250.

Has video and sega-type games and pinball machines.

Fun Fact'ry:
- 256 Hampton Road, Fremantle. Phone: 08 9335 2227.
- 7 Townsend Road, Malaga. Phone: 08 9249 6090.

Open: 10.00 am to 6.00 pm every day including weekends and public holidays, except Christmas Day, Boxing Day, New Year's Day and Easter Sunday. This is a children's (ages one to 11) physical activity centre with climbing steps, rope ladders, flying fox and tunnels to crawl through. Cost: weekends, public and school holidays $7.00 for kids five and over, and $5.00 for four years and under, for unlimited play. Other days $5.00 for unlimited time for all ages. Fully air-conditioned. Coffee shop.

Timezone Interactive Entertainment Centres: have video and sega-type games and pinball machines. They are at the following locations:

CITY:
- 181 Murray Street Mall. Phone: 08 9325 8675.
- 114 Murray Street. Phone: 08 9325 9613.
- 80 William Street. Phone: 08 9322 4364.
- 31 Lake Street, Northbridge. Phone: 08 9328 7115.

SUBURBAN:
- 34 Garden City Shopping Centre, Booragoon. Phone: 08 9364 3305.
- 2 Fremantle Malls, Fremantle. Phone: 08 9336 2329.
- Innaloo Cinema Complex. Phone: 08 9446 2440.
- Lakeside Joondalup Shopping City. Phone: 08 9300 3811.
- Warwick Entertainment Centre. 639 Beach Road, Warwick. Phone: 08 9448 3334.
- Shop 60, Southlands Boulevarde Shopping Centre, Willetton. Phone: 08 9332 0133.

ARCHERY

Archery is a sport suitable for all age groups and abilities. Altering the distance between the shooter and the target and the size of the target can keep everyone challenged. Venues include:

Archery Park Baldivis: 707 Baldivis Road, Baldivis. Phone: 08 9524 1032. Open Wednesday to Sunday and public holidays 10.00 am to 5.00 pm. Cost: Indoor or outdoor: $8.00 per round, children under 10 years, $6.00, including tuition. A round takes about an hour and a half.

Archery Park Hoddywell: 330 Clackline Road, Hoddywell. Phone: 08 9574 2410. Open daily 9.00 am to

5.00 pm. Closed Christmas Day. This archery park has 70 acres of shooting rounds and offers a variety of trails suitable for all abilities. Cost, including tuition and hire of gear: $7.50 for 9-target trail (beginners); $12.50 for 16-target trail (intermediate); and $14.50 for 20-target trail (advanced). It is cheaper if you take your own gear. You can make a day of it as BBQs are available, or take your own picnic basket. There is also a kiosk selling food and drinks.

BICYCLING

The wide expanse of the Swan River and its tributary, the Canning River, flows west to the Indian Ocean and the port of Fremantle. This enormous stretch of water, and the flat terrain surrounding it makes for easy but scenic bike riding. There are purpose built cycle/multi purpose tracks which enable recreational cyclists to ride almost completely around the river. Cycling is also very popular in Kings Park and up and down the coast.

Bikewest publishes free booklets of recreational cycle tours with excellent maps and suggested routes called *Along the Coast Ride* and *Around the Rivers Ride*. These can be obtained from the Western Australian Tourist Centre in Forrest Place, or phone Bikewest on 08 9320 9320.

For information on where to hire bikes, see Chapter 2: Getting Around, page 12.

If you like to participate in organised group rides, the Bicycle Transportation Alliance publishes a pamphlet called,

Cycling in the West, which includes the WA Rides Calendar. This lists and describes a wide range of organised rides for people of all abilities. You and your bike just turn up at the place and time indicated for a particular ride. Phone: 08 9228 4994 for a copy of the pamphlet. Cycling tours are available from:

Pedal 'n' Paddle Adventures. Phone: 08 9401 9027 or 0417 184 929. Combination cycling and canoeing tours utilise local waterways and national parks close to Perth. Half-day tours cost $40.00, full day tours $65.00, including morning tea and BBQ lunch. Pick-up from city is available. Phone for more details. See Chapter 15: Activities on the Water, Canoes and Kayaks, page 101.

BUNGEE JUMPING

Bungee West: Progress Drive, Bibra Lake, Perth. Phone: 08 9417 2500. There is a man-made tower from which adrenalin seekers can bungee jump at $69.00 per jump, or the less brave can abseil down for $30.00 per hour. There is a viewing platform for spectators. Tandem jumps are also available.

CAMEL RIDING

Calamunnda Camel Farm: 361 Paulls Valley Road, Paulls Valley. Phone/Fax: 08 9293 1156. Twenty-three kilometres from the city. Open Thursday to Sunday, and public holidays, 9.30 am to 5.00 pm. Other times and bookings by arrangement. This camel farm provides an opportunity to view Australian native bush from the back of a camel. You may see wild flowers in season and native birds and animals in a peaceful environment. Cost: a short camel ride $4.00; a 30-minute forest ride $10.00 children, $15.00 adults; one-hour forest ride $20.00 children, $25.00 adults. Half or full day rides are also available, or you can plan your own trek to forest picnic locations, or to local attractions such as Mundaring Weir. Phone for details and departure times. A minimum of four riders is required and a maximum of 10. Refreshments are available.

Cameleer Park Camel Farm:
300 Neaves Road, Wanneroo. Phone: 08 9405 3558 or 0408 094 843. Open every day except Friday, 10.00 am to 5.00 pm. This company offers professionally led camel trains with guaranteed friendly camels. You can choose from a variety of treks ranging from short rides to safaris. Prices start at $6.00 for adults, and $4.00 for children, for a short ride, up to $40.00 for adults and $35.00 for children for a two-hour ride. In summer, Camaleer offers combined camel treks and four-wheel-drive adventure weekend summer safaris. Phone for more details. Picnic, BBQ and recreation facilities are available. There is a camel museum and souvenir shop.

Steppingstone Adventures:
180 Morrissey Road, East Bullsbrook. Phone: 08 9571 2834 or 018 327 984. They offer tranquil camel rides through scenic countryside approximately 45 minutes from Perth. There are a number of packages ranging from one-hour trips ($30 per person), twilight trips ($75.00 per person including BBQ) to a day trip ($140.00 per person including lunch and dinner).

GO-KARTS

Big Track Go-Karts Hire: 26 Wotton Street, Bayswater. Phone: 08 9272 6222. Perth's largest outdoor track offering grand prix style racing in a variety of karts including dual karts. Open weekdays 1.00 pm to 9.00 pm, Saturday 10.00 am to 10.00 pm, and Sunday 10.00 am to 6.00 pm. Cost: $12.00 for 10 minutes, $6.00 for five minutes, $30.00 for half an hour. There is a kiosk and facilities for barbecuing.

Indoor Kart Hire O'Connor: Sainsbury Road (Stock Road end), O'Connor. Phone: 08 9314 2435. Open every day except Christmas Day, 10.00 am to 10.30 pm. This indoor facility offers fast, safe clean karts, on two tracks. Cost: $8.00 for five minutes, $15.00 for 10 minutes, or $35.00 for half an hour. Family passes are available and reductions may be given for group bookings. Other facilities include video driving games, air hockey, pool tables and pinball all in air-conditioned comfort.

Kart World: 136 Esther Street, Belmont. Phone: 08 9479 1200. Open daily 10.00 am to 10.00 pm. This is an indoor track with a range of go-karts to suit all drivers including kids (minimum height 1.4 metres). There are both single, and double karts with two seats and two steering wheels. Cost: $7.00 for five minutes, $12.50

for 10 minutes. There is also an amusement centre with the latest interactive machines.

Golf

Golf Escort: 70 Lockhart Street, Como. Phone: 08 9450 2046 or 018 922 554. Offers packages to suit individual requirements, at prices starting from $150.00 per player per day. Price includes: transport in a limousine or luxury coach, driven by your personal host; green fees at the course or courses of your choice; use of motorised buggy and quality golf clubs; and an interpreter if required. Arrangements can be made for lunch and dinner.

Public golf courses and driving ranges

There are numerous golf courses open to the public in the Perth metropolitan area, the majority of which are listed below. It is advisable to phone and book a tee-off time for all public courses, particularly over weekends and public holidays. Most courses offer club hire and have a kiosk selling cool drinks and snacks. Various golf courses and driving ranges include:

Araluen: Araluen Country Club Avenue, Roleystone. Phone: 08 9397 9000. An 18-hole course situated in the hills, a 50-minute drive from Perth. The course offers spectacular views and there is a very good restaurant (Verandahs) at the Country Club.

Armadale Country Club: 405 Forrest Road, Armadale. Phone: 08 9399 5377. This nine-hole course is open seven days a week.

Bayswater Public Golf Course: McGregor Street, Embleton. Phone: 08 9271 5190. This is a nine-hole course and there is a pro shop on site.

Burswood Park: Burswood Resort Hotel Complex, Great Eastern Highway, Burswood. Phone: 08 9362 7576. This is an 18-hole public course situated next to the Burswood Resort Casino on the river just three minutes from Perth City Centre. There is a day/night driving range. PGA qualified professionals are available for instruction if required.

Carramar Public Golf Course: Golf Links Drive, Neerabup. Phone: 08 9484 2311. This is an 18-hole championship course located in a scenic setting. There is also a driving range and tuition is available if required.

Collier Park Golf Course: Hayman Road, Como. Phone: 08 9450 6488. This is a 27-hole course and there is also a driving range, putting and chipping greens, and a practice bunker. Electric buggies are available for hire. Golf professionals are available for coaching.

El Caballo: Great Eastern Highway, Wooroloo. Phone: 08 9573 1288. This is a challenging 18-hole course situated an hour's drive from Perth.

Fremantle Municipal Golf Course: Montreal Street, Fremantle. Phone: 08 9336 3933. This is a hilly nine-hole course.

Glen Iris: Dean Road, Jandakot. Phone: 08 9414 1900. A 20-minute drive from Perth, this is a scenic 18-hole course with several lakes to negotiate. There is a driving range.

Hamersley Public Golf Course:
Marmion Avenue, Karrinyup. Phone:
08 9447 7137. This 18-hole course
also has a driving range and putting
green as well as a tavern.

Hillview Public Golf Course: 350
Kalamunda Road, Maida Vale. Phone:
08 9454 5554. A 27-hole course with
practice putting greens, a chipping
practice area and a driving range.
There is also a pro shop.

Jandakot Golf Centre: 23 Hope Road,
Jandakot. Phone: 08 9417 4277.
Day/night golf driving range. Open
Monday to Friday 9.00 am to 10.00
pm, Saturday and Sunday 9.00 am to
9.00 pm. A bucket of balls costs $5.00
for 50, and $9.00 for 100. There is
also a par three, nine-hole chip and
putt course which is open in daylight
hours. Cost: adults $5.00, children
and pensioners $3.50.

Joondalup Country Club: Country
Club Boulevard, Connolly. Phone:
08 9400 8811. Rated Australia's
seventh best resort course, this
breathtaking course is located 30
minutes north of Perth. There are 27
holes, some with views of the sea.
Each nine has its own characteristics.

Lake Claremont Golf Course: Lapsley
Road, Claremont. Phone:
08 9384 2887. Eighteen holes, of
which nine holes form a short par
three course, and the other nine are a
regular course. On Tuesday and
Wednesday nights, golf can be played
on the short course at night, finishing
at about 11.00 pm. Last tee-off
9.30 pm. There is a pro shop.

Maddington Public Golf Course:
Alcock Street, Maddington. Phone:

08 9459 6220. This is an 18-hole
course with a pro shop.

Marangaroo Golf Course: Aylesford
Drive, Marangaroo. Phone:
08 9484 1000. This is an 18-hole
championship course with a
driving range and professional
tuition available.

Marri Park Golf Course and Tavern:
Thomas Road, Casuarina (end of
Kwinana Freeway). Phone:
08 9419 3037. This is an 18-hole golf
course with a driving range. There is
also a tavern, TAB and pro shop.

Meadow Springs: Meadow Springs
Drive, Mandurah. Phone:
08 9581 6360. This 18-hole
championship resort course is located
45 minutes south of Perth. *Australian
Golf Digest* rates Meadow Springs
as the second best course in
Western Australia.

Peninsula: Swan Bank Road, Maylands.
Phone: 08 9370 1887. This 18-hole
course is situated on the banks of the
Swan River five minutes from Perth
city. It has pretty city and river views.
There is also a mini-golf course and a
grass driving range.

**Point Walter Public Golf Course and
Tennis Courts**: Honour Avenue,
Bicton. Phone: 08 9330 3262. This is
a nine-hole public golf course. Tuition
is available if required.

Rockingham Golf Driving Range:
Ennis Avenue, Rockingham. Phone:
08 9592 6462.

Rosehill Public Golf Course: West
Parade, South Guildford. Phone:
08 9279 5958. This is an 18-hole
course with a driving range, practice
putting greens and a pro shop.

Rottnest Island Country Club: Rottnest Island. Phone: 08 9292 5144. A nine-hole course, but phone to enquire before taking your clubs to Rottnest as it is not always open.

Secret Harbour: Secret Harbour Boulevard, Secret Harbour. Phone: 08 9524 7133. Forty minutes south of Perth, just north of Mandurah, this links-type course is designed around natural sand dunes and a lake. At present there are nine holes, with another nine on the drawing board.

Serpentine and Districts Golf Club Inc: Karnup Road, Serpentine. Phone: 08 9525 2265. This is an 18-hole course with sand greens.

Sun City Country Club: Saint Andrews Drive, Yanchep. Phone: 08 9561 1148. This is an 18-hole course through sand-hills which is situated a 50-minute drive north of Perth. Kangaroos, emus and birds are often seen on the fairways.

The Vines Resort: Verdelho Drive, The Vines. Phone: 08 9297 0222. This is Australia's Number Two resort course and is situated in the Swan Valley, about 35 minutes drive from Perth. Resort facilities include a hotel, restaurants, bars and swimming pool, but is best known for its world class 36-hole championship course along the banks of the beautiful Ellen Brook. This course is open to the public daily. The Heineken Classic, Australia's richest golf tournament, is held here every January, attracting some of the world's best players.

Wembley: The Boulevard, Floreat Park. Phone: 08 9484 2500. Situated 10 minutes drive from city centre, Wembley offers two 18-hole layouts. There is a day/night driving range, putting and pitching greens, a pro shop and tavern.

Whaleback Golf Course and Driving Range: Whaleback Avenue, Parkwood. Phone: 08 9484 1611. An 18-hole course with a driving range and pro shop.

INDOOR GOLF

Better Golf: 1st Floor, 816 Hay Street, Perth. Phone: 08 9321 4414. This is an indoor driving range in the centre of the city. It offers video appraisal and individual coaching by experienced PGA members.

Perth's Golf Centre: Basement, 790 Hay Street, Perth. Phone: 08 9322 2870. This centrally located facility has eight indoor practice ranges and a putting green. It also can provide video replay golf lessons and a computer can analyse your swing.

MINI-GOLF

Botanic Golf Gardens: 25 Drovers Place, Wanneroo (25 kilometres north of Perth). Phone: 08 9405 1475 or 0418 108 408. Open Tuesday to Sunday 10.00 am to 4.30 pm. Closed Mondays except school and public holidays. This unique 18-hole mini-golf course includes many unusual and challenging holes, such as hitting the ball into a basketball hoop. The course is picturesquely situated amongst five acres of botanical gardens. Towering trees provide plenty of shade for players and spectators and there are seats for those who just wish to relax and appreciate the surroundings. Paths meander through lush gardens, past waterfalls and frequently cross small streams. This extremely well-kept facility is recognised as one of Perth's premier gardens, with something to see and do for all ages. There is a café, kiosk and BBQ facilities. See Chapter 13: Parks and Gardens, page 84.

Heritage Golf, Peninsula Golf Course: Swan Bank Road, Maylands. Phone: 08 9370 1346. This course has 18 holes, all named after various landmarks around the Swan River. Open daily from sunrise to sunset. Cost: adults $6.00, children and pensioners $4.00.

The Great Escape: Hillarys Boat Harbour, 22 Southside Drive (off West Coast Highway), Hillarys. Phone: 08 9448 0800. Eighteen holes of mini-golf. Open daily from 10.00 am to 6.00 pm in summer, but from June to September it is usually only open at weekends. Cost: adults $5.00, students, concessions, kids $4.00. Situated next to the water slides.

GOLF WITH A DIFFERENCE

The Great Australian Hole-in-One Company: next to Barrack Street Jetty, Perth. On the edge of the Swan River just to the west of Old Perth Port, is a raised platform with a tee on it, from which you drive out over the water onto a floating platform which has different size holes on it. Great prizes to be won: Cost: $1.00 per ball, $10.00 for 12 balls, $20 for 25 balls. or, don't win a prize but hit a bucket of 50 balls for $10. Open 9.00 am until late afternoon, 7 days a week.

Supa Golf: Swan Valley Oasis Resort, 10 250 West Swan Road, Henley Brook. Phone: 08 9296 1166. This nine-hole golf course (about 900 metres long) suits all age groups and golfing abilities. It is similar to a traditional golf course but is played with four over-sized clubs and much larger balls, making a round of golf quicker and much less frustrating. Cost per game: adults $10.00, children under 16, $8.00 on weekends and public holidays (15 percent discount on weekdays). Group discounts are available. There is also a kiosk, restaurant and horse riding.

GYMS/HEALTH AND FITNESS CENTRES

For those wishing to keep fit, there are gyms and health clubs all over the metropolitan area. To find the one nearest you, consult the *Yellow Pages*, however, some of the bigger chains are:
Aspire Fitness. Phone: 08 9227 1206.
BC The Body Club.
  Phone: 08 9385 5452.
Lords Sports Club.
  Phone: 08 9381 4777.
Nuwave Health Clubs.
  Phone: 08 9362 6066.
Renouf Personal Training Centre.
  Phone: 08 9228 3188.

HORSE RIDING

The *Yellow Pages* lists a large number of horse riding facilities, which have horses or ponies available for private hire in and around Perth. Many offer scenic bush trails, night rides, beach rides and camps. Here are a small selection of those available:

Brown's Horse Hire: Lot 11 Hammond Road, Success (Jandakot). Phone: 08 9417 9143. Approximately 20 minutes south of Perth, Brown's offer trail rides around lakes and nature reserves for beginners and experienced riders. Evening and beach rides are also available. There are kangaroos and emus in an enclosure which may be fed by hand. All riding tack including helmets is provided. There is a BBQ and picnic area, also refreshments available for purchase.

Ron's Riding Ranch: 1451 Wanneroo Road, Wanneroo. Phone: 0412 922 588. Open every day of the year. Half-hour to all day trail rides through natural bushland, for beginners and experienced riders. Native animals may be seen in their natural habitat. Night rides are available by arrangement. Free pick-up from Currumbine Railway Station.

Swan Valley Trails and Horse Riding Centre: Swan Valley Oasis Resort, 10 250 West Swan Road, Henley Brook. Phone: 08 9296 2601 or 0418 681 529. In summer, you can experience a weekend twilight or breakfast ride, and meal at $30.00 per rider. Alternatively, a river and vineyard scenic ride costs $25.00 per rider. Phone for more information and bookings. On Sunday for $50.00 per person, you can ride to a vineyard for lunch and wine-tasting, then on to a tearoom for afternoon tea. This tour can also be taken by horse and cart.

Tapper's Horse Hire: Lot 8 Hammond Road, Jandakot. Phone: 08 9417 9272. Approximately 20 minutes south of Perth, and open seven days, they offer bushland bridle trails with free escort. There is a large selection of horses available for beginners and experienced riders.

The Stables Yanchep: Yanchep Beach Road, Yanchep. Phone: 08 9561 1606. Cost: $30.00 for two hours. Experience some of the finest horse trail rides in WA. The Stables also offer twilight rides, overnight camps and two-day expeditions to Moore River. Pick-up from Joondalup Train Station can be arranged.

ICE SKATING

Cockburn Ice Arena: 239 Barrington Street, Bibra Lake. Phone: 08 9434 4066. Cost: adults $13.00, children $12.00 which covers skate hire and use of rink per session. Wear thick socks! Phone for session times.

Skaters on Ice (formerly Ice World): Yirrigan Drive, cnr Mirrabooka Avenue, Mirrabooka. Phone: 08 9344 4400. Open daily. Sessions run at 10.00 am, 1.00 pm, 4.00 pm and 7.30 pm except there is no 4.00 pm session on Tuesday and Thursday. Cost: adults $8.95, children $6.95, for a two and a half hour skating session, $25.00 for a family pass (two adults, two children) Saturday and Sunday at 4.00 pm only. Skate hire: $4.95 for all sizes. Phone to check session times.

INTERACTIVE LASER GAMES

If your idea of fun is running around wearing a sensor vest, shooting at an opposing team with laser guns, and trying to avoid enemy fire, then try the following three centres:

Q-Zar: 19 Essex Street, Fremantle. Phone: 08 9430 5404. Seven days per week, from 9.00 am until late. The more games played, the cheaper Q-Zar gets, however, the most you will pay for a game is $5.00.

Zone 3 Laser Sport: 448 Murray Street, Perth. Phone: 08 9322 4440. Open seven days per week. Hours vary, but weekends open from 10.00 am until midnight. Cost: $7.00 for one game, $5.00 for second game.

Zone 3: 260 Newcastle Street, Northbridge. Phone: 08 9227 1511. Open daily: 10.00 am to 10.00 pm, Sunday to Thursday; 10.00 am to midnight, Friday and Saturday. Also takes bookings for Friday and Saturday nights, midnight to 6.00 am. Cost: $7.00 for one game, $12.00 for two games, and $16.00 for three games.

MINIATURE AND TOURIST RAILWAYS

Castledare Miniature Railway: 100 Fern Road, Wilson (end Bungaree Road). Phone: 08 9375 1223. Open first Sunday of each month, 11.00 am to 4.00 pm, and every Wednesday in school holidays, 11.00 am to 3.00 pm. Situated on the banks of the Canning River, about 15 minutes from the city centre, Castledare offers over five kilometres of 7.25 inch gauge miniature railway. There are real steam and diesel outline locomotives hauling open passenger carriages. Cost: adults $4.00, children $2.00, multirider (10 kids' rides or five adults') $12.00. There are BBQs, large grassy picnic areas and a playground for children.

Hotham Valley Tourist Railway: Commonwealth Bank Building (2nd Floor), 86A Barrack Street, Perth. Phone: 08 9221 4444. Office hours: 9.00 am to 5.00 pm Monday to Friday, 9.00 am to 12.00 noon Saturday. Hotham Valley offers a variety of day and evening trips in old coaches hauled by steam or diesel locomotives. These are usually on weekends or Wednesdays, and are often planned to coincide with festivals or events in particular country towns. For example, the Dwellingup Log Chop Explorer, Donnybrook Apple Festival Explorer, Harvey Show Steam Explorer or the Balingup Tulip Festival Explorer. There are also some dinner tours, including a murder mystery tour and two, three or four day tours to Wave Rock, Narrogin, Bunbury and Geraldton. Phone for more information and brochures.

PEDAL CAR HIRE

About Bike Hire: has three branches:
- Activity Booking Centre, Kiosk 3, Old Perth Port, Barrack Street Jetty, Perth. Phone: 08 9221 1828. Open seven days: 8.00 am to 6.00 pm. View the river by pedal car. Easy pedalling along wide flat tracks on the foreshore of the Swan River or, for the energetic, cycle up to Kings Park for scenic views of Perth City and water. For the even more energetic, you can cycle the 56-kilometre return journey to Fremantle.
- No.4 Car Park, Riverside Drive, Perth (near the Causeway). Phone: 08 9221 2665. Weekdays 10.00 am to

4.00 pm; Saturdays 10.00 am to
5.00 pm; Sunday and public holidays
9.00 am to 5.00 pm.

■ Perry Lakes Park, Floreat. Phone:
08 9221 2665. Open Saturdays
1.30 pm to 4.30 pm and Sunday
11.30 am to 4.00 pm. Baby seats
provided. Maximum two adults, two
small children. Cost: $10.00 for half
an hour, $18.00 for one hour.

Jolly Jalopy's Australia. Phone:
08 9335 3965 or 0148 954 158. Pedal
cars for hire at Whiteman Park and
Mews Road, Fremantle at weekends
and school and public holidays. Cost
is $6.00 (three people in pedal car)
for 15 minutes. See Chapter 13, Parks
and Gardens, page 84.

ROCK CLIMBING

The Climbers Association of WA:
Stephenson Avenue, Mount
Claremont. Phone: 08 9387 8100.
Information and guidance on climbing
and related activities around Perth
and Western Australia.

Adventure Out Australia: 2/55 Cargill
Street, Victoria Park. Phone:
08 9472 3919. Introductory rock
climbing courses less than an hour
from Perth. Experienced instructors
help you gain hands-on experience.
Cost: about $200.00 for a two-day
course.

For indoor rock climbing, see Wall
Climbing, page 128.

ROLLER-SKATING/BLADING

Astroskate: Kwinana Recreation and
Leisure Centre, cnr Chisham and
Gilmore Avenues, Kwinana. Phone:

08 9419 4444. This indoor skating
facility is open Friday evenings
7.30 pm to 9.30 pm, and Saturdays
10.00 am till 12 noon. Cost: $4.00
and $1.00 to hire skates. Roller-
skating and roller-blading lessons are
also available.

Blade Skate Australia: 2/8 Gugeri Street,
Claremont. Phone: 08 9384 2427. Cost:
skate hire $9.00 for two hours, $15.00
per day or $20.00 over night. Branches
also at Warwick, phone: 08 9246 9200;
and Fremantle, phone: 08 9430 4082.
Tuition is available and there is a wide
range of equipment for sale.

Rollarama Kalamunda: 3 Collins Road,
Kalamunda. Phone: 08 9293 2969.
Roller-skating and in-line hockey.
Open Monday, Wednesday, Friday
10.00 am to 12.00 noon and Friday
7.00 pm to 10.00 pm. Weekend
sessions: 10.00 am to 12.30 pm,
1.30 pm to 4.00 pm, and 7.30 pm to
10.00 pm (Saturday evening). Cost:
morning session $4.50, afternoon
session $5.00, evening session $6.00.
Skate hire: $1.00. Blade hire: $3.00.
Closed on public holidays.

Rollerdrome Balcatta: 8 Gibberd Road,
Balcatta. Phone: 08 9345 3166. Main
sessions are on Friday evenings and
weekends. Cost: $6.00 for a two-hour
session, including skate hire if
necessary. Night sessions cost $8.00.
There is also in-line hockey. Phone to
check session times.

Rollerdrome Morley: 95 Catherine
Street, Morley. Phone: 08 9276 9870.
Main sessions are on Friday evenings
and at weekends. Cost: day sessions
$5.00, night sessions $7.00. Hire of
roller skates 50 cents; roller blades

Cameleer Park Camel Farm is one of the companies offering camel treks, rides or safaris through the Australian native bush. The camels are guaranteed to be friendly!

River cruises up to the Swan Valley often include a stop at historic Woodbridge House, as in the cruise pictured here, run by Boat Torque 2000.

The calcified limestone pillars of the Pinnacles can be found in the Nambung National Park about 250 kilometres north of Perth.

The aptly named Wave Rock is composed of an enormous piece of ancient granite 15 metres high and 100 metres long. It is situated 350 kilometres south-east of Perth.

Hillarys Boat Harbour has many attractions including a boardwalk with restaurants and shops as well as accommodation, beaches, water slides and mini golf.

Underwater World is a spectacular oceanarium where visitors can journey under the sea and view sharks, stingrays and other sea creatures, or visit the dolphins in their unique sea pen.

Cottesloe Beach is one of Perth's best known beaches and is visited by families, surfers and people who enjoy fishing.

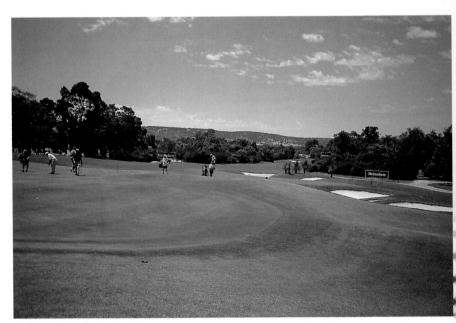

The Vines in the Swan Valley is just one of the numerous public golf courses in and around Perth and Fremantle. The Heineken Classic is played at the Vines every January.

Many wildflowers bloom in Kings Park in spring including masses of pink and white everlastings (straw flowers). The Wildflower Festival is held here in late September.

Perth's waterways are a popular place to sail catamarans and enjoy an array of water sports on a hot summer's day.

Houghton Winery Estate is one of the oldest and best known of the Swan Valley vineyards. As with many of the vineyards in this area, it is open for wine tastings and lunch.

The Mediterranean climate and loamy soils of the Swan Valley combine to make it an ideal place to cultivate many different varieties of grapes, including the cabernet grapes pictured here.

The War Memorial in Kings Park overlooks the city of Perth and the Swan River. It commemorates Western Australians killed in both World Wars and other conflicts.

Kangaroos may be seen at most wildlife parks as well as at Perth Zoo. At the Cohunu Koala Park, pictured here, kangaroos may be hand fed.

$3.00. Phone to check session times. Lessons available.

Rolloways: 352A South Street, O'Connor (near Hinds Road). Phone: 08 9337 9444. Their speciality is roller disco on Friday and Saturday nights and birthday parties. General sessions are mainly on Friday evenings and at weekends. Cost: $5.00 for two hours, $1.50 skate hire, or $3.00 blade hire. Special sessions run for toddlers, mothers and specialised age groups. Phone for session times.

Skate About: Unit 1, 1 Langley Place, Innaloo. Phone: 08 9445 1069 or 019 110 676. Learn to rollerblade or skate or improve your existing skills. Private tuition and skate hire for up to three people costs $40.00 per hour.

Star Skates: Star Surf Shop, 332 Murray Street, Perth. Phone: 08 9321 6230. In-line skates for hire. Skate where you want (river foreshore recommended). Cost: $9.00 for two hours, half day $15.00, full day $20.00. Includes all safety gear.

SKATEBOARDING

Vertigo Skate Park: 87 Forsyth Street, O'Connor. Phone: 08 9331 7006. Open Tuesday to Friday 12 noon to 10.00 pm; Saturday 10.00 am to 10.00 pm; and Sunday 10.00 am to 8.00 pm. Rollerblading and skateboarding facility. Bring your own equipment (no hire). Cost: $6.00 for a two-hour session.

SLING SHOT

Cables Water Ski Park: 8 Troode Street, Spearwood. Info Line: 08 9418 6111. Enquiries:

08 9418 6888. This is like a bungee jump in reverse, except that you are in a spherical cage. Cost: $20.00.

SNOOKER/POOL

Specialist pool places are listed below, however most hotels/pubs have a bar with pool tables available to clients.

Billy Weston's Pool and Snooker: 64 Scarborough Beach Road, Scarborough. Phone: 08 9245 3939.

The Cue Club: Unit 2, 800 Beaufort Street, Mount Lawley. Phone: 08 9370 3161. Open 12.00 noon to 11.00 pm, with slightly longer hours over the weekends.

Hot Shot Pool and Snooker: 560 Beaufort Street, Mount Lawley. Phone: 08 9227 5706.

Pot Black has 8 centres around the metropolitan area. Phone administration: 08 9430 7304 for more details. They offer pool, snooker, American Nine Ball and Billiards.

STRAWBERRY PICKING

Strawberry Fields and Tea Rooms: 2024 Wanneroo Road, Neerabup. Phone: 08 9407 5358. Forty kilometres north of the city centre. Open seven days a week. Pick your own strawberries in season (generally October/November) or buy ready-picked along with honey and assorted jams, wines, ports, liqueur, apple cider and honey mead. Tasting of products is available.

TEN PIN BOWLING

Cannington Lanes: Burton Street, cnr Chapman Road, Cannington. Phone:

08 9451 7333. Open 9.00 am to midnight. This centre has 24 lanes with computer scoring, arcade games and pool tables. It is air-conditioned and there is a café.

Fairlanes City: 175 Adelaide Terrace, East Perth. Phone: 08 9325 3588. Open seven days from 9.00 am until late. This bowling centre has 24 lanes and facilities including computer scoring, bumpers for the kids, a café, Internet café and a bar. It offers social bowling as well as glow bowling from 9.00 pm Fridays and Saturdays.

Fairlanes Craigie Bowling Centre: 9 Perilya Road, Craigie. Phone: 08 9307 6633. This centre has the same facilities as Fairlanes City above.

Kelmscott Ten Pin Bowl: 265 Railway Avenue, Kelmscott. Phone: 08 9399 4400. Open seven days 9.00 am until late. This centre is air-conditioned and has fully automatic scoring.

Morley Bowl: 176 Walter Road, Morley. Phone: 08 9275 1258. Open 8.30 am to midnight. This centre is air-conditioned and has 24 bowling lanes with computer scoring. There are pool tables and video games.

Rosemount Bowl: 464 Fitzgerald Street, North Perth. Phone: 08 9328 7246. Facilities include a fully licensed café and bar, computer scoring and bumper bowling. There are eight lanes. Open: 9.30 am to 11.30 pm, Monday to Saturday, 9.30 am to 10.00 pm Sunday.

Super Bowl Warwick Grove: 12 Dugdale Street, Warwick. Phone: 08 9246 5088. Open 8.30 am to midnight every day, except Christmas Day. This air-conditioned centre has 24 lanes with computer scoring, a pool and snooker room upstairs and a café.

Super Bowl Melville: 248 Stock Road, cnr Leach Highway, Melville. Phone: 08 9330 7466. Open seven days, 8.45 am until late. Twenty-four lanes with computer scoring and air-conditioning. A café is on site.

TENNIS

The State Tennis Centre of Western Australia. Phone: 08 9361 1112. Thirteen plexicushion courts with Perth's most powerful court lighting are available for hire, $10.00 per hour before midday, $12.00 per hour after midday. Professional tennis coaches are available. Licensed bar facilities are available in the Centre Court Café.

Alternatively, Perth has numerous tennis clubs in all suburbs, most of which are very happy to have non-members play for a small visitors' fee, or to negotiate a temporary membership. Tennis West on 08 9361 1112 can advise on your nearest club. Many local councils also have public courts available for hire. Phone the local council for information.

WALKS

The following are organised walking tours:

City Walking Tours: Phone: 08 9293 3054. These guided walks take in the main attractions of the city of Perth, and their history. Cost: $9.00 or $7.00 concession for a two-hour walk, commencing at 9.30 am Tuesdays and Thursdays. Tours leave from the WA

Tourist Centre, Forrest Place.

Fremantle Ghost Walks: Phone: 08 9484 1133 or 1800 193 300 (toll free). Cost: adults $12.00, concession $10.00, children $8.00.

There are two tours:

Ghosts of the Asylum: on Thursday at 7.30 pm and Friday and Saturday at 7.30 pm and 9.30 pm. A one hour ghost tour of the building which now houses the Fremantle Museum and Fremantle Arts Centre. It was originally the colony's first lunatic asylum and women's home and is reputed to be one of Australia's most haunted buildings.

Ghosts of the West End: on Wednesday at 7.30 pm, visits 10 different haunted buildings, including the old Round House, the colony's first prison. Tours are led by master storyteller, Alex Marshall.

Fremantle Historic Walking Tours. Phone: 08 9336 1906. Cost: adults $7.50; concession, or for 4 or more people, $6.00. Two different one and a half hour tours, describing the early development of Fremantle. By appointment only.

Kings Park Free Guided Walks. Meet at the Karri Log in Fraser Avenue (opposite the War Memorial). There are a variety of tours most lasting an hour to an hour and a half, though the Bush Walk lasts two to two and a half hours. There are tours every morning, commencing at 10.00 am and some afternoons, commencing at 2.00 pm. Tours include the Botanic Garden Walk, the Wildflower Trail, the Bushwalk and the Heritage Walk. The information office in Fraser

Avenue has a brochure entitled *Free Guided Walks*, with times and descriptions of each of the walks. There are also some excellent maps for those wanting to undertake these tours by themselves, with details of the flora and fauna you will encounter. The information office also has pamphlets on various trees and shrubs, including wattles, she-oaks, the West Australian Christmas Tree and the Zamia. There is a fascinating pamphlet on the origins of the names of some of the plants, revealing how many plants were named after early explorers and botanists, for example, the Banksia after Joseph Banks.

There are also several bushwalking clubs such as:

Perth Bushwalkers Club.
Phone: 08 9362 1614.

Bushwalkers of Western Australia.
Phone: 08 9457 1772.

Western Walking Club.
Phone: 08 9276 1419.

The West Australian Family Bushwalking Club.
Phone: 08 9337 2080.

Action Outdoors Association.
Phone: 015 341 617.

The Department of Conservation and Land Management: 50 Hayman Road, Como. Phone: 08 9334 0333. Their excellent bushwalking books are available on request.

The Heritage Council of WA: 108 Adelaide Terrace, East Perth. Phone: 08 9221 4177. Provides information on heritage trails in and around the city and further afield, such as the Bibbulman Track and Rottnest Island.

Pamphlets provide information on points of historical and cultural interest.

The Bibbulmun Track runs for 650 kilometres from Kalamunda (in the Darling Ranges) to Walpole on the south coast of Western Australia. The track runs through unspoilt forest and bush and is designed so that walks of varying lengths may be undertaken, for example circuit walks enable you to enjoy the experience of a one day forest walk which will bring you back to your starting point. There are campsites every 15 to 25 kilometres apart, approximately one day's walk.

CALM (Department of Conservation and Land Management). Phone: 08 9334 0265. Bibbulmun Track Project Office manages the track and produces a guidebook and maps. Apart from summer, when it is very hot and dry, the Bibbulmun Track may be enjoyed most of the year, particularly from August to November when the wildflowers are out.

If you're into less serious walking, interesting destinations for a wander and a coffee are Hillarys Boat Harbour/ Sorrento Quay, Fremantle, Subiaco and Northbridge. There are also dual-purpose walking/bicycle trails that almost completely encircle the Swan and Canning Rivers. There are children's playgrounds and picnic areas, some with BBQs, as well as kiosks, cafés and restaurants dotted around the edge of the river. For more information on picnic and BBQ areas in Perth, see page 144.

WALL CLIMBING (INDOOR)

Indoor wall climbing involves climbing a vertical wall with man-made hand-holds and foot-grips, whilst securely harnessed. Venues include:

The Hangout Rock Climbing Gym: 12 White Street, Bayswater. Phone: 08 9371 9939. Open: weekdays 4.00 pm to 10.00 pm; weekends: 10.00 am to 6.00 pm. Cost: adults $14.00, concession $12.00, children $10.00. Includes harness hire, and unlimited climbing.

The Overhang: 4/8 Cohn Street, Carlisle. Phone: 08 9470 6980. Open daily, except Christmas Day, New Year's Day and Good Friday. Weekdays: 10.00 am to 10.00 pm, Saturdays and Sunday: 10.00 am to 6.00 pm, public holidays: 12.00 noon to 6.00 pm. Cost: adults $12.00, students under 15 $10.00, children $8.00. Includes harness hire, instruction and unlimited climbing.

Rockface: 63B John Street, Northbridge. Phone: 08 9328 5998. Open: weekdays 4.00 pm to 10.00 pm, weekends 10.00 am to 10.00 pm. Cost: adults $10.00; students and under 18's $8.00. Harness hire: $4.00. Climbing shoes: $5.00.

WA Indoor Climbing Gym: cnr 131 Salvado Road and Jersey Street, Jolimont. Phone: 08 9383 7747. Open: weekdays 4.00 pm to 10.00 pm; weekends 10.00 am to 8.00 pm; weekdays school holidays 10.00 am to 10.00 pm. Cost: adults $9.00, concession $8.00, children $7.00. Harness hire: $3.00. Climbing shoes: $4.00. Special prices for groups, and during school holidays. On summer weekends and school holidays the gym only opens at 12.00 noon.

CHAPTER 18

ORGANISED TOURS

There are numerous companies in and around Perth and Fremantle which organise a variety of tours to all the major local tourist attractions in the region. These tours might include trips by ferry or coach to wineries, cruises on the Swan River, exploring Perth and Fremantle, visiting wildlife parks or four-wheel-driving in the Pinnacles Desert. This chapter also includes details of companies which offer organised tours further afield to destinations such as Margaret River, Albany, Wave Rock and even a 24-hour trip to Monkey Mia.

CAR TOURS

Chauffeur Affair: Phone: 08 9371 2220 or 0419 934 580. Visit the Swan Valley vineyards by chauffeur driven luxury air-conditioned vehicle and enjoy sampling some of Western Australia's finest wines. This company will take you to numerous other destinations. Cost: from $50.00 per hour for up to four people.

Response Limousine Service: Phone: 08 9310 3618 or 0408 433 272. Can arrange personalised tours of Perth and surrounding areas for four, six or 10 passengers. Tours can include escorted shopping trips, silver service picnics, airport transfers or anywhere else you might like to visit.

Two's Company Tours: Phone: 08 9246 9499. Chauffeur driven luxury car tours can be tailor made to suit you. Costs start from $90.00 a car. They could include wildlife park

visits, wine tasting in the Swan Valley or a visit to the Darling Range. This company is run in conjunction with Palms Bed and Breakfast. See page 18 in Chapter 3: Accommodation.

COACH TOURS

Australian Pacific Tours: Pinnacles Travel Centre, cnr Hay and Pier Streets, Perth. Phone: 08 9221 5477. Examples of one-day coach tours are to Wave Rock (including York, Hyden, caves and Aboriginal Paintings); Margaret River (including winery, caves, eagles, surfing beaches, karri forests and possibility of seeing dolphins); Albany (including jarrah forests, whaling museum, spectacular coastal scenery); Pinnacles (including wildlife park, seeing wildflowers (in season), historic towns, four-wheel-drive vehicle on the beach), and Valley of the Giants Tree Top Walk (including dolphins and karri forests). There are several half-day and full-day tours of Perth and Fremantle, including river cruises. Half-day tours start at $33.00 for adults, and the most expensive full-day tours are the Albany and the 'Tree Top Walk' trips, costing $107.00 (including lunch). This company also offers tours lasting up to four days.

Australian Pinnacle Tours: Pinnacles Travel Centre, cnr Hay and Pier Streets, Perth. Phone: 08 9221 5411 for more information and costs.

As well as tours lasting several days, this company has one-day coach tours to: the Pinnacles Desert (taking in a wildlife park, wildflower viewing (in season) and one of the tours includes four-wheel-driving on the beach and over sand dunes); Wave Rock (including seeing aboriginal paintings and caves); Margaret River (including wineries, caves, karri forests, eagles and wildflowers (in season); Albany (including the whaling museum, jarrah forests and spectacular coastline). The most expensive day tours are to Albany and the Valley of the Giants Tree Top Walk (including seeing dolphins and karri forests). Costs $108.00 (including lunch).

There are also several half-day tours either of Perth and Fremantle or to the Swan Valley, a wildlife park, Hillarys Marina/Underwater World and Rottnest Island. Half-day tours start at $35.00 for adults.

Feature Tours: Phone: 08 9479 4131. A good selection of day and half-day trips to see the sights of Perth and Fremantle and further afield:

Full-day excursions include trips to the Pinnacles and Wave Rock or to Albany, Margaret River and the Tree Top walk.

'The Mariners', includes a cruise down the Swan River, then a coach ride around Fremantle's historic city centre and harbours, before returning to Perth. Some Fremantle trips allow free time at Fremantle Markets (Friday and Saturday only). This is a half-day tour. There are also half-day tours to the Swan Valley wineries; Underwater World; Tumbulgum Farm; a wildlife park; New Norcia (including wildflowers).

Evening tours include a Perth by Night tour where participants enjoy a progressive dinner whilst being introduced to the Northbridge nightlife area, city views from Kings Park and South Perth, with a visit to the Burswood Casino.

Feature Tours also run the Airport/City Shuttle bus, connecting with all interstate and international flights. See Chapter 20: General Information, page 151. In addition, they offer 24-hour tours where you travel overnight to either Monkey Mia or Kalgoorlie and the Goldfields with a stop at Wave Rock.

Great Western Coach Tours: Phone: 08 9490 2455. Great Western have approximately 12 different trips that you can take on their air-conditioned 17 to 22 seat coaches. There are day tours, half-day tours and evening tours. As well as the normal tours of Perth, Fremantle, Underwater World and the wineries, some different tours include trips to:

New Norcia and the Chittering
Valley (adults $80.00).
The Murray River and the jarrah
forests (adults $80.00).
Dinner in the Hills (adults $50.00).
Two-hour forest walk through the
Australian bush with a specialist guide
(adults $45.00).
The wildflower tour in spring.
Outstanding Tours: Phone:
08 9368 4949. Offer a wide variety of
tours by luxury 16-seater coaches or
new model Range Rovers. Some of
the tours include a Swan River Cruise.
Their wide range of tours can include
visits to the wineries, Caversham
Wildlife Park, Tumbulgum Farm and
Underwater World, as well as Perth
and Fremantle by day or night.
Planet Perth Tours: Phone:
08 9276 5295. This tour company is
mainly used by backpackers, students
and younger tourists but all are
welcome. Their Wines and Vines tour
visits four wineries and costs $29.00;
or visit Caversham Wildlife Park and
Kings Park after dark for $25.00
including a BBQ dinner. You can take
horse rides through the Australian
bush either in the morning or at
sunset. This eight-hour trip includes a
BBQ meal and swimming at a
waterfall in the Serpentine Falls
National Park. Cost: $65.00.
Red Carpet Day Tours: Phone: 08
9367 7797. Luxury half-day tours of
the Perth hills for groups of 15 or
less. Includes visiting Mundaring
Weir, and viewing Perth and the Swan
coastal plain from the Darling Scarp.
You also visit an orchard and an art
and craft shop. Cost: adult $45.00

(includes afternoon tea). They also
have a day tour to Margaret River.
Cost: adult $130.00 including wine-
tasting and lunch at a winery.
Swan Gold Tours:
Phone: 08 9451 5333. Tours include:
Have half-day tours visiting Perth,
Fremantle and major attractions in
between. Costs: adult from $35.00 or
$45.00 if you choose to return by
boat to Perth from Fremantle.
Dolphins, Koalas and Kangaroos.
This four-hour tour visits Underwater
World and a Wildlife Park. Cost:
$45.00 adults.
Tumbulgum Farm and Aboriginal
Show. Visit an Australian farm and see
Aboriginal dancing and didgeridoo
playing. Cost: adults $45.00 (includes
billy tea and damper).

DISABLED TOURS
Able Tours: 565 Kilburn Road,
Parkerville. Phone: 08 9295 4965.
Specialise in four-wheel-drive
adventure tours for disabled people.
Phone for information.

FOUR-WHEEL-DRIVE TOURS
Safari Treks Four-wheel-drive Tours:
Phone: 08 9271 1271. Tours include:
Pinnacles Day Tour: (runs daily):
Includes Yanchep koalas, Australian
bush and four-wheel-driving along
white beaches, viewing the unique
Pinnacles. Cost: $98.00 adults; $66.00
children; $91.00 YHA, students,
pensioners, includes morning tea,
lunch and afternoon tea.
Wave Rock Day Tour: (Monday,
Wednesday, Saturday). Tour passes
through historical York and the

Wheatbelt to Wave Rock, Hippo's Yawn and Mulka's Cave, where there are Aboriginal paintings. Wildflowers may be seen in spring. Cost: $82.00 adults; $80.00 YHA, students, pensioners; $60.00 children. They also offer one-day trips to Margaret River and wildflower tours in spring.

Travelabout Four-wheel-drive Tours: Phone: 08 9244 1200 or 1800 621 200. Tours include:

One Day Pinnacles Desert, Sand Dunes and Beaches Four-wheel-drive Fun Tour. Visit koala park, have picture taken with a koala, view wildflowers in spring and wander through the limestone spires of the Pinnacles Desert in the Nambung National Park. Return via sand-dune tracks and deserted beaches for a refreshing swim in summer. Daily departures. All inclusive cost approx $95.00 (with lunch).

Red Back Safaris: Phone: 08 9275 6204. Tours run by this company include: **Pinnacles One Day Tour**. Departs 7.30 am every day of the year. Pick-up at all city hotels, Perth Train Station and all hostels. Travel by luxury air-conditioned four-wheel-drive vehicle through the Swan Valley, viewing the outback en route to the Nambung National Park and its unique limestone formations, the Pinnacles. Then on to Hangover Bay for a swim before lunch at Cervantes. Drive through bush tracks, viewing Australian wildlife, to magnificent sand dunes for some four-wheel-driving and sand-surfing. Return to Perth 6.30 pm. Cost: $80.00 adults, $75.00 YHA/BRA, pensioners and

students, $65.00 children, including a delicious lunch.

Western Geographic Eco Tours: Phone: 08 9336 4992. This company specialises in trips highlighting the unique geographical features, wildlife and wildflowers of Western Australia. Tours include:

Pinnacles Four-wheel-drive Eco Tour is a full day (12 hours) tour introducing participants to four-wheel-driving over sand dunes and through bush tracks to visit the weird formations of The Pinnacles. On the way, learn about the flora and fauna of the area and enjoy a swim in the Indian Ocean. Home-made lunch and morning tea are provided. Cost: adults $88.00. Also on offer is a Pinnacles Moonlight tour for $95.00 which includes a BBQ dinner with wine (November to May at full moon only).

MOTOR BIKE TOURS

All American Motorcycle Tours: Phone: 015 080 081 or after hours on 08 9277 1259. Be taken for a ride on a Harley Davidson from one hour to a full day or more. Tours from $60.00 for an hour. Choose your own route. Also have bikes with sidecars. Cost: $100.00 for an hour. Airport pick-ups can be arranged as they have a trailer.

Down Under Motorcycle Tours: Hillarys Boat Harbour, Sorrento Quay, Perth. Phone: 08 9307 4608 or 0407 078 990. Organise your own half an hour, to full-day tour, on a Harley. Gift vouchers and T-shirts available. Half an hour costs $40.00, $330.00 for a full day.

Low Rider Motorcycle Tours: Phone: 08 9418 3210 or 0408 955 667. Tours cost from $60.00 for one hour. A variety of organised tours, or choose your own itinerary. Sidecar available at $100.00 per hour.

RIVER CRUISES

Boat Torque Cruises: Pier 4, Barrack Street Jetty, Perth. Phone: 08 9221 5844. Cruises run by this company include:

Lunch with the Ducks. Departs from Barrack Street Jetty daily at 10.30 am, returning at 1.00 pm. The cruise includes full commentary, a light lunch, tea, coffee and cake. It takes you up the Swan River past Heirisson Island, Burswood Casino and on to Tranby House where you stop to feed the ducks. Cost: adults $29.00, students/concessions $25.00, children $15.00.

River Lunch and Vineyard Cruise. Departs from Barrack Street Jetty daily at 1.45 pm and returns at 5.30 pm. This cruise includes morning tea and lunch on board and a stop at Olive Farm vineyard for wine-tasting. Cost: adults $45.00, students/concession $35.00, and children $25.00.

Swan Valley River and Vineyard Cruise. Departs Barrack Street Jetty at 9.45 am returning at 4.45 pm. Cost: $75.00 or $85.00 per person for deluxe seating. Includes Swan river cruise and commentary, morning tea, visit to Woodbridge House (built in early 1880s and classified by the National Trust), wine tasting at Sandalford or Houghton Vineyard,

two-course lunch and wine at Mulberry Farm restaurant (situated on the banks of the Swan River with sweeping views of surrounding vineyards) and entertainment from the crew.

Wildflower Vineyard and Afternoon Cruise. Departs Barrack Street Jetty at 1.45 pm, Tuesday, Wednesday, Thursday, Friday and Sunday. September to November only. Return 6.00 pm. Cost: adults $40.00; students, seniors, backpacker $30.00, children (four to 12) $25.00. This tour includes a Swan River cruise, wine-tasting at a vineyard, a coach trip to see wildflowers and afternoon tea.

Captain's Seafood Dinner Cruise. Departs from Barrack Street Jetty on Wednesdays and Sunday at 7.00 pm. Cruise along the Swan River to the Swan Valley, enjoying a seafood dinner and live music. The boat returns at 10.00 pm. Cost: adults $49.00 (lobster dinner is $10.00 extra). There is an alternative meal for those who do not like seafood.

Dinner in the Valley Cruise. Departs Barrack Street Jetty at 6.00 pm returning at midnight. Saturday nights all year round, except August; Friday nights November, December and January. Cost: $65.00 or $70.00 per person for deluxe seating. Cruise the Swan Valley by night, enjoy hors d'oeuvres, light beer, wine and soft drink. At the Mulberry Farm restaurant enjoy a three-course buffet dinner followed by dancing and floor show. Dancing and refreshments continue on the cruise home. A courtesy bus will collect you from your hotel.

Starlight Dinner Cruise. Departs Barrack Street Jetty on Saturday night at 7.30 pm returning at 11.30 pm. This cruise takes you past Kings Park and several yacht clubs and offers spectacular views of the city. It includes entertainment and a full buffet meal as well as beer, wine and soft drinks. Cost: adults $58.00, in November to December $68.00.

Captain Cook Cruises: Pier 3, Barrack Street Jetty, Perth. Phone: 08 9325 3341. Cruises include:

Swan River Scenic Cruise. Departs Perth at 9.45 am and 2.00 pm and Fremantle (East Street Jetty) at 11.00 am daily all year round. Cruise duration two hours 45 minutes. Cost: adults $24.00, seniors $20.00, children (four to 14) $12.00, family (two adults, two children) $60.00. One way trips (in either direction). Cost: adults $13.00, seniors $11.00, children (four to 14) $9.00, family $40.00. Tram transfers between jetty and city centre are available.

Tourist Trifecta. Consists of the above return cruise from Perth to Fremantle, plus tram tours of both cities, with three hours free to lunch or shop in Fremantle. Perth tram will pick you up at or near your city hotel. Cost: adults $45.00, children (four to 14) $22.50 or for $75.00 (adults) and $37.50 (children, four to 14). You can experience the above tour plus a guided tour of Fremantle Prison and lunch at the Esplanade Hotel.

Twilight Cruise. Seasonally, September to April, Wednesdays and Fridays only, departs Perth at 5.30 pm, returns 7.00 pm. Cost $12.00 (all ages). Cruise includes complimentary drink and snacks. There is a well stocked bar on board.

Luncheon Cruise. Seasonally, September to May, Wednesdays, Fridays and Sunday only, departs Perth at 11.00 am, returns 1.45 pm or departs Fremantle 12.15 pm and returns 3.15 pm. Cost: adults $37.00, seniors $32.00, children $25.00, family (two adults, two children) $99.00. Morning tea and buffet lunch with wine is served whilst the boat cruises between Perth and Fremantle.

Evening Dinner Cruise. Departs 8.00 pm every Saturday night, also Fridays October to April, and Wednesdays, November to January. Returns 11.30 pm. Cost: adults $58.00, children (four to 14) $45.00. Cruise the Swan River by night, enjoying a buffet dinner with beer, wine and soft drinks. Dancing and full bar facilities are available.

Golden Sun Travel and Cruises: Barrack Street Jetty 2, Perth. Phone: 08 9325 1616 or 018 917 316. Cruises include:

Perth to Fremantle. Cruise the Swan River from Perth to the port of Fremantle viewing riverside mansions. Departs Barrack Street Jetty twice a day in the morning and afternoon. Cost: $15.00 return (ex-Perth only), $9.50 one way. A chicken and salad lunch ($8.00) may be pre-booked if required, otherwise the bar is open and snacks are available.

Perth to Tranby House. Departs Barrack Street Jetty, Perth at 2.00 pm.

Cruise up river past Burswood to Tranby House (Cost: $22.00 return, excluding entry fee to Tranby House) or continue on up river to historical Guildford (for $28.00 return). Pre-book and pay for chicken and salad ($8.00) or snacks and bar are available at extra cost.

Perth to Swan Valley Vineyards. Groups of 20 or more. Partake of a buffet lunch with wine whilst cruising up the Swan River past the city, Burswood and Tranby House and enjoy wine-tasting at the vineyards. Commentary provided by the captain.

Oceanic Cruises: Barrack Street Jetty, Perth; or East Street Jetty, East Fremantle. Phone: 08 9325 1191 (Perth) or 08 9430 5127 (Fremantle). Tours available include:

City Scenic River Tour. Departs daily from Barrack Street Jetty, Perth at 2.00 pm, returning 3.30 pm. Cruise on the Swan River. Complimentary tea and coffee are provided. Commentary will highlight some Perth landmarks, e.g. Royal Perth Yacht Club and Millionaires' Row. Cost: adults $10.00, children $5.00 (six to 14 years).

Up River Swan Valley Luncheon Cruise. Departs Barrack Street Jetty, Perth at 9.45 am, returning 4.15 pm. Cost: adults $60.00 return, children $30.00 (six to 10). Cruise on fully licensed and air-conditioned boat. The cruise includes morning tea served on board, guided tour of Tranby House, buffet luncheon at Caversham House, and one complementary glass of wine on the return cruise. This cruise only operates with a minimum of 30 people.

Super Special Cruises to Fremantle. Departs daily 10.00 am from Barrack Street Jetty, or at 11.45 am from East Street Jetty, Fremantle. Cost: $8.00 one way, $14.00 return for adults; $5.00 one way, $8.00 return for children (six to 14). View the Swan River while travelling to Fremantle. Complementary tea or coffee and an extensive commentary are provided. Free coach transfer from ferry to Fremantle town centre.

Swan River and Fremantle Inner Harbour Cruise plus Historical Tour of Fremantle by Tram. Cost: adults $16.00, children $8.00 (six to 14 years).

Paddle Steamer Decoy: Mends Street Jetty, South Perth. Phone: 08 9581 2383 or 0418 906 419. This paddle steamer is usually available for charter, but there is a jazz cruise every Sunday afternoon during the summer (early November to early May). Departs Mends Street Jetty at 2.00 pm, cruising down the river to Point Walter, and returns at 5.00 pm. Cost: adults $15.00, children (five to 12) $10.00, under five free.

TRAM TOURS
See page 13, Chapter 2: Getting Around.

WALKING TOURS
See Walks on page 126, Chapter 17: Activities on the Land.

WILDLIFE/ECO TOURS
Eco Bush Tours: Phone: 08 9336 3050. A variety of ecologically oriented tours, ranging from one to four days exploring the local flora and fauna,

Aboriginal culture and unusual land forms such as The Pinnacles and Wave Rock. For $120.00 the Perth One Day Nature Tour (covering approximately 290 kilometres) visits botanical gardens, wetlands, a wildlife park, vineyards, forests, ancient granite outcrops and offers numerous chances to view wildflowers in season and birds in their natural environment. This extremely comprehensive tour even offers a walk on the Bibbulmun Track and includes a picnic lunch.

Coates Wildlife Tours.

Phone: 08 9455 6611. A wide range of nature tours, most of which are about a week long. These tours include visits to anywhere from Ningaloo Reef and Monkey Mia to the Kimberleys, Broome or south-west National Parks. In fact, anywhere in Western Australia.

ARRANGE YOUR OWN DAY OUT

For those who have access to a vehicle, Perth and its environs provide many interesting places to visit and explore. Generally speaking, roads are well maintained and uncrowded. Most trips need a whole day, especially if you incorporate some of the attractions mentioned elsewhere in this book. In addition, this chapter also includes many of the popular places for a BBQ or stroll in the Perth/Fremantle area.

CHITTERING TOURIST WAY

A brochure which describes this scenic drive on Route No. 359, is available from the Chittering Tourist Centre (Great Northern Highway, Bindoon. Phone: 08 9576 1100.) or the WA Tourist Centre in Perth. It runs from Pinjar Road (turn right off Wanneroo Road) to Bindoon, passing through some of the prettiest countryside near Perth. As well as forests of wandoo, marri and jarrah, the route takes you past sheep and cattle farms, vineyards and orchards set amongst rolling hills and valleys. For animal lovers this route passes close to The Maze and Llama Encounters (see Chapter 14: Wildlife, page 92 and 94), Camaleer Park Camel Farm and Steppingstone Adventures (see Chapter 17: Activities on the Land, page 117). You could return to Perth via the Swan Valley Vineyards.

DARLING RANGE

The hills you can see to the east of the city, known to locals as 'the Hills', are part of the Darling Range and can be reached in an easy half-hour drive from the city. Follow either the Albany or Great Eastern Highways from the Causeway end of the city.

The hills are still largely covered in unspoilt bushland, including several National Parks, and a wide variety of wildflowers can be seen there in the spring. The area is popular for bushwalking, and CALM (Department of Conservation and Land Management, phone: 08 9334 0333) publishes a large number of books and pamphlets detailing various walks and trails suitable for people of all ages and abilities. See Darling Range map on page 139.

Darlington, Kalamunda, Roleystone, Mundaring and Armadale are communities established in the hills. Many residents are artists and craftspeople, hence there are numerous studios and galleries to visit, as well as vineyards, restaurants, produce stalls, and tearooms.

SOME BETTER KNOWN GALLERIES INCLUDE:

Mount Olive Stained Glass Studio and Gallery: 610 Mons Road, Hovea.

Craft Partners and Garden Shop: Railway Parade, Glen Forrest.

Chidlow Farm Herbs and Gemstones: 4310 Elliott Road, Chidlow.

Keane Street Pottery and Art: 24 Keane Street, Mount Helena.

Mundaring Arts Centre: 7190 Great Eastern Highway, Mundaring.

Mundaring Weir Gallery: Mundaring Weir Road, Mundaring.

Hills Art Gallery: 55 Railway Road, Kalamunda.

The Signal Box Arts and Crafts Centre: 40 Jull Street, Armadale.

Water Wheel Gallery and Tea Rooms: cnr Albany Highway and Waterwheel Road, Bedfordale.

Bickley Valley Gallery: 116 Glenisla Road, Bickley.

The Hills provide fertile ground for growing fruit, flowers, vegetables and herbs. Try visiting:

The Lavender Patch: Mundaring Weir Road, Mundaring (a tearoom set amongst a myriad of lavender bushes).

Herb Circle: cnr Railway Road and Haynes Street, Kalamunda (a shop using herbs to make foods, crafts and beauty and health products).

The Packing Shed: Lawnbrook Estate, 101 Loaring Road, Bickley. Tea and lunch is available on weekends from this orchard/vineyard. Taste local produce.

Kooralbyn Orchard: 101 Lawnbrook Road East, Bickley. A good selection of home-made jams and tasty preserves and fruits available seasonally.

Bickley Valley Herb Farm: 46 First Avenue, Bickley. Large numbers of herbs and lavenders grow here, and you can buy their herbal products and garden accessories from the gift shop.

Willow Springs Orchard and Winery: 541 Canns Road, Bedfordale. Buy fruit at wholesale prices and taste fruit wines and ports.

Raeburn Orchards: 95 Raeburn Road, Roleystone. This orchard sells fruits in season and home-made preserves. Also do tractor tours of the orchard.

The Rose Heritage Tea Rooms, and Melville Nurseries: 40 Masonmill Road, Carmel. Offers delicious teas and lunches in a delightful setting overlooking the Melville Rose Nursery and its magnificent rose gardens.

Tourist Drive No. 207 along Mundaring Weir Road has many picnic sites set amongst unspoilt forest offering a chance to view some of Australia's unique flora and fauna.

Tourist Drive No. 205 is a 44-kilometre scenic drive commencing at Armadale and passing many popular tourist areas such as Araluen Botanic Park, Churchman's Brook and Canning Dam (popular picnic spots).

DARLING RANGE

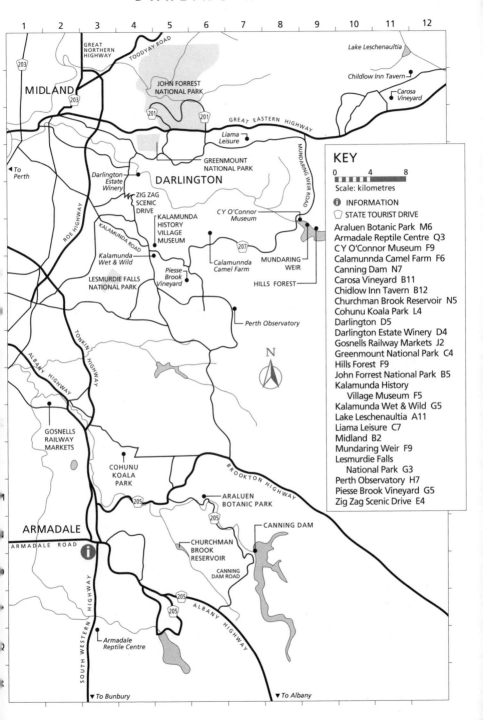

KEY

0 ▦▦▦▦ 4 ▦▦▦▦ 8
Scale: kilometres

🛈 INFORMATION

◌ STATE TOURIST DRIVE

Araluen Botanic Park M6
Armadale Reptile Centre Q3
C Y O'Connor Museum F9
Calamunnda Camel Farm F6
Canning Dam N7
Carosa Vineyard B11
Chidlow Inn Tavern B12
Churchman Brook Reservoir N5
Cohunu Koala Park L4
Darlington D5
Darlington Estate Winery D4
Gosnells Railway Markets J2
Greenmount National Park C4
Hills Forest F9
John Forrest National Park B5
Kalamunda History
    Village Museum F5
Kalamunda Wet & Wild G5
Lake Leschenaultia A11
Liama Leisure C7
Midland B2
Mundaring Weir F9
Lesmurdie Falls
    National Park G3
Perth Observatory H7
Piesse Brook Vineyard G5
Zig Zag Scenic Drive E4

The Zig Zag scenic drive at Gooseberry Hill, is a one way road of hairpin bends, with a lookout providing clear views over Perth and its coastal plain.

Greenmount Hill (in the Greenmount National Park) also offers wonderful views over the city and beyond. John Forrest National Park has similar views.

The Hills Forest: Mundaring Weir Road, Mundaring. Phone: 08 9295 2244. This is a nature-based activity centre offering outdoor activities for all ages at low cost, all year round. There are also walking trails and picnic areas in the jarrah forest.

A day trip to the Darling Range could include attractions which have been described in other chapters of this book (see Index).
They include:
John Forrest National Park (Tourist Drive 201)
Darlington Estate Winery
Llama Leisure
Lake Leschenaultia
Mundaring Weir and C.Y. O'Connor Museum
Calamunnda Camel Farm
Perth Observatory
Carosa Vineyard
Gosnells Railway Markets
Cohunu Koala Park
Araluen Botanic Park
Armadale Reptile Centre
Piesse Brook Wines
Kalamunda History Village
Kalamunda Wet and Wild

TWO WELL-KNOWN PUBS IN THE AREA ARE:
The Chidlow Inn Tavern: Lot 4

Thomas Street, Chidlow. Phone: 08 9572 4154. This 90-year-old pub has log fires in winter and serves counter lunches from Thursday to Sunday.
Mundaring Weir Hotel: Mundaring Weir Road, Mundaring. Phone: 08 9295 1106. Built in the late 1890's this pub has been extensively renovated and offers counter lunches every day of the week from 12 noon to 2.30 pm. On Sunday they have a bush band, and there are craft stalls in the grounds. The Mundaring Weir Gallery is across the road.

MANDURAH

Mandurah is situated 74 kilometres south of Perth and you can reach it in about an hour by car. Take the Kwinana Freeway out of the city and follow the signs to Mandurah.

The Peel Inlet and Harvey Estuary combine to form one of the largest inland waterways in Australia and this, along with the Murray and Serpentine Rivers, several inland lakes, and fine beaches, make the town very popular with day trippers and holiday makers.

The Mandurah Tourist Bureau (phone: 08 9550 3999), situated on the right of Mandurah Terrace as you enter town, is open daily and has a huge range of brochures and pamphlets on things to see and do in the area. It also houses the Peel Discovery Centre, which displays some of the attractions of the Peel region, with several hands-on and interactive exhibits.

Places described in detail elsewhere in this book (see Index), could be visited as part of a day trip to Mandurah:

Peel Estate Winery
Baldivis Estate Winery
Marapana Wildlife World
Linga Longa Park
Western Rosella Bird Park
Parrots of Bellawood Park

Other activities and places of interest you might like to combine with a day trip to Mandurah, include:

BOATING

There are several boat ramps in the area and boating along the vast Peel Inlet and Harvey Estuary and the Murray and Serpentine Rivers is a very popular pastime. If you wish to hire a boat, try:

Blue Manna Boat Hire: Mandurah Ocean Marina (Dolphin Pool). Phone: 08 9535 5399. Open seven days per week, 7.00 am to 6.00 pm. Cost for a motorised self-drive boat: $20.00 to $27.00 per hour, with special half- and full-day rates. You can view the luxury canal-side homes, or cruise on the vast waterways seeing a huge variety of bird life and, hopefully, some dolphins. If you wish to go fishing or crabbing, nets, bait and ice are available.

Mandurah Boat Hire: Peninsula Hotel Jetty, Ormsby Terrace, Mandurah. Phone: 08 9535 5877. Six- or 12-seater pontoon boats or dinghies for hire, all surrounded by safety mesh, so ideal for families with young children. Special rates are available for half-day or full-day hire. Enjoy fishing, crabbing and picnicking in the Inlet or on the Murray or Serpentine Rivers. Dinghies costs $25.00 per hour, six-seater pontoons $30.00 per hour and 12-seater pontoons $40.00 per hour with special half- and full-day rates.

Southern Cross Boat Hire: 20 Sunland Avenue, South Yunderup. Phone: 08 9537 6909 or 0418 920 213. Situated 12 kilometres from the Mandurah Forum shopping centre. Fully equipped modern runabouts for hire, from $150.00 per day, to $650.00 for a week. They can also provide do-nuts and knee-boards, and for a small extra charge, overnight camping equipment.

BUS TOURS

Mandurah Bus Charters: Phone: 08 9581 6555. Full-day tour of Mandurah on Tuesdays and Saturdays. Cost: $48.00 for adults, concession rates for children, includes morning tea, lunch and all entrance fees. The bus takes you to see attractions such as The Parrots of Bellawood Park, a Super Cat Estuary and Canal Cruise, and Marapana Wildlife World.

CRABBING

In summer and autumn, crabbing is particularly popular in the Peel Inlet and Peel/Harvey Estuary. You can wade out and catch blue manna crabs with a scoop net right in front of the town centre. The Mandurah Tourist Bureau has information on rules for crabbing such as minimum size and bag and boat limits, or you can contact the Fisheries Department of WA, on 08 9482 7333.

CYCLING

There is a brochure published by Bikewest which you can obtain from the Mandurah Tourist Bureau. This shows dual-purpose paths which you can use to see the Mandurah Estuary and Indian Ocean in safety. If you wish to hire a bike try:

Cycles Mandurah: Shop 2, 152 Mandurah Terrace, Mandurah. Phone: 08 9535 3490. Hires out near-new mountain bikes for $15.00 per day (with $50.00 deposit) or $45.00 per week ($100.00 deposit). Both prices include helmets and locks. Open every day except Sunday, unless prior arrangements have been made.

DIVING

The Mandurah Tourist Bureau can provide information on the many great dive sites in this area and have a pamphlet entitled *The Mandurah Wreck Trail*. Since 1851, over 17 ships have sunk here, and the pamphlet details the position of nine of them. Access to wrecks requires a boat. You can hire diving equipment from:

Mandurah Diving Academy: Unit 1, 17 Sholl Street. Mandurah. Phone: 08 9581 2566.

ENVIRONMENTAL TOUR

Alcoa of Australia offers free environmental tours of its bauxite mining and refining operation and mine site rehabilitation every Wednesday at 1.00 pm. Book by phoning 08 9531 6752. A coach takes you on the 45-minute journey from Mandurah to Pinjarra.

FISHING

There are many popular fishing spots to try: the Dawesville Channel at Dawesville, Falcon Bay, Blue Bay, and the Groynes at Silver Sands, to name a

few. You can also fish from the Old Mandurah Traffic Bridge. At night-time, in summer, prawning in the Estuary is very popular and you can also catch cobbler, tailor, garfish, herring, silver bream, mulloway, mullet and whiting. In some places, especially The Dawesville Channel and Tim's Thickett, salmon can be caught. Further afield, there is some very good deep-sea fishing and there are charter companies which will take you out for a day. You might be lucky and catch jewfish, cod, King George Whiting, southern bluefin tuna and pink snapper. Book at:

Aqualib Marine Charters: PO Box 495, Mandurah. Phone: 08 9535 6553 or 018 956 684. Offer deep-sea and game fishing (marlin are tagged and released once you have had your photo taken with your catch) as well as tours through the local canals and Peel Inlet, and whale watching (in season).

FOUR-WHEEL-DRIVING

Registered four-wheel-drive vehicles are permitted on the beaches at Tim's Thickett and Whitehills, which are situated off the Old Coast Road, south of the Dawesville Channel. You can drive through the dunes and along the beaches until you find a quiet spot for a swim or to fish. Care should be taken not to damage the fragile sand dunes.

FUN FAIR AND FUN PARK

Castle Fun Park. Phone: 08 9535 6930 or 08 9535 7240. This fun park is set around a miniature Bavarian village, the castle being a scaled down version of Neuschwanstein Castle in the

Bavarian Alps. There is also a mini-golf course, a large swimming pool in the shape of Australia, a mini grand prix track and pleasant picnic and BBQ areas with play equipment. A good place to take younger children.
King Carnival is situated on the foreshore near the old bridge and has a ferris wheel, dodgem cars, octopus and numerous kids' rides. Open Saturdays 1.00 pm to 11.00 pm, Sunday 1.00 pm to 6.00 pm, and also on public holidays.

HORSERIDING

Peel Horseback Adventures: Herron Point Road, Coolup. Phone: 08 9530 3217 or 015 084 784. A variety of half-day or full-day tours along early Western Australian pioneering tracks, as well as longer adventures. Suitable for beginners or experienced riders.

INDOOR FAMILY FUN

Mandurah Funhouse: 96 Mandurah Terrace, Mandurah. Phone: 08 9535 7721. Has an indoor play area with bouncy castles, tubes, an amusement arcade and mini-golf.

KAYAKING

Mandurah Kayak Sports. Phone: 0411 112 742 or 1800 634 665. Located on the western foreshore at the northern point of Hall Park. Open from 9.00 am to 5.00 pm, Saturdays and Sunday. Sit-on-top kayaks are available for hire to explore the Mandurah Estuary. No previous experience is required. A single kayak costs $12.00 per hour, $45.00 for half a day; a double costs

$18.00 per hour, $60.00 for half a day.

MANDURAH HERITAGE TRAIL

Mandurah is one of Western Australia's earliest settlements and there is a heritage trail covering the most significant of its historic sites, some of which are well over 100 years old. A brochure with a detailed map of all the attractions on the heritage trail is available from the Mandurah Tourist Bureau. Halls Cottage, which is open on Sunday from 1.00 pm to 4.00 pm, is the oldest building in Mandurah. It was built by Henry Hall in 1832 and has now been totally restored, and heritage listed.

MOTOR CYCLE RIDES

Legend Motorcycle Tours: 4 Egret Place, South Yunderup. Phone: 08 9581 6690 or 019 110 444. Tour the Mandurah and Peel areas on a Harley Davidson. Tours start from $30.00 for one hour. Choose from selected tours or design your own.

RIVER CRUISES

Avocet Wildlife Cruises: Phone: 0412 159 397. Cruises on the Murray River, where you can see over 135 species of birds. This is the most significant area for birds in south-west Australia, and many migrating birds from the Arctic stop here to feed. The skipper is a member of Birds Australia and offers informative commentary, and there are books on board to help you identify the birds and wildlife. There are two main cruises to choose from: The Murray Meanderer (two and a half hours long), and the Wetlands Wildlife Cruise (one and a half hours long). The Murray Meanderer costs $25.00 for adults, $20.00 for concessions and $10.00 for children. The Wetlands Wildlife Cruise costs $10.00 for adults, $8.00 for concession and $5.00 for children. There are also seasonal twilight cruises, costing $18.00 for adults, $15.00 for concession and $10.00 for children, which includes a seafood platter.

Mandurah–Murray River Cruises:
Phone: 08 9535 3324 or 0417 180 784. Cruises available include:
The Dolphin Discoverer: is a one-hour canal and estuary cruise which leaves four times a day from the Boardwalk Jetty next to the Mandurah Tourist Bureau. It takes you past luxury canal-side homes and into the estuary. You may well see dolphins swimming around the boat. Cost: $8.00 for adults, $5.00 for children, or a family ticket is $24.00 (two adults and two children).
The Twilight Dinner Cruise: is available on Friday evenings. It takes you along the estuary, Peel Inlet and Murray River, for dinner at the Murray River Lodge. Cost: $38.00.
The MV Princess: has cruises to see the bird life and dolphins of the Peel Inlet and Murray River on Tuesdays, Wednesdays, Thursdays and Sunday. Departs at 10.00 am and returns at 3.00 pm, stopping for lunch at a restaurant on the Murray River. Cost: $30.00 for adults, $16.00 for children, or a family ticket is $85.00 (two adults and two children).

Peel Supercat. Phone: 018 900 243. Daily canal and estuary cruises leave from the town and pass through luxurious canal developments with spectacular waterfront homes. You often see dolphins!

SURFING
There are many good surfing beaches, especially to the south of Mandurah at Avalon Point, Pyramids and Melros Beach.

SWIMMING
Among the most popular swimming beaches are Blue Bay, Doddi's, Falcon Bay and Silver Sands, but there are many other fine beaches.

Mandurah also has an Aquatic and Recreation Centre (on Pinjarra Road) which has a heated indoor pool as well as outdoor heated children's adventure pool and adult fitness pool.

TEN PIN BOWLING
Mandurah Ten Pin Bowling Centre:
96 Mandurah Terrace. Phone: 08 9535 5766.
Fully automated computerised scoring and open every day from 9.00 am until late.

PERTH AND THE SWAN RIVER
As previously mentioned, there are many things to see and do in and around Perth. An inexpensive way to enjoy the scenery is to explore the roads and dual purpose tracks that run around the foreshore of the Swan and Canning rivers. All of these are free, offer places to picnic and BBQ as well as great views of the city and suburbs.

SOME OF THE BETTER KNOWN PLACES TO VISIT ARE:

Burswood Park: Resort Drive (off Great Eastern Highway) Burswood. See page 85 in Chapter 13: Parks and Gardens.

Deepwater Point: The Esplanade, Mount Pleasant. The boat ramp here is very popular with water skiers, rowers, sailboarders and canoeists. The beaches offer safe swimming/paddling areas for children, and there is a grassy area with picnic facilities and a kiosk. Many water birds can be seen here.

The Esplanade, Peppermint Grove. Shady lawns under peppermint trees overlooking Freshwater Bay. Popular for picnics and champagne breakfasts.

Keane's Point, Mosman Bay; and Lilla Street, off The Esplanade, Peppermint Grove. Grassy areas with shady trees and views over Freshwater Bay to Claremont and Point Resolution. There are picnic spots, and the beaches are safe for children.

King's Park: The Lookout, on Fraser Avenue; The DNA Observation Tower, off Forrest Drive; and The Law Walk, on the river side of the park, all offer scenic views of the city and river. In the park, there is a top-class restaurant, Frasers, several kiosks, and numerous picnic and BBQ areas, for example, on both sides of Saw Avenue; at the Children's Playground and lake, off May Drive; and the grassy slopes near the Pioneer Women's Memorial.

Matilda Bay: the foreshore in front of Hackett Drive offers grassy, scenic picnic areas under shady trees with views over the river to the city, with the yachts of Royal Perth Yacht Club in the foreground. This is a popular spot for small children and their families to swim in summer.

Perth City: Riverside Drive and Narrows Open Space. On the south side of Riverside Drive is a narrow grassy area with a dual-purpose track, offering views over the river to South Perth. Running westward, it passes the Old Perth Port (Barrack Street Jetty) and extends round to the Narrows Open Space, which is reclaimed land with several lakes, fountains, water birds and so on.

Point Resolution: in Dalkeith, on the corner of Victoria Avenue and Jutland Parade, gives views across a narrow stretch of the river to Point Walter and overlooks Melville Water, Freshwater Bay and Mosman Bay.

Point Walter Reserve: off Burke Drive or Honour Avenue, Attadale. This is a very popular area for picnics, barbecues, boating and swimming and there is a large sand spit which at low tide runs hundreds of metres out into the river. A café serves light meals, including breakfasts.

South Perth: The Esplanade and Sir James Mitchell Park look over Perth Water to the City centre.

PINNACLES DESERT

The Pinnacles are situated in the Nambung National Park, about 250 kilometres north of Perth near the coastal town of Cervantes. The Pinnacles are calcified limestone pillars, which have been exposed by erosion over a period of 30,000 years. These pillars are of varying heights and shapes, some up to five metres tall and two metres thick. They stand erect in a lunar-like desert landscape. The contrast between the yellow of the terrain and the brilliant blue of the sky is very striking and provides an excellent photographic opportunity. Early morning and late afternoon light is particularly good for photography and there are usually less people present then. The best time to visit the Nambung National Park is from September to May, and the wildflowers are at their best from September to November.

The uniqueness of the Pinnacles Desert makes this an extremely popular day trip from Perth. Many tour companies run either coach or four-wheel-drive trips (see Chapter 18: Organised Tours, page 130). Alternatively, if you have access to a vehicle you may like to make the journey yourself. Take Wanneroo Road (State Route No. 60), from the city and head north past Yanchep. If you have a four-wheel-drive vehicle, keep going to approximately 10 kilometres south of Lancelin, where a scenic four-wheel-drive coastal track leads past Narrow Neck and Wedge Island to Cervantes. This route should only be tackled by competent four-wheel-drivers. If you do not wish to take the four-wheel-drive option, head inland to the Brand Highway (State Route No. 1), before bearing west again to Cervantes. State Route No. 60 is considerably quicker and more interesting than the alternative of taking the Great Northern Highway, and then the Brand Highway to Cervantes.

The fishing village of Cervantes is only two kilometres west of the entrance to the Nambung National Park. The road into the park is unsealed but is passable, but bumpy, for normal vehicles. However, in the rainy season, a four-wheel-drive may be preferable. If you don't wish to take your own car into the park, the Cervantes Shell Service Station runs daily trips to The Pinnacles departing at 1.00 pm and returning shortly before 4.00 pm. This costs $16.00 for adults, and $10.00 for children, including the $2.00 park entrance fee.

A visit to the Pinnacles could include a stop off at Yanchep National Park to see the koalas or any of the other attractions listed under The Sunset Coast below.

THE SUNSET COAST

The Sunset Coast stretches northwards from Cottesloe for approximately 45 kilometres. Tourist Drive 204 is a scenic coastal drive passing some of Perth's best beaches (see page 97 for details). As you head north up the coast, any of the places below, details of which are elsewhere in this book (see Index), could be included in a day out:

Sorrrento Quay/Hillarys Boat Harbour/Underwater World
Scarborough Fair Markets
Wanneroo Weekend Market
Conti Wines
Strawberry Fields
Gumnut Factory
Camaleer Camel Farm
Joondalup Country Club
Botanic Golf Gardens
Dizzy Lamb Park
The Stables

Yanchep National Park
Sun City Country Club
Wild Kingdom Wildlife Park and Zoo
Ron's Riding Ranch

SWAN VALLEY

A day trip to the Swan Valley, an easy
30 minutes drive from Perth (leaving on
the Great Eastern Highway), might
include some of the following stops,
details of which are given elsewhere in
this book. Many of these are on the
Swan Valley Tourist Drive (No. 203), or
only a short distance away. See Swan
Valley map on page 79.

The Swan Valley Vineyards
Gomboc Gallery
The Maze
Walyunga National Park
The Vines Resort
Whiteman Park
Woodbridge House
Caversham Wildlife Park and Zoo
Midland Military Markets or Midland
   Sunday Markets
All Saints Church
Guildford Grammar School Chapel

Places to have lunch in this area include
several of the wineries, for example,
Lamonts, Jane Brook, Olive Farm,
Houghton, Sandalford, Little River
and also:

Milston Gardens: 10581 West Swan
   Road, Henley Brook. Phone:
   08 9296 1641. Lunches and
   Devonshire teas, and they also have
   a herb garden.
The Vines Resort: Verdelho Drive, The
   Vines. Phone: 08 9297 3000. Lunch,
   dinner and Devonshire teas overlooking the magnificent golf course.

Dear Friends Garden Restaurant: 100
   Benara Road, Caversham. Phone:
   08 9279 2815 (bookings essential).
   Lunches are served Wednesday to
   Friday, and Sunday, from 12 noon;
   and dinner Wednesday to Sunday,
   from 6.00 pm. This multi award-
   winning licensed restaurant has
   wonderful food and an exceptional
   range of wines from the Swan Valley
   and beyond. They include more than
   20 vintages of Grange Hermitage!
Mulberry Farm: 34 Hamersley Road,
   Caversham. Phone: 08 9379 0344.
   This restaurant overlooks the river
   and surrounding vineyards. Lunches
   from Wednesday to Sunday. A
   speciality is the Saturday night
   dinner dance. They also do breakfast
   on Sundays.
Old Cottage Café: 5601 West Swan
   Road, West Swan. Phone:
   08 9250 3638. Set in an English
   country garden, this old cottage
   serves lunches and teas.
Sugar Gum Restaurant: 105 Terrace
   Road, Guildford. Phone:
   08 9377 2262. This is an award-
   winning restaurant in the heart of
   Guildford. Open for lunch everyday
   except Monday.
The Vineyard Tea House Restaurant:
   Lot 100, Benara Road, Caversham.
   Phone: 08 9377 6432. Open every
   day for lunch and Devonshire teas.
   Country-style food is available.

WAVE ROCK

Another one of Western Australia's
unique but strange geological features is
Wave Rock, which is over 2700 million
years old. As its name suggests, this

ancient granite rock, 15 metres high and 100 metres long, is shaped like an enormous wave about to break. It is situated four kilometres to the east of the wheatbelt town of Hyden, approximately 350 kilometres south-east of Perth. It is a long way to drive just to see a rock, however there are other lesser rock formations in the area, like Hippo's Yawn, The Humps and Mulka's Cave, where Aboriginal hand paintings may be seen. Oddly enough, the Margaret Blackburn Lace Collection (one of the largest in the World and dating back to the 17th Century) may be seen at the Wave Rock Wildflower Shop, which also acts as the Tourist Office. Phone: 08 9880 5182.

This is a popular destination for coach trips from the city (see Chapter 18: Organised Tours, page 129) however if you have access to a vehicle, follow the Albany Highway out of Perth, turn onto the Brookton Highway (State Route 40), passing through Brookton, Corrigin and Kondinin to Hyden. On the way you will see numerous wheat and sheep farms.

YORK

The town of York is about 97 kilometres east of Perth. It was Western Australia's first inland settlement in 1831, only two years after the founding of the Swan River Colony. It prospered as a commercial centre during the gold rush, and is now a farming centre. York has many beautifully restored Victorian and Federation buildings (many of which are hotels). It is situated on the banks of the Avon River in gently rolling countryside. Several festivals take place annually including Jazz and Country

Music, Veteran Car Rally, a Rose Festival and Racing and Trotting. Apart from admiring the lovely restored buildings, you can enjoy refreshments at one of the numerous cafés, restaurants and tearooms, or shop for arts and crafts, antiques and woollen products.

Other things to see and do in York are:

Ambleside Ostrich and Emu Farm. Phone: 08 9641 1274. Situated eight kilometres east of York at the Quairading, Marwick Road junction. By prior arrangement, you can see these imposing birds at all stages of development. Cost: from $4.00, $10.00 for a family pass. In the shop in the town you can purchase products such as painted and carved eggs, emu oil, leather and meat.

Avon Valley Historical Rose Garden: 2 Osnaburg Road, York. Phone: 08 9641 1469. Open autumn and spring, Fridays to Mondays, 10.00 am to 4.30 pm, or by appointment. This is a formal rose garden which has a wide range of roses, from original species to modern day varieties. You can purchase old-fashioned roses from the specialist nursery.

Balladong Farm: Avon Terrace, York. Phone: 08 9641 2730. This farm, built in 1831, was Western Australia's first inland farm and is now a museum. It promotes sustainable agriculture and permaculture and is open to the public for information. You can tour the farm, which has heritage-listed buildings and an animal nursery, for $5.00 an adult, children are free. Farm tours are from Wednesday to Sunday 10.00 am to 4.00 pm.

Old Gaol and Courthouse: 130 Avon Terrace, York. Phone: 08 9641 2072. Open 10.00 am to 4.00 pm every day. You can see the old courthouse, primitive cell block, stables and Troopers Cottage, and visit the Post Office Museum and National Trust Gift Shop.

Residency Museum: Brook Street, York. Phone: 08 9641 1751. Open Tuesday to Thursday 1.00 pm to 3.00 pm; Saturday 1.00 pm to 5.00 pm; and Sunday 11.00 am to 5.00 pm. This old colonial house was built in the 1850's and now houses a collection of antiques and memorabilia from that time.

Skydive Express. Phone: 1800 355 833. See page 113 in Chapter 16: Activities in the Air, for details of skydiving in York.

York Mini-golf: cnr Pool and Lowe Street, York. Phone: 08 9641 2188. This course is set in a native garden on the banks of the Avon River.

York Motor Museum: 116–124 Avon Terrace, York. Phone: 08 9641 1288. Open 9.00 am to 5.00 pm every day. This museum has over 100 vehicles and is Australia's finest collection of veteran, vintage, classic and racing cars. A must see for the vintage car enthusiast. You can also have a tour of York in a vintage Charabanc.

GENERAL INFORMATION

MAJOR SOURCES OF INFORMATION INCLUDE:

The WA Tourist Centre: Albert Facey House, Forrest Place, cnr Wellington Street. Phone: 1300 361 351; 24-hour recorded information: 08 9246 9977. Tourist information and booking service. Open Mondays to Fridays 8.30 am to 5.30 pm, Saturdays 8.30 am to 1.00 pm.

Fremantle Tourist Bureau: Town Hall, Kings Square, Fremantle. Phone: 08 9431 7878. Tourist information and booking service. Open Mondays to Saturdays 9.00 am to 5.00 pm, Sunday 10.30 am to 4.30 pm.

Yellow Pages Talking Guide. Phone: 13 16 20. Recorded information about entertainment, special events and tourist attractions. If you wish, consult the *Yellow Pages*, one to 17, for specific information numbers and a brief item by item description. However, you can access all the information you need by phoning the above number.

INFORMATION: A–Z

AIRLINE AND AIRPORT INFORMATION

Perth Domestic Airport is situated about 11 kilometres from the city centre, while the International Terminal is another five kilometres further out. Shuttle buses connect the two airports and there are also services to Perth and Fremantle. See details below.

Recorded information on international flight arrivals and departures, and also Qantas domestic flight arrivals and departures, can be obtained 24 hours a day by dialling: 13 12 23. For Ansett flight arrivals and departures, phone 13 15 15.

Reservations (phone numbers):
Air New Zealand 13 24 76

Ansett 13 13 00 (Domestic); 13 14 14 (International)

British Airways 08 9425 7711

Cathay Pacific 13 17 47

Garuda Indonesia 08 9481 0963

Malaysia Airline 13 26 27

Qantas 13 12 11 (International); 13 13 13 (Domestic)

Royal Brunei 08 9321 8757

Singapore Airlines 13 10 11

South African Airways 08 9321 2435

Thai Airways International 1300 65 1960

United Airlines 13 17 77

OTHER USEFUL NUMBERS:

Airport Duty Free Hotline 1800 805 141

Baggage Enquiries 08 9270 9433

Customs Information 1300 363 263

Quarantine Enquiries 1800 020 504

AIRPORT SHUTTLE BUSES

Feature Tours: Phone: 08 9479 4131
(24-hour booking and enquiry service),
runs a bus service from both the domestic
and international airports to the city and
return. Buses meet every interstate and
international flight and leave from outside
the Arrivals Hall. To return to either
airport, phone Feature Tours the day
before departure to arrange to be
collected from any hotel or hostel in the
city. Cost: $7.00 to the domestic airport,
$9.00 to the international airport. Buses
depart every hour from 3.00 am to
6.00 pm, and at 8.00 pm and 10.00 pm.
A shuttle service runs between the
domestic and international airports at a
cost of $5.00.

Fremantle Airport Shuttle: Phone:
08 9383 4115 or 0417 171287, runs a bus
service between Fremantle and the two
airports. It costs $12.00 per person to the
domestic airport and $15.00 to the
international airport, but there is a $25.00
family rate. Will pick up from the
Fremantle Railway Station, from your
hotel or any other major landmark by
prior arrangement.

AUTOMATIC TELLER MACHINES (ATMs)/EFTPOS

Numerous ATMs are located in central

Perth and in all suburban shopping centres
and can be accessed 24 hours a day.
International credit cards can be used at
most of these machines. Most shops,
supermarkets and service stations have
EFTPOS (Electronic Funds Transfer)
facilities where you can not only pay for
your purchases but in many cases, withdraw
a limited amount of cash at the same time.

BAGGAGE REPAIRS

The Leather and Luggage Repair Centre:
15 Woodroyd Street, Mount Lawley.
Phone: 08 9271 7941.

Mallabones Luggage and Leather:
Shop M21, City Arcade, Perth.
Phone: 08 9322 3240.

Trinity Leather Travel Goods: Shop 112,
Trinity Arcade, Perth. Phone: 08 9321
5106 and 720 Hay Street Mall, Perth.
Phone: 08 9226 1818.

Lynn's Leather and Luggage: Shop 3,
24 St Quentin Avenue, Claremont.
Phone: 08 9284 2147.

BANKING HOURS

Monday to Thursday: 9.30 am to 4.00 pm.

Friday: 9.30 am to 5.00 pm.

Saturdays, Sunday and public holidays: closed.

BOOKING SERVICES (INCLUDING THEATRES AND SPORTS EVENTS)

BOCS: Phone: 08 9484 1133 or
1800 193 300 (for calls from outside the
metro area). Tickets for theatres, the
Concert Hall, some rock concerts (but not
those at the Entertainment Centre), the
Hopman Cup (tennis), all the University
Theatres including tickets for the
Somerville (outdoor cinema).

Red Tickets: Phone: 08 9484 1222 or

1902 291 502 (enquiries) or 1800 199 991 (for calls from outside the metro area). Tickets for events at the Entertainment Centre, sporting events and live bands at some of the nightclubs.

BYO stands for Bring Your Own (usually alcohol). Many cheaper restaurants are BYO and even at some licensed restaurants it is possible to BYO and still pay a corkage fee per person. If you are invited to a BBQ or picnic and told to BYO this frequently means bring your own food as well as drinks. Best to check. Bring a plate does not mean an empty one! Bring a plate of snacks or something to share around.

CAR RENTAL

See page 10 in Chapter 2: Getting Around, for car rental companies.

CLIMATE

Perth has a Mediterranean climate. Summer temperatures average 29°C during the day and 17°C at night. Most years there are a few days when the maximum temperature is over the old century, 100°F, usually in January or February. It rarely rains in the summer months, November to March. The wettest months are in winter in May, June, July and August, however it only rains for about half the number of days and the rest are clear and sunny. In winter temperatures average 18°C during the day, and 9°C at night. Perth's average annual rainfall is 974.4 millimetres.

CONSULATES

Austria 08 9261 7070

Belgium 08 9321 4067

Canada 08 9322 7930

China 08 9321 8193

Croatia 08 9321 6044

Denmark 08 9335 5122

Finland 08 9321 2100

France 08 9386 9366

Germany 08 9325 8851

Greece 08 9325 6608

India 08 9221 1485

Indonesia 08 9221 5858

Ireland 08 9385 8247

Italy 08 9367 8922

Japan 08 9321 7816

Malaysia 08 9325 9146

Mauritius 08 9430 5872

Nepal 08 9386 2102

Netherlands 08 9381 3539

Pakistan 08 9444 3648

Philippines 08 9367 4189

Portugal 08 9335 9458

Seychelles 08 9291 6570

Spain 08 9322 4522

Sri Lanka 08 9263 3598

Sweden 08 9244 3699

Switzerland 08 9293 2704

Thailand 08 9221 3237

UK 08 9221 5400

USA 08 9231 9400

CREDIT CARDS

For lost or stolen cards, phone:

American Express: 1800 230 100

Bankcard: 1800 224 402

Diners Club: 1300 360 060

MasterCard: 1800 120 113

Visa Card: 1800 125 440

CURRENCY EXCHANGE

Dial It Service (for daily exchange rates): Phone: 08 9482 6311.

Most banks will exchange foreign currency into Australian dollars.

The following companies specialise in foreign exchange:

Thomas Cook: 704 Hay Street (cnr Hay Street Mall and Piccadilly Arcade), Perth. Phone: 08 9481 7900. They also have several other city and suburban branches. Thomas Cook is also at the International Airport.

Interforex: Shop 24, London Court, Perth. Phone: 08 9325 7418; and cnr William and Adelaide Streets, Fremantle. Phone: 08 9431 7022.

Travelex Australia: Domestic Airport. Phone: 08 9479 7644.

CUSTOMS

National information line: 1300 363 263.

If calling from outside Australia, phone: +612 6275 6666.

WARNING! There are severe penalties for not declaring prohibited or restricted items and goods on which you must pay duty. If you are in doubt, ask a Customs officer. Trained dogs may be used to detect drugs or prohibited imports.

DUTY FREE CONCESSIONS

All travellers aged 18 or over can bring the following items into Australia duty free:

- $A400.00 worth of goods such as electronic equipment, cameras, watches, jewellery, sporting goods and so on (gifts given to you or intended for others are included in this $400.00). Travellers under 18 are entitled to $200.00 worth of the above goods.
- 1125 ml alcohol (spirits, beer, wine)
- 250 cigarettes or 250 grams of cigars or other tobacco products
- clothes, shoes, personal items
- goods owned and used for at least 12 months (you may be asked to provide proof of date of purchase).

What you must declare on arrival in Perth:
- animal, plant material or their derivatives
- food
- protected wildlife and products made from protected wildlife
- drugs (medications) and medicines
- currency (amounts of $A10 000 or more, or equivalent in foreign currency)
- firearms, weapons and ammunition
- goods in excess of the duty free concessions described above.

   Note: The above items will be inspected by customs or quarantine officers. Some goods, such as objects made of wood, straw or hide, may be treated and returned. Other items such as fruit, vegetables, meat and live plants will be confiscated.

What you must declare on departure from Perth:
- heritage items (certain works of art, stamps, coins, minerals and archaeological items)

- firearms and ammunition
- animal or plant material
- currency: amounts of $A10 000 or more or equivalent in foreign currency.

DEPARTURE TAX

A $27.00 (adult) departure tax is usually included in the cost of the air ticket.

ELECTRICITY

The current in Australia is 220–240 volts and transformers are needed for any appliance using 110 volts, for example, hair dryers and shavers. However, most hotels have universal outlets. The three pin Australian plug is not the same as that used in other countries and you will require an adaptor.

EXCHANGE RATES, SEE CURRENCY EXCHANGE

FISHING LICENCE AND RESTRICTIONS

The Fisheries Department of WA (phone: 08 9482 7333) can provide you with a brochure outlining the fish you are likely to catch and also what the bag limits and legal sizes are. You must have a Recreational Licence from the Fisheries Department for: abalone, rock lobster, marron, net fishing and south-west freshwater angling.

Furthermore, there are particular seasons for prawning and crabbing, minimum sizes for crabs caught, legal ways of catching them, and a daily limit per person or per boat. Contact the Fisheries Department for details, otherwise you may inadvertently be breaking the law. There are also Marine Conservation Areas where special fishing rules apply.

GENERAL WARNINGS

Mosquitos are more prevalent in the evening and in damp, shady places. Use a personal insect repellent and cover as much of the body as possible (wear long sleeved shirts and long pants) if mosquitos are evident. There are some viruses which are transmitted by mosquitos, the most notable being the Ross River Virus which can be quite debilitating. There are no malaria-carrying mosquitos in Perth or Western Australia.

Petty Crime. As in all large cities, take precautions, for example, never leave your bag or wallet unattended in a public place, lock your car and don't leave valuables on the beach or in the car while you swim. Car theft is quite prevalent.

Safety on the Beach. See under Beaches, page 97 for basic safety rules for the beach.

Snakes. Poisonous snakes are sometimes seen, especially in sandy areas and bushland. The dugite is the most common. Generally, snakes are shy and will try to avoid you. Do not provoke them. If bitten, keep the patient calm and still, if possible firmly bandage or bind the affected limb, and send for medical assistance immediately. Fatalities are extremely rare as antivenenes are normally available.

Spiders. The female Red-back Spider is poisonous and you should seek medical assistance if bitten. Antivenene is readily available. Symptoms usually include a sharp stinging sensation, followed by redness and swelling in the area where the bite has occurred; and sweating. The spider is usually dark brown to jet-black with a very obvious orange/red stripe down its back. It is not aggressive and will only bite when cornered. Red-backs are usually found under logs or bark on the ground or in empty containers or woodsheds away from the light.

Sunburn. The sun in Perth is extremely strong and the UV rating very high. Wear maximum protection sunscreen and apply regularly, especially when on the beach. Wearing a hat and sunglasses is advisable during the day. Drink plenty of fluids.

HEALTH AND VACCINES

Western Australia has a clean and healthy environment and it is quite safe to drink water out of the tap although bottled water is also readily available. Perth has world class medical facilities and should you require medical attention, either use a locum service or contact one of the hospitals listed below.

Vaccinations are not required when visiting Perth from overseas, unless you have visited an infected country in the last 14 days.

HOSPITALS WITH ACCIDENT AND EMERGENCY FACILITIES

Fremantle Hospital: Alma Street, Fremantle. Phone: 08 9431 3333.

Princess Margaret Children's Hospital: Roberts Road, Subiaco. Phone: 08 9340 8222.

Royal Perth Hospital: Wellington Street, Perth. Phone: 08 9224 2244.

Sir Charles Gairdner Hospital: Verdun Street, Nedlands. Phone: 08 9346 3333.

Saint John of God Hospital (Private): Murdoch Drive, Murdoch. Phone: 08 9366 1111.

Swan District Hospital: Eveline Road, Middle Swan. Phone: 08 9347 5244.

Other Medical Facilities include:

Dental Hospital. Phone: 08 9220 5777; a/h emergency service: 08 9325 3452.

Doctor Locum Service. Phone: 08 9328 7111.

Poisons Information Centre. Phone: 13 11 26.

Ambulance. Phone: 000 (emergencies only)

INTERNET CAFÉS

Captain Munchies: 2 Beach Street, Fremantle. Phone: 08 9430 4321.

Indigo Net Café and Lodge: 256 West Coast Highway, Scarborough. Phone: 08 9245 3388.

Net Trek Café: 8 Bannister Street Mall, Fremantle. Phone: 08 9336 4446.

The Planet Café: 264 Newcastle Street, Northbridge. Phone: 08 9227 9399.

Tropicana Café: 177 High Street, Fremantle. Phone: 08 9336 6693.

Many of the larger hotels have a business centre in which guests can gain access to the Internet, however this can be expensive. Quite a few Youth Hostels and budget hotels also have Internet access. At some, guests can use the service at no cost, though if you are not a guest you may have to pay a low fee to access the Internet. You can also log on at the following places:

Fairlanes City: 175 Adelaide Terrace, East Perth. Phone: 08 9325 3588.

Pot Black Centre: 106 James Street, Northbridge. Phone: 08 9227 7422.

Smiley's Internet Services: 337 Stirling Highway, Claremont. Phone: 08 9385 5520.

The Perth Tourist Lounge: Level 2, Carillon Arcade, 680 Hay Street Mall, Perth. Phone: 08 9481 8303.

The Travellers Club and Information Centre: 499 Wellington Street, Perth. Phone: 08 9226 0660.

LICENSING HOURS

Pubs and bars are usually open Monday to Saturday 10.00 am to 12 midnight, Sunday noon to 9.00 pm.

LIBRARIES

In the telephone directory, look under individual local councils for information on public libraries in particular areas.

The Alexander Library is in the Perth Cultural Centre, Francis Street, Perth. Phone: 08 9427 3111. It is open seven days a week: Monday to Thursday 9.00 am to 9.45 pm, Friday 9.00 am to 5.30 pm, and Saturday and Sunday 10.00 am to 5.30 pm.

MEDIA

Newspapers. The *West Australian* newspaper comes out every day except Sunday. Entertainment details are printed every day. The Sunday newspaper is *The Sunday Times*. *The Australian* is the national newspaper, which has daily editions: Monday to Friday, and there is a *Weekend Australian*.

Television channels. There are five: the ABC, SBS (multicultural); and three commercial stations, Channels Seven, Nine and Ten.

MOBILE PHONE RENTALS

Vodafone Rental: Perth International

Airport. Phone, toll free: 1800 245 001 or 08 9477 1600.

PHARMACIES

In the City Centre, the following pharmacies are open seven days a week:

Forrest Chase Pharmacy: Shop 54, Forrest Chase, 425 Wellington Street, Perth. Phone: 08 9221 1691.

Barrack Street Chemist: 87 Barrack Street, Perth. Phone: 08 9325 3242. Not open on public holidays.

Throughout the suburbs many pharmacies are open seven days a week and close around 8.00 pm or 9.00 pm. A few which stay open later, are:

Claremont SDIP Chemist: 234 Stirling Highway, Claremont. Phone: 08 9384 2292. Open 9.00 am to 11.00 pm every day of the year.

Botts Drive in Chemist: 1098A Albany Highway, Bentley. Phone: 08 9458 1515. Open 8.00 am to 11.00 pm every day of the year.

Midnight Chemist: 647 Beaufort Street, Mt.Lawley. Phone: 08 9328 7775. Open until midnight seven days per week.

Fremantle Drive in Pharmacy: 197 High Street, Fremantle. Phone: 08 9335 9633. Open Monday to Saturday 8.00 am to 10.00 pm, Sunday/holidays 8.00 am to 9.00 pm

For others, consult the *Yellow Pages*.

POPULATION

The population of Western Australia is about 1.8 million, with about 1.3 million people living in the Perth metropolitan area. Over the years, Perth has become a multicultural society, with a huge diversity of nationalities.

POST OFFICE

The General Post Office is situated at 3 Forrest Place, Perth. Phone: 13 13 18 for all information. Open Monday to Friday 8.00 am to 5.30 pm, Saturday 9.00 am to 12.30 pm, Sunday noon to 4.00 pm.

Suburban post offices are open Monday to Friday 9.00 am to 5.00 pm. The General Post Office and all suburban Post Offices have a poste restante service and will hold mail for visitors.

PUBLIC HOLIDAYS

1st January: New Year's Day

26th January: Australia Day

1st Monday in March: Labour Day

March/April: Good Friday/Easter Monday

25th April: Anzac Day

1st Monday in June: Foundation Day

Last Monday in September: Queen's Birthday

25th December: Christmas Day

26th December: Boxing Day

ROAD RULES/DRIVING INFORMATION

The blood alcohol limit in Western Australia is 0.05. Random breath testing is very prevalent. Penalties for being over the limit are harsh.

Speed cameras are widely used, so be constantly aware of the speed limits. On normal roads in the metropolitan area, the speed limit is 60 km/h. Fines and other penalties are severe.

Keep left except when overtaking.

Correct wearing of seat belts by all passengers is compulsory.

When driving in country areas after dark, take care as animals, especially kangaroos, often wander onto the roads.

Most petrol stations are open seven days a week, with normal hours being 7.00 am to 6.00 pm, though many remain open till later. 24-hour petrol stations are becoming more and more common.

SHOPPING HOURS

Perth

Monday to Thursday: 8.30 am to 5.30 pm

Friday: 8.30 am to 9.00 pm

Saturday: 8.30 am to 5.00 pm

Sunday: noon to 6.00 pm

Fremantle

Monday to Friday, except Thursday: 8.30 am to 5.30 pm

Thursday: 8.30 am to 9.00 pm

Saturday: 8.30 am to 5.00 pm

Sunday: 10.00 am to 4.00 pm

Suburban

Monday to Friday, except Thursday: 8.30 am to 5.30 pm

Thursday: 8.30 am to 9.00 pm

Saturday: 8.30 am to 5.00 pm

The above hours apply, except for public holidays, although shops in the city and major shopping centres may open on public holidays other than Christmas Day, Good Friday and Anzac Day. Delicatessens and fresh produce markets can be open 12 hours a day, seven days a week. Times may vary.

TAXIS

Swan Taxis (Perth): Phone: 13 13 88

Coastal Cabs (Fremantle): Phone: 13 10 08

Black and White Taxis: Phone: 08 9333 3333

Yellow Cab Company: Phone: 13 19 24

TELEPHONES

The first few pages of the *White Pages* telephone directory have many useful numbers to help you make local, interstate and overseas calls.

Public telephones can be found on the street and in hotels, shops and cafés. Local calls cost 40 cents and you can talk as long as you like. You can use a phonecard (available at newsagents), cash, or in some cases, a credit card.

When phoning Perth from outside the State, use the prefix 08. STD calls to places outside Perth are charged according to length of call, time of day and so on.

Overseas calls. You can dial direct to most overseas countries, however Country Direct is a service which enables you to gain direct access to telephone operators in the country you wish to ring. You can then make a collect (reverse charge) call, or telephone credit card call. For country collect, dial: 1800 881 followed by the country code of the country you wish to call. For an operator assisted call phone 1234.

Emergency Telephone numbers:

Ambulance: 000

Fire: 000 (life threatening emergencies only)

Police: 000 or 08 9222 1111 (to request police presence, Perth); 08 9430 1222 (Fremantle)

Other useful telephone numbers:

Directory Assistance
Perth: 1223
Country and Interstate: 1223
International: 1225

Interpreter Services: 13 14 50 (24 hour number)

Public Transport Information: 13 62 13 (bus, train, ferry)

Weather Forecast: 08 9263 2222; or 1196 (recorded information for Perth metropolitan area)

TIME

Australia has several time zones, with Perth being eight hours ahead of GMT (Greenwich Mean Time). Adelaide is one and a half hours ahead of Perth, Brisbane, Sydney and Melbourne are two hours ahead of Perth. However, when the Eastern States are on daylight saving Adelaide is two and a half hours ahead of Perth, and most other cities three hours ahead.

TIPPING/TAXES

Tipping is not expected in and around Perth. However, if you are particularly impressed with the service obtained, a tip would be gratefully accepted.

In shops and restaurants you pay marked prices. As yet there is no value-added tax, goods and services tax, or sales tax to be added on.

VIDEOS

Australia uses the PAL system.

VISAS

Visitors of all nationalities, except New Zealanders, need to obtain a visa prior to coming to Australia. These can be obtained at Australian Embassies, High Commissions and Consular Offices.

WEIGHTS AND MEASURES

The metric system is used in Australia.

INDEX